CAMBRIDGE TEXTS IN TI
HISTORY OF PHILOSOPH

—

FRIEDRICH SCHLEIERMACHER
Hermeneutics and Criticism

CAMBRIDGE TEXTS IN THE
HISTORY OF PHILOSOPHY

Series editors
KARL AMERIKS
Professor of Philosophy at the University of Notre Dame
DESMOND M. CLARKE
Professor of Philosophy at University College Cork

The main objective of Cambridge Texts in the History of Philosophy is to expand the range, variety and quality of texts in the history of philosophy which are available in English. The series includes texts by familiar names (such as Descartes and Kant) and also by less well-known authors. Wherever possible, texts are published in complete and unabridged form, and translations are specially commissioned for the series. Each volume contains a critical introduction together with a guide to further reading and any necessary glossaries and textual apparatus. The volumes are designed for student use at undergraduate and post-graduate level and will be of interest not only to students of philosophy, but also to a wider audience of readers in the history of science, the history of theology and the history of ideas.

For a list of titles published in the series, please see end of book.

FRIEDRICH SCHLEIERMACHER

Hermeneutics and Criticism
And Other Writings

TRANSLATED AND EDITED BY
ANDREW BOWIE
Anglia Polytechnic University, Cambridge

CAMBRIDGE
UNIVERSITY PRESS

CAMBRIDGE UNIVERSITY PRESS
Cambridge, New York, Melbourne, Madrid, Cape Town, Singapore, São Paulo

Cambridge University Press
The Edinburgh Building, Cambridge CB2 2RU, UK

Published in the United States of America by Cambridge University Press, New York

www.cambridge.org
Information on this title: www.cambridge.org/9780521591492

First published 1998

A catalogue record for this publication is available from the British Library

Library of Congress Cataloguing in Publication data

Schleiermacher, Friedrich, 1768–1834.
[Selections. English 1998]
Hermeneutics and criticism and other writings / Friedrich
Schleiermacher; translated and edited by Andrew Bowie.
   p.   cm. – (Cambridge texts in the history of philosophy)
Includes index.
ISBN 0 521 59149 X hardback
ISBN 0 521 59848 6 paperback
1. Hermeneutics. 2. Criticism. I. Bowie, Andrew, 1952–
II. Title. III. Series.
B3092.E5S34   1998
121'.68-dc21   98-12846 CIP

ISBN-13 978-0-521-59149-2 hardback
ISBN-10 0-521-59149-X hardback

ISBN-13 978-0-521-59848-4 paperback
ISBN-10 0-521-59848-6 paperback

Transferred to digital printing 2006

Contents

Introduction

Hermeneutics, the 'art of interpretation', has moved in recent years in the English-speaking world from being regarded as a subsidiary aspect of European philosophy to being one of the most widely debated topics in contemporary philosophy. Almost every account of the history of modern hermeneutics pays some kind of tribute to the founding role played by the German Protestant theologian and philosopher Friedrich Daniel Ernst Schleiermacher (1768–1834). The tribute is, though, usually significantly double-edged: very many of these accounts reiterate the conception of Schleiermacher as the 'Romantic' theorist who thinks of interpretation as an 'intuitive', 'empathetic' identification with the thoughts and feelings of the author of a text. This has often led to his being written off as part of the history of psychologistic textual interpretation that has been discredited by approaches to language and meaning in existential hermeneutics, analytical semantics, and structuralism and post-structuralism. However, as the texts translated here demonstrate, Schleiermacher never in fact saw interpretation in empathetic terms, seeing it rather in terms that now sound surprisingly relevant to contemporary philosophical accounts of language and epistemology.

Understanding Schleiermacher's hermeneutics is, though, made difficult by the fact that there are hardly any texts by Schleiermacher that exist in a version of which he would finally have approved: the work on hermeneutics in the present volume, for example, dates from as early as 1805 and as late as 1833, although the underlying conceptual framework does not change as much as some commentators have suggested.[1] *Hermeneutics and Criticism* (*HC*) (published posthumously in 1838 and mainly containing work dating from 1819 onwards) appeared in the *theological*, not the philosophical division of the first edition of Schleiermacher's complete works, and is particularly concerned with the interpretation of the New Testament. However, hermeneutics evidently plays a central role in Schleiermacher's philosophy as a whole, which he expressly separates in certain respects from his theology. He also repeatedly insists that there should be no difference in the principles of interpretation for religious and for secular texts.

HC must therefore be seen both in terms of its relation to preceding traditions of Biblical and philological interpretation and in relation to the philosophical challenges to theories of interpretation posed by the new views of culture, history and language which develop in the wake of J.-J. Rousseau, J. G. Hamann, J. G. Herder and others at the end of the eighteenth century.[2] The status of *HC* is, as such, thoroughly ambiguous. The supposedly new idea of a universal hermeneutics, with which Schleiermacher begins, is, for example, as Jean Grondin suggests, not necessarily new at all: 'in a little-known piece of 1630, *The Idea of the Good Interpreter*, [the Strasbourg theologian Johann Conrad Dannhauer] had already projected a universal hermeneutics under the express title of a *hermeneutica gener-alis*';[3] on the other hand, some of the key assumptions of *HC* are turning out to be startlingly relevant to contemporary philosophical debate.

Despite the problems over the exact status of *HC*, Schleiermacher's work on hermeneutics clearly remains of major importance for a whole variety of disciplines. One needs, though, to be aware of how the hermeneutics relates to his other work, and to the intellectual contexts of that work if this is to be appreciated. Without this awareness it is easy to gain a false impression of the texts translated here, which can seem at times to be merely manuals for the praxis of interpretation and for textual criticism, rather than properly philosophical texts. The fact is also that the significance of Schleiermacher's philosophical conception only really becomes apparent

---

[1] The problem in the hermeneutics emerges over the relative weight attached to 'grammatical' interpretation, which relies on systematic knowledge of the language in which the text is written, as opposed to 'technical' and 'psychological' interpretation, which rely on non-systematisable investigation both of the contexts of the text and of other texts and utterances by the author. The simple answer is that Schleiermacher thought both types essential, but tended to change his mind on certain aspects of how each was to be carried out.

[2] See Andrew Bowie, *From Romanticism to Critical Theory. The Philosophy of German Literary Theory*, London 1997.

[3] Jean Grondin, *Introduction to Philosophical Hermeneutics*, Yale 1994, p. 48.

when it is considered in relation to the increasingly manifest deficiencies of some of the dominant trends in philosophical reflection on language and knowledge in the twentieth century, particularly in the analytical tradition.[4] These two perspectives might seem to point in opposing directions, but this is not in fact the case. The reasons why the two perspectives converge offer a way of approaching Schleiermacher's thought as a whole that enables his hermeneutics to be seen in an appropriate light. Instead, then, of situating Schleiermacher exclusively within some of the very specific historical contexts in which his ideas developed, or of seeing him predominantly in terms of the theology which formed the main basis of his professional career, this introduction will also locate his thought in relation to some key issues in modern philosophy.

Spontaneity and receptivity

There has been a growing interest in the Anglo–Saxon world in the tradition of Kantian and post-Kantian German philosophy, in which Schleiermacher plays an important but neglected role. John McDowell's *Mind and World*, for example, at times strikingly parallels ideas central to Schleiermacher's philosophy. McDowell suggests, in the light of Kant's *Critique of Pure Reason*, which was also the main point of philosophical orientation for Schleiermacher, that in our cognitive relations to the world 'the deliverances of receptivity already draw on capacities that belong to spontaneity',[5] so that 'We must not suppose that receptivity makes an even notionally separable contribution to its co-operation with spontaneity' (ibid.). Related locutions are common in Schleiermacher: 'the original being-posited of reason in human nature [in the sense of that part of nature which is human] is its incorporation into the receptivity of this nature as understanding and into the spontaneity of this nature as will'.[6] 'Spontaneity', the activity of the mind which renders the world intelligible by linking together different phenomena, and 'receptivity', the way the world is given to the subject, therefore cannot be finally separated. In consequence, the link between the subject and the world cannot be conceived of in terms of a dualism which gives rise to all the problems of how the two relate to each other in

---

[4] See Beate Rössler, *Die Theorie des Verstehens in Sprachanalyse und Hermeneutik*, Berlin 1990; Andrew Bowie, 'The Meaning of the Hermeneutic Tradition in Contemporary Philosophy', in ed. Anthony O'Hear, *'Verstehen' and Humane Understanding*, Cambridge 1996, pp. 121–44.

[5] John McDowell, *Mind and World*, Cambridge, Mass., and London 1994, p. 41.

[6] Friedrich Schleiermacher, *Ethik (1812–13)*, Hamburg 1990, p. 14.

an intelligible manner that so troubled Kant's successors, including Schleiermacher, with respect to Kant's incoherent separation of knowable 'appearances' and unknowable 'things in themselves'.[7] Neither can the relationship be seen in terms of how we gain an accurate 're-presentation' of a 'ready-made' world of pre-existing objects: that would require a complete account of the difference between what is passively received from the 'outside' world and what is actively generated by the 'inside' mind. There is, simply, no location which would make such an account possible. We can *neither* wholly isolate the world from what our minds spontaneously contribute to it, *nor* wholly isolate our minds from their receptive involvement with the world. Many of the points of this kind made by contemporary philosophers in relation to the Idealist tradition are also made by Schleiermacher, sometimes in a more convincing manner than they are in either Kant or Hegel.[8]

Attention to the relevance of German Idealist epistemology to contemporary philosophy might seem to leave one at some remove from the specific issue of Schleiermacher's hermeneutics. There is, though, an important way of establishing a link between the two topics, which further opens up the route into Schleiermacher's thought as a whole. Once the role of the 'spontaneity' of the subject in the constitution of an objective world is established the world cannot be said to be reducible to the objective physical laws which govern it. Establishing *objective* laws which could explain why the world becomes *subjectively* intelligible at all, rather than just consisting in the interaction of physical processes, involves the problem of how to objectify that which is inherently subjective, thus of how to come to knowledge of what is already supposed to be the prior *condition* of knowledge. This is the fundamental problem with which, in the wake of Kant, German Idealist and Romantic philosophers try to come to terms. Importantly, the underlying problem here also appears at the level of language, the means by which we can be said to 'objectify' the subjective. It is Schleiermacher who first realises this in a fully elaborated manner.

Natural languages can be treated like law-bound objects, not least because they are physically instantiated. For Schleiermacher this aspect of

---

[7] As Schelling, who, along with Leibniz and Spinoza, was the other major philosophical influence on Schleiermacher, would put it in 1833, the thing in itself is 'an impossible hybrid, for to the extent to which it is a *thing* (object) it is not in itself, and if it is in itself it is not a thing' (F. W. J. Schelling, *On the History of Modern Philosophy*, Cambridge 1994, p. 102).

[8] See Andrew Bowie, 'John McDowell's *Mind and World*, and Early Romantic Epistemology', *Revue internationale de philosophie* 1996 197, pp. 515–54.

language is what can be 'mechanised', and he sees it in *HC* in terms of 'the grammatical'. The vocabulary, syntax, grammar, morphology and phonetics of a language are initially given to those who use that language in an 'objective' form, which is evident in the fact that they can now be successfully programmed into a computer. I cannot use a language as a means of communication and at the same time ignore these 'mechanisable' aspects. However, my *understanding* of what others say about the world cannot be said to result solely from my knowledge of objective rules of the kind that can be programmed into a computer, because it relies on my *making* sense of an ever-changing world which is not reducible to what can be said about it at any particular time. I can, for example, spontaneously generate intelligible sentences that have never been said before, and I can understand new metaphors which are meaningless in terms of the notional existing rules of a language.[9]

Schleiermacher often points out that this ability is most manifest in the inventive way children acquire language. The initial acquisition of a linguistic rule necessarily entails that the child has already understood something about the way language and the world relate without employing any rule, otherwise the result is a regress of rules for the understanding and acquiring of rules which would render our acquisition of language incomprehensible. As he puts it in the *Ethics*: 'If language appears to come to [the child] first as receptivity, this only refers to the particular language which surrounds it; spontaneity with regard to being able to speak at all is simultaneous with that language' (*Ethik (1812–13)* p. 66). The regress these ideas are intended to circumvent will be what leads Schleiermacher in *HC* to his notion of 'divination', the ability to arrive at interpretations without definitive rules, and to his terming hermeneutics an 'art', because it cannot be fully carried out in terms of rules. We live, then, in a world which is bound by deterministic laws that also apply to our own organism, yet are able to choose between alternative courses of action and generate new ways of understanding. In the same way our understanding and use of language involve a relationship between what Schleiermacher often refers to as 'bound' activity, based on the acknowledgement of the rules involved in any natural language, and 'free' activity, which allows us to transcend such rules in order both to understand in a new context where it is not

---

[9] On this issue, see Manfred Frank, *The Subject and the Text. Essays in Literary Theory and Philosophy*, Cambridge 1997, and *Das Individuelle-Allgemeine. Textstrukturierung und -interpretation nach Schleiermacher*, Frankfurt am Main 1977.

self-evident from the context that the rule is applicable, and to articulate the world in new and individual ways.[10] A complete philosophical account of language would have to explain how these two aspects relate, just as a complete philosophical account of knowledge would have to explain exactly how the spontaneous and the receptive, the active and the passive, the subjective and the objective relate. The question that recurs in the most important philosophy of the period is whether such accounts are actually possible. Schleiermacher's conviction is that a final account is not possible. It is this which separates him, like his friend Friedrich Schlegel, from Fichte's and Hegel's Idealism (and, at times, from Schelling),[11] and which leads him to his most important insights in the hermeneutics.

The philosophical era inaugurated by Kant's *Critique of Pure Reason* in 1781 is, then, defined by the attempt to understand the relationship between the spontaneous and the receptive aspects of an 'autonomous' subject that is freed both from complete natural determinism and from subjection to a divine authority. Schleiermacher's most notable and influential contributions to the history of philosophy lie in his integration of reflection upon language into the issue of spontaneity and receptivity, but understanding just how he carries out this integration presupposes an adequate account of why hermeneutics plays a role in his wider philosophical project.

'Feeling' and 'intuition'

Schleiermacher's arrival on the intellectual scene was announced in 1799 by the publication of *On Religion*, written at the instigation of his friends from the Romantic circle, such as Friedrich Schlegel, who are the 'cultured despisers' of religion of the book's subtitle. *On Religion*, whose effects on Protestant theology are even now by no means exhausted, is generally seen as a rhapsodic counter to rational theology, which insists, in the wake of Kant's refutation of the philosophical proofs of God's existence that had sustained the tradition of rational theology, on the centrality of individual 'feeling' as the basis of religion. For a period, beginning with the *Sturm und*

---

[10] This distinction is central to Schleiermacher's *Aesthetics*, perhaps the most unjustly neglected work on aesthetics of the nineteenth century: see Andrew Bowie, *Aesthetics and Subjectivity: from Kant to Nietzsche*, Manchester 1993, Chapter 6.

[11] On the critique of Idealism, see Manfred Frank, *Der unendliche Mangel an Sein*, Frankfurt am Main 1975; Andrew Bowie, *Schelling and Modern European Philosophy*, London 1993, and Manfred Frank, 'Philosophische Grundfragen der Frühromantik' in *Athenäum* iv, Paderborn, Munich, Vienna, Zürich 1994.

Drang movement, in which the centrality of individual feelings epitomised by Werther's assertion in Goethe's *The Sufferings of Young Werther* that 'What I know, everyone can know, my heart is mine alone', has become almost a commonplace, this approach to religion might not seem that surprising. However, if one sees *On Religion* as at least to some extent continuous with Schleiermacher's and his contemporaries' ideas about the philosophy of the time, matters are not that simple.

The key terms in Schleiermacher's contentions are 'intuition', '*Anschauung*', and 'feeling', '*Gefühl*', which seem to suggest that the widespread mistaken image of Schleiermacher the theorist of empathetic interpretation may at least be valid here. But take the following passage, addressed to his imagined philosophical interlocutor, which points to the essential theoretical focus of *On Religion*: 'I ask you, then: what does your ... transcendental philosophy do? It classifies the universe and divides it into this kind of being and that kind of being, it pursues the bases of what is there and deduces the necessity of the real, it spins from itself the reality of the world and its laws.'[12] In the same year as Schleiermacher published *On Religion* F. H. Jacobi published his letter *Jacobi to Fichte*, which articulates a philosophical tension central to the period that is apparent in the passage just cited.[13] Jacobi takes up ideas in the letter from his contributions to the 'Pantheism Controversy' which began in 1783 between himself and Moses Mendelssohn, the leader of the Berlin Enlightenment. The controversy arose over whether G. E. Lessing was a Spinozist (and thus, in the view of the time, an atheist), and became the matrix from which many of the major problems of modern philosophy first emerged (see Bowie, *From Romanticism to Critical Theory*). The letter contains the famous ironic image, coincidentally echoed in Schleiermacher's remarks on transcendental philosophy's spinning 'from itself the reality of the world and its laws', of Fichte's philosophical system as a sock which has to knit itself. Jacobi's essential insight was into the problem of grounding any philosophical system, and Schleiermacher's remarks on transcendental philosophy relate to his documented awareness of Jacobi's decisive interventions.

Spinoza's key idea in this context, which was part of what led to his being thought an atheist, was that the determination of each thing in the universe is only possible via its not being other things, so that, in Jacobi's

---

[12] Friedrich Schleiermacher, *Über die Religion. Reden an die Gebildeten unter ihren Verächtern*, Berlin n.d., p. 47.
[13] Friedrich Heinrich Jacobi, *Jacobi an Fichte*, Hamburg 1799.

phrase, the Spinozist universe is a universe of 'conditioned conditions', each thing depending upon its determining 'condition' within a self-relating whole. What, though – and this was the issue that most concerned Jacobi and Schleiermacher – prevented this just being a universe which consisted of an endless regress of chains of causality, and of things which had no essential identity, because their having an identity depended upon their relations to other things, thus upon what they themselves are not? This would be a universe of what Jacobi termed 'nihilism': instead of establishing a 'ground', a '*Grund*', the 'principle of sufficient reason', the '*Satz vom Grunde*'– which Jacobi reformulates as 'everything *dependent* is *dependent upon* something'[14] – actually led to an '*Abgrund*', an 'abyss'. The view based on the 'principle of sufficient reason', which can be seen as corresponding to the underlying structure of the scientistic world view, failed to come to terms with the contingent fact that things were intelligible at all, with the fact that we live in a world which in many ways *does* evidently already hang together and make sense. Because it leads to a regress, a mere chain of conditions does not explain what makes the world intelligible, and so intelligibility must depend on the 'unconditioned', or what the thinkers of the period often termed the 'Absolute'. For Spinoza God, as that which is cause and ground of itself, has precisely this status. This conception, though, Jacobi shows, poses the problem of how, if all we know has to be known in terms of its conditions, the *un*conditioned could be known at all, without contradicting its very nature by seeking its *condition*. Jacobi himself does not think the unconditioned can be known and thinks it must be presupposed via a '*salto mortale*', a leap of faith which takes the place of a philosophical explanation of why things are intelligible. He therefore calls what he is engaged in '*Unphilosophie*', there being no point in pursuing the *philosophical* task of completely grounding what is held as true.

Although these arguments are vital to the development of his own position, Schleiermacher, for his part, is still happy in *On Religion* to embrace Spinoza as someone for whom the universe was 'his sole and eternal love' and for whom 'the infinite was his beginning and end', because 'intuition of the universe', of the kind he sees in Spinoza, 'is the hinge of my whole speech' (*Über die Religion* p. 56). 'Intuition' plays this role, Schleiermacher explains, because the aim of *On Religion* is, in a manner analogous to Jacobi, to separate religion from metaphysics and morality: religion's 'essence is

---

[14] In Scholz, Heinrich, ed., *Die Hauptschriften zum Pantheismusstreit zwischen Jacobi und Mendelssohn*, Berlin 1916, p. 271.

neither thought nor action, but intuition and feeling' (ibid. p. 53). The wider context is once again important here if such assertions are not to appear merely vague.

One of the most influential philosophical attempts to shore up the new foundations of knowledge in the subject rather than in objectivity initiated by Kant was Fichte's attempt from the 1794 *Doctrine of Science* onwards to ground both knowledge and ethics in the spontaneity of the I. Fichte's philosophy wished to establish the primacy of the practical I as unconditioned '*Tathandlung*', as the 'deed-action' which was the condition of the world being intelligible rather than remaining a mere chaos of – unknowable – causally linked events. This had led Fichte to the position from which Jacobi distances himself in the letter, and which is the target of Schleiermacher's notion of 'intuition', namely a position in which human subjectivity, as Schleiermacher puts it, is 'condition of all being and cause of all becoming' (ibid. p. 53). As opposed to this 'philosophical', Idealist position, Schleiermacher maintains the following:

> the universe is uninterruptedly active and reveals itself to us at every moment. Every form which it produces, every being to which it gives a separate life in accordance with the fullness of life, every occurrence which it pours out of its rich, ever-fruitful womb, is an action of the universe on us; and in this way, to accept everything individual as a part of the whole, everything limited as a presentation of the infinite, is religion. (ibid. p. 57)

Schleiermacher's rhetoric should not conceal the philosophical significance of the point being made. The individual's ability actively to determine the universe in cognition and action, which Fichte's Idealism makes the very ground of being's intelligibility, depends upon the prior 'activity' of the universe itself, which was present before any individual subject was alive. Schleiermacher is influenced by Spinoza's notion of *natura naturans*, and by the development of this notion in Schelling's *Naturphilosophie* of 1797 into the idea of nature as a 'productivity' which comes to 'intuit' itself both in its transient differentiated 'products' – specific natural objects and organisms – and, at a higher level, in our thinking about those products. The controversial issue is how the notion of 'intuition' is conceived, because it is here that the threatened split between mind and world is addressed.

Fichte resolves the split on the subjective side, grounding his philosophy in his version of 'intellectual intuition' – 'that through which I know something because I do it'[15] – in which the split between receptivity (intuition) and the spontaneity of the 'intellect' is overcome in terms of the prior activity of the I, which splits *itself* into knowing I and known not-I. The identity of mind and world is therefore guaranteed at the very outset by the primacy of active mind, without which the world would be merely inert and opaque. Epistemology and ontology are equally grounded in a spontaneous activity: this is best understood by the way philosophical reflection can take the I beyond thinking about causal relations between things to consideration of its very ability to reflect upon itself and the world at all. Schleiermacher's version of 'intuition', on the other hand, though in some ways linked – not least via the mutual relation to Kant – to Fichte's, overcomes the split by suggesting that it is only by an acceptance of an inherent link of ourselves to a world which transcends *both* our cognitive and practical activity that we can really comprehend our place in the universe. It is no coincidence that, as Theodore Kisiel has demonstrated,[16] Martin Heidegger arrived at his idea of 'being in the world', which is prior to any epistemological attempt to ground knowledge in an account of the relationship of subject to object, and at his desire to deconstruct previous metaphysics, in part via his reading of *On Religion*.

In Schleiermacher's 'religion', then, as in Jacobi's '*Unphilosophie*', there is an immediate significance inherent in the very fact of being at all: each experience, intuition and feeling is 'a work which stands for itself without connection with others or dependence on others; it knows nothing of deduction and connection . . . everything in it is immediate and true for itself' (*Über die Religion* pp. 58–9). If, for example, the individual's meaningful relationship to the beauty of nature – which in Schleiermacher's terms is already religious – is thought in fact to be ultimately the result of an explicable concatenation of deterministic natural events, its meaningful 'immediacy' would become reduced to a meaningless 'mediation'. Such an explanation would lead, though, Schleiermacher suggests, to an unfulfillable endlessly regressing attempt to come to terms with all the related factors that would need to be explained on both subjective and objective sides in order to complete the 'mediation'. The point about the meaningful 'intuition' is that it does not require this: its 'infinity' lies in its unique individuality, the completely individual, yet immediate feeling of being part of a whole that transcends one. Schleiermacher insists (and this will

---

[15] J. G. Fichte, *Werke* I, Berlin 1971, p. 463.
[16] Theodore Kisiel, *The Genesis of Heidegger's 'Being and Time'*, Berkeley, Los Angeles, London 1995.

be vital for his hermeneutics) that each person can intuit in ways which are incommensurable, without this necessarily damaging the idea that they partake of 'religious' unity. – He also notoriously insists, it should be remembered, that, as such, 'a religion without God can be better than one with God' (ibid. p. 108).

It is no exaggeration to suggest that some of the most significant problems in modern philosophy are inherent in this issue. Soon after the publication of *On Religion* Hegel makes, in his 1802 *Belief and Knowledge*, one of his early attacks on the notion of 'immediacy', precisely in relation to Jacobi and Schleiermacher. Such attacks will become one of the essential sources of Hegel's main philosophical ideas, culminating in the claim of the *Science of Logic* that there is nothing in heaven and earth that is not mediated. Just how virulent Hegel's antipathy to the idea of the immediacy of 'feeling' is becomes apparent in his later attack, in 1822, on its successor notion, in Schleiermacher's *The Christian Faith* of 1821, of the 'feeling of radical dependence' (*'Gefühl der schlechthinnigen Abhängigkeit'*). Schleiermacher insists on this aspect of self-consciousness in order to come to terms with the fact that for our spontaneous autonomy to escape solipsism it must yet be dependent upon effects of the world on ourselves in receptivity, in a manner over which we have no final control, because these effects begin before the development of reflexive self-consciousness. At the same time, though, the effects of the world on the individual also depend on the spontaneity of that individual, as the differing ways in which individuals respond to the same aspects of the world suggest. As always in Schleiermacher, the total preponderance of one side of any conceptual opposition is relativised by revealing how it cannot ultimately be separated from its opposite. The feeling of dependence is the source of the notion of God in *The Christian Faith*: it reveals a ground of the relationship between mind and world which cannot be 'mediated', which is not available to cognition or articulation in philosophy. It is precisely this inarticulable ground that Hegel attempts to obviate in the *Logic*, by claiming that even immediacy must actually be mediated for it to be intelligible as immediacy at all (see Bowie *Schelling*, Chapter 6). Schleiermacher also refers to the feeling of dependence as a '*Grundton*',[17] a 'tonic', in the musical sense, that is occasioned by the world's evoking a response in the individual, and which must always precede our mediated knowledge as the way in which we are first 'attuned'

---

[17] Ed. H. Peiter, F. D. E. Schleiermacher, *Der christliche Glaube*, Berlin, New York 1980, p. 253.

to the world at all. Whether the argument that the ground of our being in the world cannot be articulated in philosophy necessarily leads in a theological direction is, of course, debatable: aspects of the thought of Heidegger, in his insistence on the prior 'disclosure' of the world before any particular scientific articulation, and of certain kinds of pragmatism, which often echo aspects of Schleiermacher's thought, suggest it does not.[18]

Hegel maintains against Schleiermacher that 'If religion in man is founded only on a feeling, then it rightly has no other determination than to be the feeling of his dependence, and in this way the dog would be the best Christian, for it carries this most strongly in itself' (cit. in *Der christliche Glaube* p. lvii). What appears as immediate is, then, merely that which has not been subjected to the 'exertion of the concept'. In a sense, therefore, Hegel is quite happy with nihilism, because for him anything particular, including the individual subject, only gains its truth if it becomes part of the universal by being conceptualised, and is thus dissolved into the articulation of its relations to other things. Hegel is aware that we must relate to the world in some immediate sense, of the kind suggested in the notion of 'intellectual intuition', for there not to be a dualism between mind and world. However, he thinks this initial immediacy is merely the kind of consciousness one might attribute to animals, such as dogs, which are unable to 'reflect' and thereby move to the higher stages of properly philosophical thinking which culminate in a complete account of the mind-world relationship, into which everything particular has been '*aufgehoben*'.

This might seem to locate Schleiermacher firmly in the camp of a reactionary 'Romanticism' which is more concerned with a mystical sense of intuitive 'Oneness' than, for example, with the real solutions to human misery that can be provided by the progressing work of the modern sciences. Schleiermacher's work is, though, thoroughly compatible with a positive, if potentially critical, attitude to the scientific and technical advances of modernity: indeed, he was more insistent than either Schelling or Hegel upon the need to avoid philosophical speculation which failed to take the results of the sciences seriously. The main point is that Schleiermacher's separation of theology from philosophy leads him to assign different roles to each, without devaluing either. In certain key respects Schleiermacher and Hegel actually share many of the same post-Kantian assumptions

---

[18] On the relation to pragmatism, see Christian Berner, *La philosophie de Schleiermacher*, Paris 1995, pp. 168–70.

about the need not to separate mind and world, and about the need for new kinds of philosophically justified rational accountability in modernity. Where they part company is over the relation of the contingency of the individual subject to the whole in which it is located, and over the possibility of 'absolute knowledge'. This divergence is apparent in the fact that Schleiermacher's central philosophical ideas lead him to hermeneutics, and to very different conceptions of 'dialectic' and 'ethics' from those of Hegel.

Dialectic and hermeneutics

One way of suggesting why a new kind of hermeneutics came to play a central role in Schleiermacher's work is to show, as I shall in a moment, that it follows from the structure of his main philosophical assumptions. Another, intriguing way has been proposed by Stephen Prickett.[19] The usual biographical story is that Schleiermacher's pioneering work on translating and editing Plato and his work on Biblical criticism, along with the demands of an academic post – as late as March 1805 he says in a letter that he will soon have to lecture on hermeneutics while as yet having no real idea about it – led to his working on hermeneutics for the first time in 1805. Prickett, though, points out another element in the story which suggests a further motivation for Schleiermacher's new approach. Around the time of the appearance of *On Religion* Schleiermacher was asked to translate David Collins' *Account of the English Colony in New South Wales*, which he decided, of his own accord, to supplement with further research into New Holland (the project was never published). In Collins' text, as Prickett puts it, 'What [Collins] records is a classic encounter with the "other" in its most extreme and uncompromising form', namely with an aboriginal tribe living in great misery whom Collins (implausibly) regarded as being devoid of any kind of religion at all. For Schleiermacher, in the terms of *On Religion*, the tribe could yet have religious consciousness via their particular sense of participation in the universe. How, though, would we be able to understand their apparently wholly alien religious sentiments?

The attempt to demonstrate how this question could be answered helps to establish the relationship in Schleiermacher's thought between 'dialectic' and hermeneutics. The first move would obviously be to learn the

---

[19] Stephen Prickett, 'Coleridge, Schlegel and Schleiermacher: England, Germany (and Australia) in 1798', forthcoming in *1798*, London 1998.

tribe's language, but here all the now familiar problems arise with regard to translation that have, via the influence of Quine, also played such a role in recent analytical semantics, which Schleiermacher very evidently foresaw. How can one be sure which part of one's own language is the correct translation of a part of another, initially wholly alien language? Even apparently successful translation does not necessarily answer all the problems entailed in understanding the 'other'. How can we be certain that, by being at least able to translate their utterances, we actually understand how the people in question think? – Computers, after all, can now quite often translate with some degree of accuracy in certain contexts. – The crude answer would be that we 'empathise' with the people in an 'intuitive' manner, and this has often been assumed to be Schleiermacher's position. Consideration of Schleiermacher's view of truth and language in his dialectic shows just how mistaken this view is.

Schleiermacher defines hermeneutics as 'the art of understanding ... the ... discourse of another person correctly',[20] and dialectic as the presentation of 'the principles of the art of philosophising',[21] or 'the foundations for the artistic (*kunstmäßige*) carrying out of dialogue in the domain of pure thought'.[22] The former is concerned with the meaning of utterances, the latter with their truth, which might seem just to repeat the difference between *doxa* and *episteme*. Schleiermacher, though, is a thoroughly post-Kantian thinker, and his development of Kantian themes actually brings him, despite his attachment to Plato, much closer to issues in contemporary philosophy than to Platonic metaphysics, at least as it is traditionally understood.

The notorious problem here, which still vitiates many positions in the analytical philosophy of language – particularly in its regular failure to account for linguistic innovation – is the relationship between what the world gives to the speaker, which includes what is, in one sense at least, an already constituted language, and what the speaker herself contributes to meaning and truth. In naturalistic terms the effects of the world on the speaker are simply causal, the impact of indeterminate numbers of different stimuli on the nerve ends. However, given the further factor of the

---

[20] Friedrich Schleiermacher, *Hermeneutik und Kritik*, Berlin 1838, p. 4.
[21] Friedrich Schleiermacher, *Dialektik (1811)*, Hamburg 1986, p. 4.
[22] Friedrich Schleiermacher, *Dialektik (1814–15). Einleitung zur Dialektik (1833)*, Hamburg 1988, p. 117. As will be apparent in *HC*, Schleiermacher's use of words based on '*Kunst*' involves both the sense of 'method' or 'technique', which entails the application of rules, and of 'art' as that which cannot be bound by rules.

irreducibly different physical constitution of each organism, this obviously offers no way of showing how these impacts result in identity of *meaning* between speakers. The aspect of endless difference in the way the world affects each organism in receptivity is what Schleiermacher refers to as the 'organic function'. Meaning and truth, though, rely upon the establishing of identities from what is given as difference in the organic function. The 'formal', in Schleiermacher's terms, is the 'intellectual' 'principle of unity' (*Dialektik (1811)* p. 16), as opposed to the organic, the principle of 'multiplicity', and knowledge is constituted by the intellectual activity underlying the principle of unity. The formal and the organic meet in the judgement.

As is well known, Kant makes a radical distinction between purely formal 'analytic' and 'synthetic' judgements, but Schleiermacher, well before Quine, rejects this distinction: 'The difference between an analytical and a synthetic judgement cannot be held on to, and is not a difference at all, because identical judgements are not judgements but only empty formulae if they are not founded in the complete concept, in which that difference alone is founded' (*Dialektik (1814–15)* p. 33). A (supposedly) analytic judgement like 'all men are mortals' is, then, either an empty, merely formal judgement, like 'a=a', in which case we learn nothing, or it already involves 'intuition' and is contingent on what we know from the world. This knowledge will, though, always remain open to revision, so that the 'organic function' must play a role even in an apparent tautology, because we never in fact arrive at the 'complete concept' and thus cannot get beyond synthetic judgements. Even operations in logic, which come closest to the purely 'intellectual', involve the activity of thinking of real people, and rely on a history of previous acts of thought. Although we may think of 'reason' in the logical sense as the universally valid formal rules of thought, it is, Schleiermacher maintains, never actually available in its pure form: there is always an aspect of the 'organic function' in anything that can count as knowledge. This means that 'No knowledge in two languages can be regarded as completely the same; not even . . . A=A' (ibid. p. 25). The only way we can try to establish such identity of knowledge is pragmatic, via linguistic communication. This raises precisely the issues later associated with the problems for semantics which result, for example, from Frege's Platonic notion of the 'sense' a word is supposed to possess independently of the often contingent, revisable ways it is actually used or understood, and which are suggested by Quine and Donald Davidson in the idea of the 'indeterminacy of translation/interpretation'. Reason for Schleiermacher, then, is really the *potential* for using the principle of unity to arrive at true knowledge, a potential which relies on the organic function as well as on the activity of the formal, synthesising capacity of the mind. Both the organic and the formal, of course, are necessary for language, which must be instantiated as object in the physical world that is given in the organic function. This means, therefore, that language blocks the possibility of access to 'pure reason': pure reason would entail a 'purely formal', 'general' language, but how would we ever learn it?[23]

The core of Schleiermacher's view is summarised in the claim, which introduces a key term in his arguments, that 'the schematism of all true concepts is only innate in reason as a living drive' (*Dialektik (1814–15)* p. 41): the true concepts do not pre-exist in a 'Platonic' manner; they are, rather, the normatively constituted aim of the activity of thought in a community. In the *Critique of Pure Reason* Kant called the 'universal procedure of the imagination to provide a concept with its image' the 'schema'.[24] Kant's schema, which belonged to the 'productive imagination', the source of Fichte's '*Tathandlung*', provided the bridge between spontaneity and receptivity, between what Schleiermacher sees as the never directly accessible chaos of pure receptivity, and never directly accessible pure spontaneity. He regards such limit notions as 'regulative ideas', in the Kantian sense that they must be presupposed if reason is to be able to assume there really is a totality within which particular cognitions are located, but, given that they play a necessary *constitutive* role in any attempt to understand the world, this distinction as well is seen as ultimately untenable (See *Dialektik (1814–15)* p. 8, and Berner, *La philosophie de Schleiermacher* pp. 108–9).

A schema for Schleiermacher is a 'shiftable' image (*Dialektik (1814–15)* p. 145), thus a flexible framework with no definitive boundaries which enables us to establish identities between differing determinations that a thing can share with something else. The patterns of data we receive at any point in our lives cannot be shown to be absolutely the same at any two moments, but even if they appear to be identical this still would not allow one to understand how knowledge in fact comes about. This is because a single moment of receptivity can be seen in terms of a variety of differing schemata: 'at different times the same organic affection leads to completely different concepts. The perception of an emerald will at one time be for me

---

[23] See J. G. Hamann's critique of Kant in: *Schriften zur Sprache*, Frankfurt am Main 1967, pp. 224–6.
[24] Kant, *Kritik der reinen Vernunft*, B pp. 179–80, A pp. 140–1.

a schema of a certain green, then of a certain crystallisation, finally of a certain stone' (ibid. p. 39). The idea that the notion of the schema might give vital clues to the understanding of language was probably first proposed by Schelling in the *System of Transcendental Idealism* of 1800, a text Schleiermacher certainly knew, but it is Schleiermacher who really works out its implications. Before looking, in the next section, at Schleiermacher's account of schematism and language, which is central both to the ethics and to the hermeneutics, the notion of truth and knowledge in the dialectic requires further investigation.

The mutual influence between Schleiermacher and the early Romantic thinker Friedrich Schlegel (with whom he began to share a flat in 1797 in Berlin) is important here. Both Schleiermacher and Schlegel are suspicious of the correspondence theory of truth, but they are equally suspicious of the kind of scepticism which fails to account for the ways in which we do in fact engage with the world in terms of 'holding as true'. Schlegel asserts that 'One has always regarded it as the greatest difficulty to get from consciousness to reality (*Daseyn*). But in our view this difficulty does not exist. *Consciousness* and *reality* appear here as the connected parts (*Glieder*) of a whole.'[25] The real difficulty is that 'the whole' is not something which philosophy can articulate, for example in the manner Hegel wishes to, because consciousness and the object world can only be articulated as predicates of the absolute, unknowable ground which links them. While sometimes appearing to rely upon a correspondence theory, Schleiermacher is well aware of the basic problem it involves: 'One could say that correspondence of thought with being is an empty thought, because of the absolute different nature and incommensurability of each' (*Dialektik (1814–15)* p. 18). If thought is essentially synthesising activity that continually makes things given in receptivity determinate in changing ways – as suggested in the claim that 'the schematism of all true concepts is only innate in reason as a living drive' – and this activity is channelled by the finite number of words we use to articulate determinacy, how can we claim that these words 're-present', or correspond to things, without invoking a location beyond both thought and things from which their identity could be apprehended?

Schleiermacher is quite certain, therefore, that 'The idea of absolute being as the identity of concept and object' is not accessible to our knowledge,

---

[25] Friedrich Schlegel, *Transcendentalphilosophie*, ed. Michael Elsässer, Hamburg 1991, p. 74.

even though it is the 'transcendent' basis of knowledge (*Dialektik (1814–15)* p. 30). In 1800 Schlegel suggests, in a similar vein, that 'there is no absolute truth ... this spurs on the spirit and drives it to activity'.[26] Hegel seeks to show that spirit *can* ultimately understand its own activity, because it can both affect and be affected by the world, and can also be aware of being both the subject and the object of its own thinking in 'absolute knowledge'. Schleiermacher and Schlegel think that self-consciousness can only strive to achieve such understanding, with no ultimate guarantee of success, because the being of self-consciousness transcends its ability to know itself:

> as thinkers we are only in the single act [of thought]; but as beings we are the unity of all single acts and moments. Progression is only the transition from one moment to the next. This therefore takes place through our being, the living unity of the succession of the acts of thought. The transcendent basis of thought, in which the principles of linkage are contained, is nothing but our own transcendent basis as thinking being ... *The transcendent basis must now indeed be the same basis of the being which affects us as of the being which is our own activity.*[27]

Schleiermacher therefore sees an analogy between 'immediate self-consciousness', the ground of unity between different moments of thought which is not available to our reflective consciousness (which can only apprehend particular acts of thought), and the 'transcendent basis'. The latter's role is 'transcendental', albeit in an ontological rather than an epistemological sense, because it is the condition of possibility of the same self-consciousness being both spontaneous and receptive, thus of the ability of the I to move from spontaneity to receptivity while remaining the same self-consciousness.[28] Schleiermacher, then, uses 'transcendental' interchangeably with 'transcendent', which Kant reserved for what was beyond cognition.

Knowledge itself is only possible as the result of a particular intuition of the world in receptivity which is rendered identical with some other

---

26 Friedrich Schlegel, *Philosophische Vorlesungen* (1800–1807) (*Kritische Friedrich Schlegel Ausgabe* Volume 12), Munich, Paderborn, Vienna 1964, p. 95.

27 *Friedrich Schleiermachers Dialektik*, ed. R. Odebrecht, Leipzig 1942, pp. 274–5.

28 It is also the ground of the ability to recognise oneself, rather than see a mere random object or person in a mirror: without a prior pre-reflexive familiarity with oneself, what criterion could one use to know that what one sees is in fact oneself? For my memories to be in the first person at all the experiences they are based on must initially be immediately and incorrigibly mine if they are to be able to be reflexively (though now fallibly) re-identified as mine. See Manfred Frank, *Selbstbewußtsein und Selbsterkenntnis*, Stuttgart 1991.

intuition by spontaneity, so there can be no *knowledge* of the principle which creates identity, because knowledge itself depends on a prior differentiation for synthesis to be possible in the first place.[29] As Kant saw, in order for temporally differentiated receptivity to be intelligible, there must be a ground that connects its different moments. This ground prevents the moments being merely chaotic for lack of a principle that both retains a trace of them and makes their difference into identity. Kant, though, failed to show what sort of access we have to this grounding principle of our very self. Schleiermacher calls 'immediate self-consciousness', which is intended to fill the gap left by Kant, 'that which links all the moments of both functions, of thinking and willing, [it is] the identity in the linking, it is real being' (ibid. p. 291). In the same way as the world only manifests itself in differing transient moments, but must exist in a way that transcends these moments, the I can never grasp itself all at once, yet must exist in a way that transcends its access to itself at differing moments. Religious consciousness, as we saw, is the 'intuition' of such a totality, which can therefore never be achieved in the form of knowledge, because knowledge is inherently temporal, based on the linking of different aspects of what is given in the organic function: 'For just this reason Absolute, Highest Unity, identity of the ideal and the real are only schemata. If they are to become living they come again into the domain of the finite and of opposition' (*Dialektik (1814–15)* p. 67). In Jacobi's terms, we would be seeking the 'conditions of the unconditioned' by trying to know them.

Unlike Schlegel, who, until his conversion to Catholicism in 1807, cannot be said to hold firm religious beliefs, Schleiermacher thinks his position does give a way of talking about God: 'God's being is given to us in things to the extent that in each individual thing the totality is posited by dint of being and by being together, and so the transcendent basis is thereby also posited' (ibid. p. 66), and 'Just as the idea of the Godhead is the transcendental *terminus a quo*, and the principle of the possibility of knowledge as such, so the idea of the world is the transcendental *terminus ad quem* and the principle of the reality of knowledge in its becoming' (ibid. p. 70). As such, 'we can say of the idea of the world that the whole history of our knowledge is an approximation to it' (ibid.). The approximation, though, can

---

[29] In a text called '*Urtheil und Seyn*' Hölderlin refers to this in 1795, via a probably fictional etymology, as the '*Ur-teilung*', the 'primary separation' which gives rise to the need for synthesis, the joining of what is separate in a judgement, an '*Urteil*'. See Dieter Henrich, *Der Grund im Bewußtsein. Untersuchungen zu Hölderlins Denken (1794-5)*, Stuttgart 1992. Schleiermacher makes the same point in the passage from the *Dialectic* translated in this volume, with reference to the 'absolute subject'.

never be said to reach its goal because it depends on a basis that transcends it, rather than on an initial *fundamentum inconcussum* on either the side of things (materialism) or the side of the subject (idealism): 'the particular is that which is purely given in being but which does not purely resolve into thought, and the universal is what is completely given in thought but which cannot be purely shown in being. So both are asymptotic and their identity can only be completed via relation to the Absolute as their necessary supplement' (*Dialektik (1811)* p. 41). For Schlegel this transcendence of the Absolute leads to 'the higher scepticism of Socrates, which, unlike common scepticism, does not consist in the denial of truth and certainty, but rather in the serious search for them' (*Philosophische Vorlesungen*, p. 202). Both Schleiermacher and Schlegel agree that the consequence of this position is, as far as knowledge is concerned, that 'Beginning in the middle is unavoidable' (*Dialektik (1814–15)* p. 105). For Schleiermacher our knowing consists in an 'oscillation' between the organic and the intellectual function, neither of which can be purely present as itself. This idea will be vital for the hermeneutics.

Hermeneutics and ethics

Given these anti-foundational arguments, it might seem rather surprising that Schleiermacher and Schlegel share the conviction that the inaccessibility of the Absolute to knowledge is not a reason for abandoning the pursuit of truth. Hilary Putnam comes very close to Schleiermacher when he maintains that 'The very fact that we speak of our different conceptions as different conceptions of *rationality* posits a *Grenzbegriff*, a limit-concept of the ideal truth' (Hilary Putnam, *Reason, Truth and History*, Cambridge 1981, p. 216). In the light of the post-modern desire to say good-bye to such notions, talk of the Absolute as the 'limit-concept of the ideal truth' might seem merely a pious attempt to defend the no longer defensible. Schleiermacher is interesting not least because his approach to truth and understanding already opposes, in the name of a rationality that aims to be universal, the kind of arguments against universalism that have become familiar again from Lyotard, Rorty and others, while still sustaining a sense of the potential for irreducible alterity which he regards as inherent in the way any individual relates to the world.[30]

[30] See Manfred Frank, *Grenzen der Verständigung*, Frankfurt am Main 1988, and *Das Individuelle-Allgemeine*.

Donald Davidson has maintained in his account of interpretation, which shares several features with Schleiermacher's, that 'The method is not designed to eliminate disagreement, nor can it; its purpose is to make meaningful disagreement possible, and this depends on a foundation – *some* foundation – in agreement'.[31] In the 1833 *Introduction to the Dialectic* Schleiermacher already makes Davidson's point when he argues that 'Disagreement of any kind presupposes the acknowledgement of the sameness of an object, as well as the necessity of the relationship of thought to being . . . For if we take away this relationship of thought to being there is no disagreement, rather, as long as thought only remains purely within itself, there is only difference (*Verschiedenheit*)' (*Dialektik (1814–15)* pp. 132–4). Against idealism Schleiermacher insists that our thinking be of something that is not itself reducible to determinate thought, in order for the dialectical process via which knowledge develops to begin. However, this does not give a foundational point from which to proceed, such as the 'self-certainty' of the subject, 'observation reports', 'stimulus meanings', or whatever, so 'we must be satisfied with arbitrary beginnings in all areas of knowledge' (ibid. p. 149). Despite this, the process of knowledge acquisition itself is not merely arbitrary because there must always be some ground of agreement, rather than mere random difference, among those who seek the truth. In the extreme case, instead of conflicting judgements about the same thing – which Schleiermacher puts in the form 'A is b', 'A is not b', such as 'This substance is phlogiston', 'This substance is not phlogiston' – we might have 'A is' and 'A is not' (ibid. p 135), such as 'Phlogiston exists', 'Phlogiston does not exist'. The only presupposition in this latter case is the fact of being itself, as that which can be differentiated in judgements, and 'this would no longer be a disagreement within our area, but a disagreement about the area itself' (ibid. p. 136). What remain, therefore, are the conflicting orientations towards the truth that are seen as already inherent in language, and this takes one back to the issue of schematism and its relation to hermeneutics.

The section of *Friedrich Schleiermachers Dialektik* translated in this volume gives the most condensed account of Schleiermacher's fundamental assumptions about language. These should now make it clear why hermeneutics plays such an important role in his thought. Even though we 'cannot know whether the other person hears or sees as we do' (*Friedrich*

---

[31] Donald Davidson, *Inquiries into Truth and Interpretation*, Oxford 1984, pp. 196–7.

Schleiermachers Dialektik p. 371), we assume that knowledge is constituted in the same way in everyone for there to be knowledge at all. The key difference is between the organic function, which we can never prove to be the same in others and which involves different 'input' for each individual and each culture, and the intellectual function, which is assumed to structure the organic in the same way despite these differences. Whether what the intellectual function produces is in fact the same must be established by 'exchange of consciousness . . . this presupposes a mediating term, a universal and shared system of designation' (ibid. p. 372), namely language, which is made possible by schematism, the establishing of relative identities (ibid. p. 373).

In the *Ethics* Schleiermacher claims:

> Every person is a completed/closed-off (*abgeschlossen*) unity of consciousness. As far as reason produces cognition in a person it is, qua consciousness, only produced for this person. What is produced with the character of schematism is, though, posited as valid for everyone, and therefore being in one ['*Sein in Einem*' – by which he means individualised self-consciousness] does not correspond to its character [as schematism]. (*Ethik (1812–13)* p. 64)

Schleiermacher defines language as the 'system of organic movements which are simultaneously the expression and the sign of the acts of consciousness as cognitive faculty, seen in terms of the identity of schematism' (ibid. p. 65). The identity of knowledge articulated in language is, though, only a postulate which must be continually confirmed in real processes of communication. These processes take place in natural languages, so we cannot even maintain that all languages 'construct' in the same way, because we lack a 'universal language' (*Friedrich Schleiermachers Dialektik* p. 374). At the same time we must presuppose a universal 'innate' capacity for reason that is ultimately identical in all language users, for if this were not so, 'there would be no truth at all' (ibid. p. 375). This may sound 'Platonic', but what is being sought is an answer to how it is that we can translate between languages and cultures, and come to understand and agree with the 'discourse of the other'. A pure form of reason is, as we saw, never directly available, precisely because of the difference of languages. As such, 'pure reason' functions as a regulative idea, which has an *ethical* basis in the demand to acknowledge the other. In reality we continually seek the general truth via the particular, in an '*oscillation between the determinacy of the particular and the indeterminacy of the general image*' (ibid. p. 372), where the identity of the universal (which is unstable because of the role of the organic) is fixed by the sign that comes repeatedly to stand for it. The sign can, of course, be revealed as inadequate and change its sense or be replaced by another sign. For Schleiermacher the main source of such changes is the fact that we will each, because of the organic function, schematise in different ways, some of which may become universally accepted. The awareness of the different ways in which individuals schematise 'coincides with the attempt to resolve conflicting ideas. We must come to know the individual difference itself and thus remain with our task, namely the task of wishing to know' (ibid. p. 378). Schleiermacher does not, however, think 'knowing the individual' is 'intuitive' or 'empathetic', as many commentators suggest. Instead, access to individuality requires a *method* which will enable it to become accessible. It is the inherent generality of language resulting from the fact that any language involves only a finite number of elements for the articulation of a non-finitely differentiated world which makes such a method necessary.

These arguments should make it clear that Schleiermacher's underlying conception is primarily ethical, in a way which is echoed in those areas of contemporary philosophy which have abandoned the analytical project of a theory of meaning based on the kind of 'regulist' explanation used in the natural sciences.[32] The desire for agreement is founded both in the need to take account of the possibility of the individual being right against the collective, and in the need to transcend the individual which results from the realisation that truth cannot be merely individual. The locus of the ethical is therefore the relationship between language and the individual: 'thought is only ethical to the extent to which it is inscribed in language, from which teaching and learning develop', but, crucially, 'the common possession of language is only ethical to the extent to which individual consciousness develops by it' (*Ethik (1812–13)* p. 264).

The relationship between dialectic and hermeneutics is, therefore, based on the relationship between the universal aspect of language and the fact that individuals can imbue the same universally employed words with different senses. As such: 'Language only exists via thought, and vice versa; each can only complete itself via the other. The art of explication and translation [hermeneutics] dissolves language into thought; dialectic dissolves

---

[32] See, e.g., Robert Brandom, *Making it Explicit*, Cambridge, Mass., and London 1994.

thought into language.'[33] Hermeneutics moves towards the specific intentions of the individual in the contexts of their utterances, which are not exhausted by the possible general validity of those utterances; dialectic moves towards general validity, in the name of universal agreement:

> Looked at from the side of language the technical discipline of hermeneutics arises from the fact that every utterance can only be counted as an objective representation (*Darstellung*) to the extent to which it is taken from language and is to be grasped via language, but that on the other side the utterance can only arise as the action of an individual, and, as such, even if it is analytical in terms of its content, it still, in terms of its less essential elements, bears free synthesis [in the sense of individual judgement] within itself. The reconciliation (*Ausgleichung*) of both moments makes understanding and explication into an art [in the sense of that whose 'application is not also given with the rules']. (*Ethik (1812–13)* p. 116)

It is, then, 'clear that both [hermeneutics and dialectic] can only develop together with each other' (*Dialektik* (Jonas) p. 261), so that the division between apprehension of the individual and of the universal must be continually re-examined. The ongoing obligation to attend to the conflict between these two aspects of thought is the foundation not only of hermeneutics but also of dialectic, which both result from the inaccessibility of absolute knowledge.

The methodological divisions in the hermeneutics follow from this basic opposition: 'grammatical' interpretation, in which 'the person ... disappears and only appears as organ of language', is distinguished from 'technical interpretation', in which 'language with its determining power disappears and only appears as the organ of the person, in the service of their individuality'.[34] The crucial point is that successful understanding requires the completion of both kinds of interpretation. This is, though, necessarily an 'infinite task', for the kind of reasons which precluded absolute knowledge in the dialectic: the two sides cannot be reduced to each other from a finite perspective. There is, therefore, an ethical obligation to come to terms with the fact that we can never claim fully to understand the other, even though we always must understand in some measure if we can engage in dialogue or attempt to translate.

---

[33] Friedrich Schleiermacher, *Dialektik*, ed. L. Jonas, Berlin 1839, p. 261.
[34] Friedrich Schleiermacher, *Hermeneutik und Kritik*, ed. Manfred Frank, Frankfurt am Main 1977, p. 171.

This position contrasts sharply with some still dominant contemporary approaches to meaning. Analytical conceptions of linguistic meanings as 'abstract entities' existing independently of language users, and structuralist descriptions of language as a 'symbolic order' (Lacan) or 'general text' (Derrida) into which the individual is 'inserted' are often simply seen as the definitive counter to individualist intentionalism, in which words are supposed to gain their sense solely by the inner acts of the speaker. In the light of Schleiermacher's actual ideas about interpretation (rather than the ones attributed to him) both sides of this opposition involve a crucial failure to mediate between methodological extremes and thereby to appreciate the irreducible ethical dimension in all communication. The consequences of this failure are now apparent, for example, in the failure of the semiotic assumptions that underlie structuralism and post-structuralism to account for the functioning of everyday communication, in the failure of the 'semantic tradition' to arrive at convincing explanations of meaning,[35] and in the bankruptcy of purely intentionalist literary interpretation. Schleiermacher does not give final answers to philosophical questions about meaning: such final answers are, for him, an ethically based regulative idea, not something to be definitively articulated in a theory. His demonstration of the damaging results of concentration on one side of the opposition between the rule-bound and the spontaneous aspects of language is, though, now turning out to be a vital factor in the development of new philosophical approaches to language after the failure of the analytical 'linguistic turn'.

---

[35] As Putnam remarks in relation to Alfred Tarski's 'Convention T': 'The problem is not that we don't understand "Snow is white" . . . the problem is that we don't understand *what it is to understand* "Snow is white". *This* is the philosophical problem' (Putnam, Hilary, *Realism and Reason. Philosophical Papers Vol 3*, Cambridge 1983, p. 83). See also Charles Taylor, *Human Agency and Language*, Cambridge 1985, Chapters 9 and 10.

Chronology

	of Nature; Fichte publishes *The Science of Knowledge*; Friedrich Wilhelm III accedes to throne of Prussia; Schleiermacher becomes reformed chaplain at the Charité hospital in Berlin
1798–1800	Publication of the *Athenaeum*, vols. I–III, literary organ of the Berlin Romantics
1798	Schelling publishes *On the World Soul*
1799	Schleiermacher publishes first edition of *On Religion: Speeches to its Cultured Despisers*
1800	Friedrich Schlegel publishes *Lucinde*; Novalis (Friedrich von Hardenberg) publishes *Hymns to the Night*; Schleiermacher publishes *Soliloquies* and *Confidential Letters Concerning Friedrich Schlegel's Lucinde*
1803–6	Schleiermacher assumes post as university preacher at Halle
1804–28	Schleiermacher publishes German translation of Plato
1806	University of Halle overrun by Napoleon's troops; Schleiermacher publishes 2nd edition of *On Religion* and *The Celebration of Christmas: A Conversation*
1809	Founding of the University of Berlin by Wilhelm von Humboldt with Schleiermacher as secretary to the founding commission
1809–34	Schleiermacher at the University of Berlin as professor of theology, member of philosophical and historical sections of the Berlin Academy of Sciences
1810–34	Schleiermacher is preacher at the Holy Trinity Church in Berlin
1813	Birth of Kierkegaard in Copenhagen
1814	Death of Fichte at University of Berlin
1815	Congress of Vienna settles the Napoleonic wars
1818–32	Hegel at the University of Berlin
1821	Schleiermacher publishes 3rd edition of *On Religion* with "Explanations" attached to each speech
1821–2	Schleiermacher publishes 1st edition of his systematic theology, *The Christian Faith* [*Glaubenslehre*]
1830–1	Schleiermacher publishes 2nd edition of *The Christian Faith*
1832	Deaths of Goethe and Hegel
1834	Death of Schleiermacher, 6 February

Further reading

The standard new German edition of Schleiermacher's works will eventually be the *Kritische Gesamtausgabe* (a projected 40 volumes, in five divisions, Berlin, New York 1984–), which offers exemplary scholarly editions of the texts. As is the way with such editions, progress is necessarily slow, and the edition of the hermeneutics, which is being undertaken by Wolfgang Virmond, is still some years off. The first edition of Schleiermacher's works was the *Gesamtausgabe der Werke Schleiermachers in drei Abtheilungen* (Berlin 1838–64), in which the first division, where *Hermeneutics and Criticism* was located, contained the theological works, the second contained the sermons, and the third the philosophical works. The only other significant edition of hermeneutic texts is *F. Schleiermacher: Hermeneutik. Nach den Handschriften neu herausgegeben und eingeleitet von Heinz Kimmerle* (Heidelberg 1959, second, revised edition Heidelberg 1974), which was translated as: *Hermeneutics: The Handwritten Manuscripts* by James Duke and Jack Forstman (Missoula, Mont. 1977). Terrence Tice is preparing a different version from the present translation of some of *Hermeneutics and Criticism*, but, before the present edition and Tice's edition, Duke and Forstman's translation was the only substantial text from Schleiermacher's work on hermeneutics readily available in English.

Until very recently the secondary literature in English on the hermeneutics was either philosophically deficient, for lack of attention to the place of the hermeneutics in Schleiermacher's wider project, or simply beholden to the misleading accounts of Schleiermacher which began to develop with Dilthey and were rendered canonical by Gadamer's *Truth and Method*. It is only recent work that takes account of the work of Manfred Frank in particular (see below) which manages to avoid Dilthey's and Gadamer's distortions. Andrew Bowie's *Aesthetics and Subjectivity. From Kant to Nietzsche* (Manchester 1993), and *From Romanticism to Critical Theory. The Philosophy of German Literary Theory* (London 1997) both contain a substantial chapter on Schleiermacher which attempts to correct the dominant view in the light of the work of Frank and others; Bowie's 'The Meaning of the Hermeneutic Tradition in Contemporary Philosophy' in ed. A. O'Hear, *'Verstehen' and Humane Understanding*, Royal Institute of Philosophy Lectures (Cambridge 1996), pp. 121–44 uses Schleiermacher's hermeneutics against analytical semantics, suggesting ways it connects to the work of Donald Davidson, Robert Brandom and others. Jean Grondin, *Introduction to Philosophical Hermeneutics* (Yale 1994) gives a very useful condensed account of Schleiermacher in an outstanding volume on the history and theory of hermeneutics as a whole (which also contains an excellent bibliography); another useful general work is Richard E. Palmer, *Hermeneutics. Interpretation Theory in Schleiermacher, Dilthey, Heidegger and Gadamer* (Evanston 1969). Stephen Prickett, *Origins of Narrative. The Romantic Appropriation of the Bible* (Cambridge 1996) makes interesting connections between the hermeneutics and English Romanticism; and Tilottama Rajan, *The Supplement of Reading: Figures of Understanding in Romantic Theory and Practice* (Ithaca 1990) relates Schleiermacher to contemporary theoretical issues. Terrence Tice has provided a thorough *Schleiermacher Bibliography* (Princeton 1966, updated Princeton 1985).

Without doubt the best account of Schleiermacher's philosophy, and the place of the hermeneutics within it, is Christian Berner, *La philosophie de Schleiermacher* (Paris 1995), of which an English translation is in preparation. Gunter Scholtz's *Die Philosophie Schleiermachers* (Darmstadt 1984) is an indispensable guide both to the philosophy as a whole, and to the complex history of its reception. Manfred Frank's controversial *Das Individuelle-Allgemeine. Textstrukturierung und -interpretation nach Schleiermacher* (Frankfurt am Main 1977), and his introduction to his edition of *Hermeneutik und Kritik* (Frankfurt am Main 1977) brought Schleiermacher into contemporary philosophical debate, particularly on account of their refutation of Gadamer's view and of their connection of Schleiermacher to structuralism and post-structuralism. Frank's *Das Sagbare und das Unsagbare* (Frankfurt am Main 1988) made clear just how productive Schleiermacher's philosophy could be made for a whole series of issues in contemporary philosophy. Some of the essays in this volume, including an essay on Schleiermacher's hermeneutics are included in ed. Andrew Bowie, *Manfred Frank, The Subject and the Text. Essays in Literary Theory and Philosophy* (Cambridge 1997). The German literature on Schleiermacher's hermeneutics is very extensive, so the following must serve as a sample of the accounts which have helped set the main terms of the debate: ed. Hendrik Birus, *Hermeneutische Positionen. Schleiermacher – Dilthey – Heidegger – Gadamer* (Göttingen 1982); Wilhelm Dilthey, 'Die Entstehung der Hermeneutik' in *Gesammelte Schriften* Vol. 5 (Stuttgart, Göttingen 1964), pp. 317–38, and *Leben Schleiermachers* Vol. 1, ed. M. Redeker (Berlin 1970), Vol. 2, ed. M. Redeker (Berlin 1966); Hans-Georg Gadamer, *Wahrheit und Methode* (Tübingen 1975); Eilert Herms, *Herkunft, Entfaltung und erste Gestalt des Systems der Wissenschaften bei Schleiermacher* (Gütersloh 1974); Jochen Hörisch, *Die Wut des Verstehens* (Frankfurt am Main 1988); Heinz Kimmerle, *Die Hermeneutik Schleiermachers im Zusammenhang seines spekulativen Denkens* (Dissertation Heidelberg 1957); Hermann Patsch, 'Friedrich Schlegels "Philosophie der Philologie" und Schleiermachers frühe Entwürfe zur Hermeneutik' in *Zeitschrift für Theologie und Kirche* lxiii (1966), pp. 434–72; Reinhold Rieger, *Interpretation und Wissen. Zur philosophischen Begründung der Hermeneutik bei Friedrich Schleiermacher* (Berlin, New York 1988); Beate Rössler, *Die Theorie des Verstehens in Sprachanalyse und Hermeneutik* (Berlin 1990); Harald Schnur, *Schleiermachers Hermeneutik und ihre Vorgeschichte im 18. Jahrhundert* (Stuttgart, Weimar 1994); Peter Szondi, 'Schleiermachers Hermeneutik heute', in *Sprache im technischen Zeitalter* lviii (1976), pp. 95–111.

On Schleiermacher's life, see Dilthey, *Leben Schleiermachers* (which does not, though, cover Schleiermacher's whole career); B. A. Gerrish, *A Prince of the Church: Schleiermacher and the Beginnings of Modern Theology*; Friedrich Wilhelm Kanzenbach, *Friedrich Daniel Ernst Schleiermacher* (Hamburg 1989); Martin Redeker, *Schleiermacher: Life and Thought* (Philadelphia 1973); and Stephen Sykes, *Friedrich Schleiermacher* (Richmond, Va. 1971).

Note on the text and the translation

The continuing dominance of the standard misconception of Schleiermacher's hermeneutics in texts about hermeneutics is perhaps not surprising, given that one of its main sources is precisely the book which has done the most to put hermeneutics at the centre of contemporary philosophical debate, Hans-Georg Gadamer's *Truth and Method*. The reasons for the continuing influence of mistaken views of Schleiermacher, like Gadamer's, are complex, but nearly all relate to a more widespread failure adequately to engage with the philosophy of early German Romanticism, a failure which relates both to historical changes in the perception of the history of philosophy and to the fact that some of the relevant texts have not been readily accessible. The aim of the present edition is, then, to make some of the key texts on hermeneutics by Schleiermacher available in English to a general audience.

Hermeneutics and Criticism, with Particular Reference to the New Testament was first published in the edition of Dr Friedrich Lücke, four years after Schleiermacher's death, by G. Reimer, Berlin, in 1838, as Volume 7 of the First Division, *On Theology*, of Schleiermacher's *Complete Works*. This text did not appear again in print until Manfred Frank published most of it, along with a selection of other texts by Schleiermacher on hermeneutics from a variety of different sources, in 1977 (*Hermeneutik und Kritik*, Frankfurt am Main). Frank omitted the majority of the passages directly referring to the New Testament in order to be able to highlight the more philosophical aspects of Schleiermacher's hermeneutics, particularly those relating to issues in literary theory, in a text whose length would not be too taxing for the more general reader. In the present translation I have to some extent followed Frank's procedure and his choice of passages to omit.

However, in order to retain a clearer sense of the overall aims of the text, and to increase its value to theologians, I have both included significantly more of the material relating to the New Testament and given my own paraphrases of the contents of all omitted passages. Given that my expertise in German philosophy totally outstrips my expertise in Biblical scholarship, I have, though, made no attempt to point out the ways in which Schleiermacher's substantive points about the Bible have been overtaken by subsequent scholarship. This would have led to a very unwieldy textual apparatus for a text whose methodological precepts often remain valid, even though their application to actual texts by their author is sometimes mistaken.

Frank interpolates, as I also do, a manuscript on 'Technical Interpretation' taken from the edition of *F. Schleiermacher: Hermeneutik. Nach den Handschriften neu herausgegeben und eingeleitet von Heinz Kimmerle* (Heidelberg 1959).[1] As Frank suggests, useful as this edition is, the fact that it consists solely of Schleiermacher's notes for his own use for lectures makes it pretty inaccessible to the unprepared reader. Lücke's edition, on the other hand, though depending in part on others' notes taken at Schleiermacher's lectures, reads coherently and is, in the main, fairly accessible and comprehensive: it is largely based on Schleiermacher's manuscripts from 1819 that contain marginalia from 1828 and 1832–3. Lücke indicates the sources of his text in footnotes reproduced in the translation, and Wolfgang Virmond, who is producing the edited texts of the hermeneutics for the *Friedrich Schleiermacher Kritische Gesamtausgabe*, which will not appear for some years yet, regards it as a more than passable edition of most of the major aspects of Schleiermacher's mature hermeneutics. It is also, of course, the main text by Schleiermacher on hermeneutics that was actually available to readers during the history of modern hermeneutics.[2] One of the most notable results of Virmond's research for the critical edition is the revelation that the text on 'Technical Interpretation', which was generally assumed to have been a late text (and which Schleiermacher re-used for a lecture in 1832–3), is actually almost certainly from the *earliest* manuscript on hermeneutics, of 1805, suggesting a much greater continuity in Schleiermacher's conception than had hitherto been assumed. The

---

[1] This has been translated as: *Hermeneutics: The Handwritten Manuscripts* by James Duke and Jack Forstman (Missoula, Mont. 1977), but the translation in this volume is my own.
[2] For details of the latest research on the dating and status of Schleiermacher's texts on hermeneutics, see Virmond's indispensable 'Neue Textgrundlagen zu Schleiermachers früher Hermeneutik', *Schleiermacher-Archiv Band 1*, pp. 575–90 (Berlin, New York 1985).

manuscript of another complete text translated here, the *General Hermeneutics* of 1809–10, was lost by Schleiermacher, but a reliable copy was made of it in 1811 by August Twesten; it was published for the first time by Wolfgang Virmond, *Schleiermacher-Archiv Band 1*, pp. 1,271–310 (Berlin, New York 1985). Its relatively early date enables one to compare Schleiermacher's conceptions of hermeneutics from differing periods: a systematic account of the continuities and changes will, though, only be possible when the volume of the *Kritische Gesamtausgabe* appears. The final text, an extract from Schleiermacher's *Dialectic* of 1822 on language and schematism, is given as the most concise version of his basic conception of language.

My aim in the translation has been to be as literal as possible, while attempting to render the text into reasonably acceptable English. Schleiermacher poses certain problems both for translators and readers because he does not always sustain a consistent terminology. It is therefore important to follow the advice on this issue offered in *Hermeneutics and Criticism* itself, which warns against assuming that, just because one sense of a word seems to have been clearly established in some contexts, the sense will remain the same in other contexts. This even applies to the title, which I have rendered as *Hermeneutics and Criticism*, even though certain parts of the text, especially those which connect to Schleiermacher's *Dialectic*, make *Hermeneutics and Critique* more appropriate. I decided in favour of the former title because of the weight given in the last part of the text to the specific issue of textual criticism. In certain cases I have indicated in footnotes where a key problem-term is being employed, particularly with regard to words to do with '*Kunst*', which, characteristically for the time, oscillate in meaning between 'technique' or 'method', and 'art'. This apparently lax usage is not a failing on Schleiermacher's part because his theory itself depends upon the idea that the border between the rule-bound and the inventive must continually be re-negotiated. Similar problems arise over the term '*Anschauung*', and the related verb '*anschauen*'. Here I have often used the questionable *terminus technicus* 'intuition', which is familiar from translations of Kant, but sometimes I have used other terms closer to the everyday sense, which relates to 'looking at'. The point is that the word is used by Schleiermacher for all kinds of contact between 'mind' and its 'object', an object which can, for example, include itself, the meaning of a word, or what is given from the world. The notional end points of this contact are pure receptivity and pure spontaneity, which, as Schleiermacher makes clear, he thinks are merely regulative ideas that are never actually present in their pure form. An analogous issue arises over the word '*Gegenstand*'; 'object', which, informatively, could very often also be appropriately translated as 'subject', in the sense of 'the subject we will be discussing today' that is the 'object' of our conversation. I have in this case consistently used 'object', as that which 'stands against' its subject–other, which is the way the word is frequently used in the philosophy of the period. Otherwise, assuming the translation is at least initially comprehensible, I hope the reader will agree that I have attempted to follow Schleiermacher's own approach to translation, by combining the 'comparative' need to understand via the author's contexts with my own attempts, by looking for consistency of thought, to 'divine' the specific senses that cannot be derived solely from the known contexts.

My thanks go to Herr Virmond for providing me with a copy of the *General Hermeneutics*, and for his helpful advice on other scholarly matters, and, once more, to Manfred Frank, who first aroused my interest in Schleiermacher and who has been a continuing source of encouragement and inspiration to me for many years. Initial work for this project was done with the invaluable assistance of the Alexander von Humboldt Stiftung and of the British Academy Research Leave Scheme. Karl Ameriks suggested I translate and edit a text for the *Texts in the History of Philosophy* series and provided exemplary and splendidly prompt editorial advice. Anna Bristow at Anglia and my brother Angus helped me with my Latin and Greek (though any errors are my responsibility alone), and Hilary Gaskin at Cambridge University Press was unfailingly helpful at all stages of the proceedings.

Hermeneutics and Criticism

General introduction[1]

1. Hermeneutics and criticism, both philological disciplines, both theories[a] belong together, because the practice of one presupposes the other. The former is generally the art[2] of understanding particularly the written discourse[3] of another person correctly, the latter the art of judging correctly and establishing the authenticity of texts and parts of texts from adequate evidence and data. Because criticism can only recognise the weight to be attached to evidence in its relationship to the piece of writing or the part of the text in question after an appropriate correct understanding of the latter, the practice of criticism presupposes hermeneutics. On the other hand, given that explication[4] can only be sure of its establishing of meaning if the

---

[1] Summarised from various of Schleiermacher's marginalia in his notebook of 1828 and several transcripts of lectures from differing years.

[2] *Translator's note*: For Schleiermacher 'art' is any activity that relies on rules, for which there can be no rules for the applying of those rules. Schleiermacher uses 'art' (*Kunst*) both in the sense of the Greek '*techne*', meaning ability, capacity, and in a sense related to the new aesthetic notion, primarily associated with Kant, that something cannot be understood as *art* merely via the rules of the particular form of articulation. The differing senses of the word are decisive for the whole of his hermeneutics. It is vital to keep this in mind for the understanding of the rest of the text: I shall generally employ the word 'art' in translating all the words Schleiermacher uses which have to do with the '*Kunst*' of interpretation, as there is no obvious other English word to cover what he means.

[3] *Translator's note*: I shall often use the rather artificial terms 'discourse', or 'utterance' for '*Rede*', rather than referring to 'speech', because Schleiermacher often uses the term '*Rede*' for both spoken and written language, and there is no obvious English equivalent which keeps this ambiguity. At other times I shall use 'speech', or other terms, depending upon the context: where there is any significant ambiguity I will specify the German.

[4] *Translator's note*: The German is '*Auslegung*', and I shall generally use the English 'explication' for this word, as its links to 'unfolding' bring it closer to the German sense of 'laying out' the meaning of the text. This also differentiates it from '*Interpretation*', which Schleiermacher sometimes uses in different contexts.

[a] *Kunstlehren*, literally 'theories of the art of'.

3

authenticity of the text or part of the text can be presupposed, then the practice of hermeneutics presupposes criticism.

Hermeneutics is rightly put first because it is also necessary when criticism hardly takes place at all, essentially because criticism should come to an end [i.e. once the authenticity of the text is established], but hermeneutics should not.

2. In the same way as hermeneutics and criticism belong together, so too do they both belong together with grammar. Fr. A. Wolf and Ast already put all three together as philological disciplines, the former as philological preparatory sciences, the latter as an appendix to philology. Both, however, regard them in a too specialised manner, only in relation to classical languages of antiquity. The relationship of these three disciplines is rather one which is perennially valid, they are even inter-related by mutual determination when the language has not yet died out and still lacks a history of literature. Because of their inter-relatedness with each other the beginning of each individual discipline is admittedly difficult, although even children learn the three disciplines together in living communication. Hermeneutics and criticism can only be carried out with the help of grammar and they depend on grammar. But grammar can be established only by means of hermeneutics and criticism, if it does not wish to mix up the worst use of language with classical use, and mix up general rules of language with individual peculiarities of language. The complete solution of this three-fold task is only possible in an approximate manner when they are linked together, during a philologically developed era, and when the task is carried out by exemplary philologists.[5]

[5] *Translator's note*: In the text that follows the numbered passages which follow the italicised main principles generally refer directly back to the italicised passages, so that an apparently unexplained 'it' will usually refer to the activity discussed in the main principle, such as the need for a cursory reading of the whole text before engaging in detailed interpretation. In some of the more difficult cases I have made it clear what is being referred to, in more obvious cases I have not done so.

Hermeneutics

Introduction

1. Hermeneutics as the art of understanding *does not yet exist* in a general manner, *there are instead only several forms* of specific hermeneutics.

1. Only the art of *understanding*, not the *presentation* of understanding as well.[1] This would only be a special part of the art of speaking and writing, which could only depend on the general principles.

In[2] terms of the well-known etymology hermeneutics can be regarded as a name which is not yet fixed in a scientific manner: a) the art of presenting one's thoughts correctly, b) the art of communicating someone else's utterance to a third person, c) the art of understanding another person's utterance correctly. The scientific concept refers to the third of these as the mediator between the first and the second.

2. But also not only [understanding] of difficult passages in foreign languages. Familiarity with the object and the language are instead presupposed.

---

[1] *Editor's note (Lücke)*: Against the dominant definition since [J.A.] Ernesti, *Institutio interpretis Novi Testamenti*, ed. Ammon, [Leipzig 1764], pp. 7 and 8: 'Est autem interpretatio facultas *docendi*, quae cujusque orationi sententia subjecta sit, seu, efficiendi, ut alter cogitet eadem cum scriptore quoque. – Interpretatio igitur omnis duabus rebus continentur, sententiarum (idearum) verbis subjectarum intellectu, earumque idonea *explicatione*. Unde in bono interprete esse debet, subtilitas intelligendi et subtilitas explicandi.' [But interpretation is the ability to *teach*, whether the meaning is articulated in speech or actions, so that the other person may think the same as the writer. – All interpretation, therefore, consists of two things, understanding of the meanings (ideas) articulated in the words and the proper *explication* of them. Whence in a good interpreter there must be delicacy of understanding and delicacy of explication.] Earlier J. Jac. Rambach, *Institutiones hermeneuticae sacrae*, [Jena 1723] p. 2 added a third, the sapienter applicare [wisdom of application] to this, which recent authors are unfortunately stressing once again.

[2] *Translator's note*: From the lecture of 1826. As opposed to Schleiermacher's hand-written manuscripts the additions and explanations from the notes taken at lectures are printed in a smaller font.

If both are [presupposed] then passages become difficult only because one has also not understood the more easy passages. Only an artistic[a] under-standing continually accompanies speech and writing.

3. It has usually been thought that for the general principles one can rely on healthy common sense. But in that case one can rely on healthy feeling for the particular principles as well.[3]

2. It is difficult adequately to situate general hermeneutics.

1. For a time it was admittedly treated as an appendix to logic, but when everything to do with application was given up in logic, this had to cease as well. The philosopher has no inclination, as philosopher, to establish this theory, because he rarely wants to understand, but himself believes he is necessarily understood.

2. Philology has also become something positive via our history. This is why its manner of treating hermeneutics is only a collection of observations.

Addition.[4] Special hermeneutics, both as a genre and in terms of lan-guage, is always only a collection of observations and does not fulfil any sci-entific demands. To carry out understanding without consciousness (of the rules) and only to have recourse in particular cases to rules, is also an uneven procedure. One must, if one cannot give up either of them, com-bine these two points of view with each other. This happens via a twofold experience. 1) Even where we think we can proceed in a manner which is most free of art [i.e. solely via the following of rules], often unexpected dif-ficulties arise, the bases for the solution of which must lie in the earlier point of view [i.e. where there is no consciousness of rules]. We are therefore always obliged to pay attention to what can become the basis of a solution. 2) If we always proceed in an artistic manner, then we in the last analysis come anyway to an unconscious application of the rules without having left the artistic behind.

---

[3] *Editor's note (Lücke):* In the lectures on hermeneutics last held in the winter of 1832–3 Schleiermacher sought to achieve the concept and necessity of general hermeneutics in a dialectical manner by a cri-tique of the to some extent self-contradictory views, which were limited to the classical realm, of F. A. Wolf in the *Darstellung der Altertumswissenschaft* in the *Museum der Altertumswissenschaft*, Vol. 1, pp. 1–145, and Fr. Ast in the *Grundriß der Philologie*, Landshut 1808, 8.

But as everything which he says about this can be read in a much more developed version in the two academic articles on the 'Concept of Hermeneutics in relation to F. A. Wolf's Indications and Ast's Textbook' we have rightly refrained, with a few exceptions, from including here the incom-plete spoken presentation from the books of notes taken at lectures.

[4] Marginalia of 1828.

[a] *kunstmäßiges.*

3. Just as the art of speaking and understanding stand opposite each other (and correspond to each other), and speaking is only the external side of thought, so hermeneutics is to be thought of as connected to art and is therefore philosophical. In such a manner, though, that the art of explication depends on the composition and presupposes it. The parallelism consists, however, in the fact that where speech is without art, no art is needed to understand it [i.e. understanding is wholly rule-bound].

4. Speech is the mediation of the communal nature of thought, and this explains the belonging together of rhetoric and hermeneutics and their common relationship to dialectics.

1. Speech is admittedly also mediation of thought for the individual. Thought is prepared by inner discourse, and to this extent discourse is only the thought itself which has come into existence. But if the thinker finds it necessary to fix the thought for himself, then the art of discourse arises as well, the transformation of the original thought, and then explication also becomes necessary.

2. The belonging together of hermeneutics and rhetoric consists in the fact that every act of understanding is the inversion of a speech-act,[b] during which the thought which was the basis of the speech must become conscious.

3. The dependence of both [hermeneutics and rhetoric] on dialectics consists in the fact that development of all knowledge is dependent on both (speech and understanding).

Addition.[5] General hermeneutics therefore belongs together both with criticism and with grammar.[6] But as there is neither communication of knowledge, nor any fixing of knowledge without these three, and as at the same time all correct thought is directed to correct speech, then all three are also to be precisely connected with dialectics.

The[7] belonging together of hermeneutics and grammar depends upon the fact that each utterance is grasped only via the presupposition of the understanding of

---

[5] Marginalia of 1828.

[6] *Translator's note*: Lücke here interposes a misleading footnote, suggesting that Schleiermacher subsumes rhetoric into grammar, which I omit. Manfred Frank has pointed out that Schleiermacher in fact makes a strictly functional distinction between rhetoric as the discipline concerned with the spoken word and grammar as the discipline concerned with language as a system of rules.

[7] *Editor's note (Lücke)*: From the lecture of 1832. From now on the date of the lecture will only be noted if it is not this lecture.

[b] *Akt des Redens.*

language. – Both are concerned with language. This leads to the unity of speech and thought; language is the manner in which thought is real. For there are no thoughts without speech. The speaking of the words relates solely to the presence of another person, and to this extent is contingent. But no one can think without words. Without words the thought is not yet completed and clear. Now as hermeneutics is supposed to lead to the understanding of the thought-content, but the thought-content is only real via language, hermeneutics depends on grammar as knowledge of the language. If we now look at thought in the act of communication through language, which is precisely the mediation for the shared nature of thought, then this has no other tendency than to produce knowledge as something which is common to all. In this way the common relationship of grammar and hermeneutics to dialectic, as the science of the unity of knowledge, results. – Every utterance can, further, only be understood via the knowledge of the whole of the historical life to which it belongs, or via the history which is relevant for it. The science of history, though, is ethics. But language also has a natural side; the differences of the human spirit are also determined by the physical aspect of humankind and by the planet. And so hermeneutics is not just rooted in ethics but also in physics. Ethics and physics lead, however, back again to dialectic, as the science of the unity of knowledge.

5. As every utterance has a dual relationship, to the totality of language and to the whole thought of its originator, then all understanding also consists of the two moments, of understanding the utterance as derived from language, and as a fact in the thinker.

1. Every utterance presupposes a given language. One can admittedly also invert this, not only for the absolutely first utterance, but also for the whole of the utterance, because language comes into being through utterance; but communication necessarily presupposes the shared nature of the language, thus also a certain acquaintance with the language. If something comes between the immediate utterance and communication, so that the art of discourse begins, then this rests in part on the worry that something might be unfamiliar to the listener in our use of language.

2. Every utterance depends upon previous thinking. One can also invert this, but in relation to communication it remains true, because the art of understanding only begins with advanced thought.

3. According to this every person is on the one hand a location in which a given language forms itself in an individual manner, on the other their discourse can only be understood via the totality of the language. But then the person is also a spirit which continually develops, and their

discourse is only one act of this spirit in connection with the other acts.[8]

The individual is determined in his thought by the (common) language and can think only the thoughts which already have their designation in his language.[9] Another, new thought could not be communicated if it were not related to relationships[10] which already exist in the language. This is based on the fact that thinking is an inner speaking. But from this one can also positively conclude that language determines the progress of the individual in thought. For language is not just a complex of single representations, but also a system of the relatedness of representations. For they are brought into connection by the form of the words. Every complex word is a relation, in which every pre- and suffix has an individual significance (modification). But the system of modification is different in every language. If we objectify the language, then we find that all speech-acts are only a way in which the language appears in its individual nature, and every individual is only a location in which the language appears, so that we then direct our attention in relation to significant writers to their language and see a difference of style in them. – In the same way every utterance is to be understood only via the whole life to which it belongs, i.e., because every utterance can only be recognised as a moment of the life of the language-user in the determinedness of all the moments of their life, and this only from the totality of their environments, via which their development and continued existence are determined, every language-user can only be understood via their nationality and their era.

6. *Understanding is only a being-in-one-another of these two moments (of the grammatical and psychological).*

1. The utterance is not even understood as an act[c] of the mind if it is not understood as a linguistic designation, because the innateness of language modifies the mind.

2. The utterance is also not understood as a modification of language if it is not also understood as an act of the mind, because the ground of all influence of the individual lies in the mind, which itself develops by utterance.

---

[8] *Translator's note*: Schleiermacher often uses *Tatsache* and *Tat* interchangeably, in order to stress the aspect of doing in a fact concerning a person.

[9] *Translator's note*: I use the masculine third-person pronoun where Schleiermacher uses the masculine gender – here '*der Einzelne*' – even though the reference is clearly not only to the masculine gender.

[10] *Translator's note*: *Beziehungen*, though the context suggests that Schleiermacher may have actually meant '*Bezeichnungen*', 'designations'.

[c] *Tatsache*.

✱ *7. Both are completely equal, and it would be wrong to call grammatical interpretation the lower and psychological interpretation the higher.*

1. Psychological interpretation is the higher when one regards language only as the means whereby the individual communicates his thoughts; grammatical interpretation is in this case just the removal of passing difficulties.

2. Grammatical interpretation is the higher when one looks at language to the extent to which it determines the thought of all individuals, but one looks at the individual person only as the location of language and his utterance only as that in which language reveals itself. Then the psychological is completely subordinated, like the existence of the individual person.

3. From this duality complete equality follows as a matter of course.

In relation to criticism we find the use of the terms higher and lower criticism. Does this difference also occur in the area of hermeneutics? But which of the two sides should be subordinated? The business of understanding an utterance in relation to language can to a certain extent be mechanised, thus be reduced to a calculus. For if difficulties are present these can be regarded as unknown quantities. The issue becomes mathematical, is therefore mechanised, because I have reduced it to a calculus. Should this, as a mechanical art, be the lower interpretation, and the aspect based on the intuition[d] of living beings be the higher because individualities cannot be rendered numerical? But as the individual appears from the grammatical side as the location where language shows itself to be alive, then the psychological appears subordinated; his thought is determined by language and he by his thought. The task of understanding his utterance therefore includes both in itself, but the understanding of language appears to be higher. But if one now regards language as originating every time in particular speech-acts, then it also, because it goes back to individuality, cannot be subordinated to calculation; the language itself is an individual in relation to others and the understanding of the language, in the perspective of the particular mind of the speaker is an art like that other side, therefore is not something mechanical, therefore both sides are equal. – But this equality is again to be limited in relation to the particular task. Both sides are not equal in every particular task, neither in relation to what is achieved in each, nor in what is demanded. There are texts in which one of the sides, one of the interests predominates, and others where the opposite is the case. In one text one of the sides of the task will be able to be completely accomplished, the other not at all. One finds, for example, a fragment by an unknown author. There one can well recognise the period and place of the text by the language. But only if one is certain of the author via the language can the other task, the psychological, begin.

[d] *Anschauung.*

8. The absolute solution of the task is when each side is dealt with on its own in such a way that dealing with the other side produces no change in the result, or, when each side, dealt with on its own, completely replaces the other, but the other must equally be dealt with on its own.

1. This duality is necessary if each side replaces the other because of § 6 [above].

2. But each is only complete if it makes the other superfluous and makes a contribution to constructing the other side, precisely because language can only be learned by understanding utterances, and the inner constitution of a person, together with the way the outer world affects them can only be understood via their utterances.

9. Explication (das Auslegen) is an art.

1. Each side on its own. For in every case there is construction of something finitely determinate from the infinite indeterminate. Language is infinite because each element is determinable in a particular manner via the rest of the elements. But this is just as much the case in relation to the psychological side. For every intuition of an individual is infinite. And the effects on people from the outside world are also something which gradually diminishes to the point of the infinitely distant. Such a construction cannot be given by rules which would carry the certainty of their application within themselves.

2. For the grammatical side to be completed on its own there would have to be a complete knowledge of the language, in the other case [the psychological] a complete knowledge of the person. As there can never be either of these, one must move from one to the other, and no rules can be given for how this is to be done.

The complete task of hermeneutics is to be regarded as a work of art, but not as if carrying it out resulted in a work of art, but in such a way that the activity only bears the *character* of art in itself, because the application is not also given with the rules, i.e. cannot be mechanised.

10. The successful practice of the art depends on the talent for language and the talent for knowledge of individual people.

1. By the former we do not mean the ease of learning foreign languages, the difference between mother tongue and foreign tongue does not matter for the moment, – but rather the living awareness of language, the sense of analogy and difference, etc. One might think that in this way rhetoric

(grammar) and hermeneutics would always have to be together. But in the same way as hermeneutics demands another talent, so for its part does rhetoric (grammar), and they do not both demand the same talent. The talent for language is admittedly common to both, but the hermeneutic direction develops it differently from the rhetorical (grammatical).[11]

2. The knowledge of people here is primarily of the subjective element in the combination of thoughts. For this reason hermeneutics and artistic presentation of a person are just as little always together. But a large number of hermeneutic mistakes are based on the lack of this talent (of the artistic presentation of a person) or on its application [in a specific real case].

3. To the extent that these talents (to a certain extent) are universal gifts of nature, hermeneutics is also a universal activity. To the extent to which someone is lacking on one side he is indeed deficient, and the other side [where he is not deficient] can only be useful to him for choosing correctly what others give him on the first side.

Addition.[12] The *predominant* talent is not only required because of the more difficult cases, but also in order never to remain just with the immediate purpose (of the single talent), but rather always to pursue the goal of both main directions, cf. § 8 and 9.

The talent necessary for the art of hermeneutics is dual, and we have up to now not yet been able to grasp this duality in a concept. If we could completely reconstruct every language in its particular uniqueness and could understand the individual via language as we could understand language via the individual, then the talent could be reduced into one talent. But given that research into language and the grasping of the individual cannot yet do this, we must still assume *two* talents, as different talents. – The talent for language is itself a dual talent. The intercourse of people begins with the mother tongue but can also extend to another tongue. Therein lies the duality of the talent for language. The comparative grasping of languages in their differences, the extensive talent for language, is different from the penetration into the interior of language in relation to thought, the intensive talent for language. This is the talent of the real researcher into language. Both are necessary, but almost never united in one and the same subject, they must therefore mutually complement each other in different subjects. The talent for the knowledge of people also divides into two. Many people can easily grasp the particularities of other people comparatively via their differences. This (extensive) talent can easily

---

[11] *Translator's note*: cf. note 6 above: the three interpolations of 'grammar' in this section, which are by Lücke, are based on his mistaken subsumption of rhetoric into grammar, and can be ignored.

[12] Marginalia of 1828.

re-, indeed *pre*-construct the way of behaving of other people. But the understanding of the individual meaning of a person and of their particularities in relation to the concept of a human being is a different talent. This (the intensive talent)[13] goes deep. Both are necessary, but rarely combined, and must therefore mutually complement each other.

11. Not all discourse is the object of the art of explication to the same extent. Some utterances have a value of zero, others have an absolute value; most discourse lies between these two points.

1. Something has a value of zero if it possesses interest neither as a deed nor has significance for language. People talk because language only sustains itself in continual repetition. What only repeats what is already there is nothing in itself. Conversations about the weather. But this zero is not absolute nothing, but only a minimum. For what is significant develops itself via it.

The minimum is common discourse in business matters and in habitual conversation in everyday life.

2. On each side there is a maximum: on the grammatical side this is what is most productive and the least repetitious, the *classical*. On the psychological side this is what is most individual and the least common, the *original*. What is absolute is, however, only the identity of the two, the element of *genius*[14] or that which forms the primary image[e] for language in the production of thought.

3. The classical must not, though, be temporary, but must determine subsequent products. The original must also do exactly this. But even the absolute (the maximum)[15] should not be free from having been determined by what is earlier and more universal.

Addition.[16] What lies between the minimum and the maximum approximates to one of the two; a) to the common, [approximates] the relative lack of content, and the charming presentation, b) to the genial, [approximates] the classical in language, which does not, though, need to be original, and the originality in the linking (of thoughts) which does not, though, need to be classical.[17]

---

[13] Added by Lücke.
[14] *Translator's note*: The sense is clearer if one remembers that Kant refers to 'genius' as the talent which 'gives the rule to art', and is therefore not dependent upon the existing rules.
[15] Added by Lücke.   [16] Marginalia of 1828.
[17] Added by Lücke: further such additions in brackets will not be noted.

[e] *das Genialische oder Urbildliche.*

Cicero is classical, but not original; the German Hamann original, but not classical. – Are both sides of the hermeneutic procedure to be used equally in all cases? If we have a classical writer with no originality, the psychological procedure can lack any appeal, and also not be necessary; but his individuality of language must be observed on its own. A non-classical writer uses more and less bold combinations in language, and here the understanding of the expressions must be engaged with from the psychological side, but not from the side of language.

12. If both sides (of interpretation, the grammatical and the psychological) are to be applied in all cases, then they are always in a different relationship to each other.

1. This already follows from the fact that what is grammatically insignificant need not also be psychologically insignificant, and vice versa; what is significant does not, therefore, also develop equally on both sides from everything insignificant.

2. The minimum of psychological interpretation is applied when the objectivity of the matter in question predominates. (To this) belongs pure history, primarily in the details, for the whole view is always subjectively affected. Epic. Business dealings, which wish to become history. Didactic material of a strict form in every area. In all these cases the subjective is not to be applied as a moment of explication, but becomes the result of the explication. The minimum of grammatical together with the maximum of psychological explication in letters, if they are authentic. Overriding of the didactic and the historical in these. Lyric. Polemic.

Addition.[18] The hermeneutic rules must be more a method of pre-empting difficulties than observations for dissolving those difficulties.

The hermeneutic achievements of successful workers (in the details) must be considered. However, the theoretical procedure does not engage with the details, but is concerned with the discovering of the identity of the language with the thought. – The *prevention* of difficulties in the reconstruction of the utterance and the sequence of thoughts is the task of hermeneutics. But the task is not to be accomplished in this general manner. For the productions of a foreign language are always fragmentary for us. The extent of what is available to us is admittedly different in different languages. But we lack the total production of language to a greater or lesser extent, e.g. in Greek or Hebrew. No language is completely

---

[18] Marginalia of 1832.

present to us, not even our own mother tongue. For this reason we must construct the propositions of hermeneutic theory in such a way that they do not resolve particular difficulties, but so that they are ongoing instructions for the procedure, and always only have to do with the task in general. The difficulties are then regarded as exceptions and require another procedure. In this we ask only about the completion of what is lacking, from which the difficulties arise, not about the (general) type. This will be the same in both directions (the grammatical and the psychological).

13. There is no other multiplicity in the method of explication than the one above (12.).

1. For example the strange view, which arose out of the dispute about the historical explication of the N.T. [New Testament, passim.], as if there were several kinds of interpretation. The insistence on historical interpretation is only the correct insistence on the connection of the writers of the N.T. with their age. (Dangerous expression 'concepts of the time'.) But this insistence becomes mistaken if it denies the new concept-forming power of Christianity and wants to explain everything from what is already there. The denial of historical interpretation is right, if it just opposes this one-sidedness, and wrong if it wants to be universal. The whole issue then depends on the relationship of grammatical and psychological interpretation, for the new concepts arose from the particular enlivening of the mind [in Christianity].

2. Just as little (does a multiplicity arise) if one understands historical interpretation in terms of the taking account of events. For that is even something which precedes the interpretation, because thereby only the relationship between the speaker and the original listener is restored, which should therefore always be corrected beforehand.

3. *Allegorical Interpretation.* Not interpretation of allegory, where the figurative meaning is the only one for which there is no difference whether it is based on true events, as in the parable of the sower, or on fiction, as in the parable of the rich man, but instead an interpretation where the literal meaning falls in the immediate context, and yet, along with that meaning, also takes on a figurative meaning. One cannot dismiss allegorical interpretation with the general principle that every utterance could only have One meaning, the one that it is usually assumed to have in terms of grammar. For every allusion is a second meaning, and whoever fails to grasp it along with [the first meaning] can fully follow the context, but they still lack a meaning which was put into the utterance. On the other hand, who-

ever finds an allusion which was not put into the utterance has always failed to explicate the utterance correctly. Allusion takes place when one of the accompanying ideas is woven into the main sequence of thoughts, and one thinks that this idea could just as easily be aroused in the other person. But the accompanying ideas are not just single and little ideas, but in the same way as the whole world is posited in an ideal form in humankind, it is also always, albeit as a dark silhouette, thought of as real. Now there is a parallelism of the various sequences on large scale and on a small scale, so something from another sequence can always occur to one in every case: parallelism of the physical and the ethical, of the musical and the painterly, etc. Attention should only be directed to this if figurative expressions indicate it. That it has happened even without such indications particularly in relation to Homer and to the Bible has a particular reason. The reason is, in relation to Homer and the O.T. [Old Testament, passim.], the uniqueness (of Homer) as a book for universal education and of the O.T. as literature in general, from which everything had to be taken. Added to that in both cases was the mythical content, which on the one hand resulted in gnomic philosophy, on the other in history. There is, though, no technical interpretation for myth, because it cannot originate in one individual, and the wavering of common understanding between literal and figurative meaning here makes the duality most apparent. – In the case of the N.T. it is admittedly different, and in this case two reasons explain the procedure. On the one hand via its connection with the O.T., where this kind of explanation was produced and was therefore transferred to nascent scholarly explication. On the other hand via the idea, which was even more developed here than in relation to the O.T., of regarding the Holy Spirit as the author. The Holy Spirit cannot be thought of as a temporally changing individual consciousness. Whence the inclination to find everything in it. General truths or single specific prescriptions satisfy this inclination of their own accord, but the inclination is irritated by what is most isolated and essentially insignificant.

4. Here the question now imposes itself on us in passing, as to whether the Holy Books ought to be dealt with differently because of the Holy Spirit? We cannot expect a dogmatic decision about inspiration because this must itself depend upon the explication. We must *first of all* not make a difference between the speaking and the writing of the Apostles. For the future church had to be built on the first of these. But precisely for this reason we also must, *second*, not believe that in the Scriptures the whole of

Christianity was the immediate object. For they are all directed at specific people and could not be correctly understood even in the future if they had not been correctly understood by these people. But the people could not wish to seek anything but determinate individual things in the [Scriptures], because for them the totality had to result from the mass of particulars. We must therefore explicate them in the same way and thus assume that, even if the writers were dead tools, the Holy Spirit could only have spoken through them in the way they themselves would have spoken.

5. The worst deviation in this direction is cabbalistic explication, which, in the aim of finding everything in each individual thing, turns to the single elements and their signs. – One sees that in whatever can still deserve the name explication in terms of its aim there is no other multiplicity than that of the various relationships of the two sides we have established.

Addition.[19] Dogmatic and allegorical interpretation have, as the pursuit of content and significance, the common basis that the result should be as profitable as possible for Christian doctrine and that nothing in the Holy Books should be transitory or of little importance.

From this point one comes to inspiration. Given the great multiplicity of kinds of idea about this topic the best thing is first to try out what consequences result from the most strict idea. Thus the idea that the effectiveness of the Holy Spirit stretches from emergence of the thoughts to the act of writing. This no longer helps us because of the variants. These were, though, certainly already there before the putting together of the Scripture. Here criticism already becomes necessary. But even the first readers of the Apostolic letters would have had to abstract from the thought of the authors and from the application of their knowledge of the authors, and would consequently have sunk into the deepest confusion. If one now also asks why the Scripture did not arise in a completely miraculous manner without using people, then one has to say that the Holy Spirit can only have chosen this method (namely via people) if He wanted everything to be traced back to the authors indicated. For this reason only this can be the correct explication. The same is true of the grammatical side. But then everything particular must also be dealt with in purely human terms and the moving force remains only the inner impulse. – Other ideas which attribute some particular aspects, e.g. the protection against errors, to the Spirit, but not the rest, are untenable. The progress would thereby have to

[19] Marginalia 1828.

17

be thought of as inhibited, but what is correct, what remains constant, would again fall to the author. Should everything relate to the whole church because of inspiration? No. The immediate receivers [of the inspiration] would then always have had to explicate incorrectly, and the Holy Spirit would have acted much more correctly if the Holy Scriptures had not been occasional writings. In grammatical and psychological terms everything remains with the general rules. But the extent to which a special hermeneutics of the Holy Scriptures results can only be investigated later.

([Note by Lücke] In the lecture of 1832 this point is dealt with here and the border between general and special hermeneutics is determined more precisely with particular application to the N.T.[20] Schleiermacher says:) If we go back to the hermeneutic task in its original form, namely the utterance as a thought-act in a given language, then we come to the proposition: to the extent to which there is a unity of thought, there is also an identity of languages. This realm must contain the general rules of language. But as soon as there is a particularity of thought through the language, then a special hermeneutic realm emerges. In the more precise determination of the borders between the general and the particular the question first arises on the grammatical side: to what extent can the utterance be regarded as One (as a unity) from the perspective of language? The utterance must be a proposition.[21] Only thereby is something One in the realm of language. But the proposition is the relating of noun and verb, ὄνομα and ῥῆμα. *General hermeneutics certainly goes as far as the extent to which the understanding of the utterance derives from the general nature of the proposition.* But, although the *nature* of the proposition as a thought-act is the same in all languages, the *treatment* of the proposition in differing languages is different. Now the bigger the difference in the treatment of the proposition is in the languages, the more the realm of general hermeneutics is limited, the more differences come into the realm of general hermeneutics.

In the same way on the psychological side. To the extent that human life is one and the same, every utterance as the life-act of the individual is subordinated to the general hermeneutic rules. But to the extent that human life individualises itself, every life-act and thus also every speech-act[f] in which the life-act presents itself is also differently constituted in other people and connects differently to the rest of their moments of life. Here the realm of special hermeneutics enters. If we now presuppose that all differences of human nature in its life-functions also present themselves in language, then it also follows that the constitution of the

[20] Given in excerpts.
[21] *Translator's note*: the German here is *Satz*. I do not try to make any substantive distinction between 'proposition' and 'sentence'; *Satz* can also mean 'clause'.

[f] *Sprechakt*.

proposition is connected to the constitution of the life-act. This is true both for the general and for the particular. But the relationship of the general and the particular is highly nuanced. For the inequality and multiplicity in the treatment of the proposition can also be the same in different families of languages, so that groupings arise. In this way there can also be a common hermeneutics for every family of languages. Furthermore, we recognise different ways of treating language for different thought-acts. In this way linguistic differences can arise in the same language, e.g. in prose and poetry.[g] But these differences can, on the other hand, be the same in different languages. In prose I want the strict determination of thought by being, but poetry is thought in its free play. As such on this side I have far more of the psychological, whereas in prose the subject recedes more. Here two different areas of the special develop, one which relates to the difference in the construction of language, another which relates to the difference of the thought-act. – As far as the latter is concerned the general and the particular in the explication of an individual author relate in the following manner. To the extent that the thought-acts of the individual express in every case the whole determinacy of life or function of life in the same way, the laws of psychological interpretation will be the same. But as soon as I think of an inequality and do not find the key in the thought-act itself, but must also take account of other things, the realm of the special begins. As such the realm of the general is admittedly not very large. For this reason hermeneutics also always began with the special and went no further than the special. If we now begin with the fact that the utterance is a moment of life, then I must seek out the whole context and ask how the individual was moved to make the utterance (occasion) and towards which subsequent moments the utterance was directed (purpose). As the utterance is something compound it can, even in relation to the same occasion and purpose, still be something different. We must therefore analyse it and say, the general goes only as far as the laws of progression in thought are the same, where we find differences the special begins. In a didactic discussion, for example, and in a lyric poem the laws of progression are different, even though both are sequences of thoughts. The hermeneutic rules are therefore also different in relation to them, and we are in the realm of special hermeneutics.

Now the question whether and to what extent N.T. hermeneutics is a special hermeneutics is answered as follows. From the linguistic side it does not seem to be a special hermeneutics, for the linguistic side is initially to be related to the Greek language, but from the psychological side the N.T. does not appear as One, but is to be differentiated between didactic and historical writings. These are different genres, which may demand different hermeneutic rules. But that does not give rise to a special hermeneutics. Nevertheless N.T. hermeneutics is special, but only in relation to the compound language area or the hebrewising character of

[g] *Poesie*, with the wider, Greek sense of 'literature', 'creative discourse'.

language. The N.T. writers were not used to thinking in the Greek language, at least not in relation to religious matters. This qualification refers to Luke, who could have been born a Greek. But even the Greeks became Christians in the realm of Hebraism. Now in every language there are very many differences, in terms of location, different dialects in the widest sense, in terms of time, different periods of language. The language is different in each. This requires special rules which relate to the special grammar of different periods of time and different places. But this is even more generally applicable. For if there is a spiritual development in a people, then there is also a new development of language. In the way every new spiritual principle forms language, so did the Christian spirit. But from this no other special hermeneutics arises. If a people begins to philosophise it shows a great development of language, but it does not need a special hermeneutics. But in the N.T. the new Christian spirit emerges in a mixture of languages where the Hebrew is the root in which the new was first thought; the Greek was, though, grafted on. This is why N.T. hermeneutics is to be treated as a special hermeneutics. As the mixture of languages is an exception and not a natural state, N.T. hermeneutics, as a special hermeneutics, also does not emerge in a regular manner from general hermeneutics. – The fact is that the natural difference of languages does not ground a positive special hermeneutics, for this difference belongs to grammar, which is presupposed by hermeneutics and is just applied, nor does the difference between prose and poetry in one and the same language and in different languages, for the knowledge of this difference is also presupposed in hermeneutic theory. Just as little does a special hermeneutics become necessary via the psychological differences, to the extent that they emerge in an even manner in the relative opposition between the general and the special.

14. The difference between explication which is artistic and that which is free of art does not depend upon the difference between native and foreign, nor between speech and writing, but always upon the fact that one wants to understand some things exactly and others not.

1. If it were only foreign and old writings which required art, then the original readers would not have required it, and the art would therefore depend on the difference between the original readers and us. But this difference must first be cleared out of the way by knowledge of language and history; only after successful making equivalent [of the past and ourselves] does explication begin. The difference between foreign old writings and native contemporary ones consists only in the fact that the operation of being equivalent cannot completely precede explication but is only completed with the explication and during it, and this is always to be taken account of in explicating.

2. But it is not just writing [where this is the case]. Otherwise the art would only have to become necessary via the difference between writing and speech, i.e. via the lack of the living voice and via the lack of other kinds of personal influence. But the latter themselves in turn need explication, and this always remains uncertain. The living voice admittedly makes understanding very much easier, but the writer must take account of the fact (that he is not speaking). If he does this then the art of explication ought also to be superfluous, which is not in fact the case. The necessity for the art of explication therefore does not rest solely on this difference, even where he has not done this [taken account of the fact that he is not speaking].

Addition.[22] That the art of explication does, though, admittedly relate more to writing than speech results because, as a rule, oral discourse is helped by many things via which an *immediate* understanding is given, which is lacking in writing, and because one can make no use – particularly of the isolated rules which one anyway cannot keep in one's memory in passing speech.

3. If writing and speech relate in this way then there is no difference left than the one named, and it follows that even explication which does justice to the art has no other goal than we have in listening to any piece of everyday speech.

15. The more lax practice in the art assumes that understanding results as a matter of course and expresses the aim negatively: misunderstanding should be avoided.

1. Its presupposition depends upon that fact that it is primarily concerned with insignificant things, or at least only wishes to understand for the sake of a particular interest, and therefore sets itself limits which are easy to implement.

2. But even it must, however, have recourse to art in difficult cases, and that is how hermeneutics arose from the practice which is free of art. Because hermeneutics also only paid attention to the difficult cases it became a collection of observations and for the same reason straight away always special hermeneutics, because the difficult cases can be more easily investigated in a particular area. This is how theological and juridical hermeneutics arose and philologists also only paid attention to special purposes.

[22] From the marginalia and the lecture of 1828.

3. The basis of this view is the identity of language and of the manner of combination in speakers and listeners.

16. The more strict practice assumes that misunderstanding results as a matter of course and that understanding must be desired and sought at every point.

1. Based on the fact that it takes understanding very seriously and that the utterance, considered from both sides [the artistic and the 'artless'], should be completely dealt with by it.

Addition. It is a basic experience that one does not notice any difference between what is free of art and the artistic until a misunderstanding arises.

2. It [strict practice] begins with the difference of the language and the manner of combination, which must admittedly (14.) rest on identity and the difference is only the lesser aspect which eludes the practice which is free of art.

17. Two things are to be avoided, qualitative *misunderstanding of the content, and the misunderstanding of the tone or* quantitative *misunderstanding.*

Addition. The task can also be determined negatively as the avoidance of material (qualitative) and formal (quantitative) misunderstanding.

1. Looked at objectively the qualitative is the confusion of the location of one part of the utterance in the language with that of another part, like, e.g., confusion of the meaning of a word with the meaning of another word. Subjectively, qualitative misunderstanding is the confusion of the relationships of an expression, such that one gives it another relationship from the one which the speaker has given it in his context.[23]

2. Quantitative misunderstanding relates subjectively to the power of development of a part of the utterance, to the value (emphasis) which the speaker attributes to it, – analogously it relates objectively to the place which a part of speech occupies in the gradation, e.g. the superlative.

3. The qualitative always develops out of the quantitative, which is usually given less attention.

4. All tasks are contained in this negative expression [i.e. §17]. But because of their negativity we cannot develop the rules out of them, but must begin with something positive, but continually orient ourselves to this negative.

---

[23] Here the clearer expression of the thought is taken up directly from the lecture.

5. Positive and active misunderstanding are also to be distinguished as well. The latter is the imputation,[h] which is, though, the consequence of one's own prejudice, in relation to which, therefore, nothing determinate can happen, to the extent that it does not appear as a maximum, in which completely false presuppositions are the basis.

Misunderstanding[24] is either a consequence of hastiness or of prejudice.[i] The former is an isolated moment. The latter is a mistake which lies deeper. It is the one-sided preference for what is close to the individual's circle of ideas and the rejection of what lies outside it. In this way one explains in or explains out what is not present in the author.[j]

18. The art can only develop its rules from a positive formula and this is the historical *and* divinatory[25] (prophetic) objective *and* subjective reconstruction of the given utterance.

1. *Objectively historical* means realising how the utterance relates to the totality of the language and the knowledge enclosed within it as a product of language. *Objectively divinatory* means to conjecture how the utterance itself will become a point of development for the language. Without both qualitative and quantitative misunderstanding cannot be avoided.

2. *Subjectively historical* means knowing how the utterance is given as a fact in the mind, *subjectively divinatory* means to conjecture how the thoughts contained in the mind will continue to have an effect in and on the utterer. Without both misunderstanding is equally unavoidable.

3. The task is also to be expressed as follows, to understand the utterance at first just as well and then better than its author. For because we have no immediate knowledge of what is in him, we must seek to bring much to consciousness that can remain unconscious to him, except to the extent to which he himself reflectively becomes his own reader. On the objective side he has even here no other data than we do.

4. The task is, put like this, an infinite task because it is an infinity of past and future that we wish to see in the moment of the utterance. For this reason this art is as capable of enthusiasm[k] as every other art. To the extent to

---

[24] From the lecture of 1826.
[25] *Translator's note*: 'Divinatory' replaces 'prophetic', which is crossed out in the manuscript.

[h] *Einlegen*, in the sense of 'putting the sense into' the utterance.
[i] *Befangenheit*.
[j] *So erklärt man hinein oder heraus was nicht im Schriftsteller liegt.*
[k] *Begeisterung* in the sense of 'inspiration'.

which a text does not arouse this enthusiasm it is insignificant. – But how far and on which side in particular one wishes to go with the approximation must be decided practically in every case and belongs at best in a special hermeneutics, not in general hermeneutics.

19. Before the application of the art one must put oneself in the place of the author on the objective and the subjective side.

1. On the objective side, then, via knowledge of the language as he possessed it, which is therefore more determinate than putting oneself in the place of the original readers, who themselves must first put themselves in his place. On the subjective side in the knowledge of his inner and outer life.

2. But both can only be completely achieved by the explication itself. For it is only from the texts of each particular author that one can get to know their vocabulary and just as much their character and their circumstances.

20. The vocabulary and the history of the era of an author relate as the whole from which his writings must be understood as the part, and the whole must, in turn, be understood from the part.

1. Complete knowledge is always in this apparent circle, that each particular can only be understood via the general, of which it is a part, and vice versa. And every piece of knowledge is only scientific if it is formed in this way.

2. The putting oneself in the place of the author is implicit in what has just been said, and it follows first of all that we are the better equipped for explication the more completely we have assimilated it, but second that nothing which is to be explicated can be understood all at once, but that it is only each reading which makes us capable of better understanding by enriching that previous knowledge. Only in relation to that which is insignificant are we happy with what has been understood all at once.

21. If knowledge of the specific vocabulary is only to be cobbled together during explication via lexical help and isolated observation, no independent explication can result.

1. Only direct tradition[1] from the real life of the language gives a source for the knowledge of the vocabulary which is more independent of explication. In Greek and Latin we only have such tradition in an incomplete

---

[1] *Überlieferung*, in the sense of 'transmission'.

manner. This is why the first lexical works stem from those who had worked their way through the whole of the literature for the purposes of knowledge of the language. For this reason, though, these works require continual correction by the explication itself and every artistic explication must for its part contribute to this.

2. By specific vocabulary I understand dialect, period and language area of a particular genre, the last beginning with the difference between poetry and prose.

3. The beginner must take the first steps with the help of those aids, but independent interpretation can only rest on the relatively independent acquisition of that previous knowledge. For all determinations of language in dictionaries and observations must begin with particular and often uncertain explication.

4. In the area of the N.T. one can say in particular that the uncertainty and arbitrariness of the explication rests in the main on this deficit. For opposed analogies can always be developed from single observations. – But the path to the vocabulary of the N.T. goes from classical antiquity through Macedonian Hellenism, the Jewish profane authors Josephus and Philo, the deuterocanonical writings and LXX [Septuagint] as the strongest approximation to the Hebrew.

As[26] far as the contemporary manner of academic study of N.T. exegesis is concerned, there is a lack of sufficient preparation. Usually one comes directly from grammar school education in classical philology to the artistic explication of the N.T. That is an unfavourable situation. But we do not therefore wish to agree with the wish that, for the sake of theological education, the present scholarly education in school should be changed, and that instead of the classics the church fathers should be read in grammar schools with future theologians because the language and the body of ideas of the former are supposed to be too dissimilar. That would have negative consequences. It would be bad if theologians were only taught patristically. Our general education is already too much defined by classical antiquity, so that a damaging difference between the education of theologians and the others would necessarily occur. One can have very honest intentions with regard to the Christian cause, be very Christian-minded without wishing to break off the connection with pagan antiquity. The period in which the most educated church fathers wrote was, after all, the period of decline. But this period cannot be understood on its own, but only by comparison with the preceding point of culmination of the literature. If someone comes to the Christian monuments with real love, the

---

[26] From the lecture of 1826.

more he will understand them from out of the knowledge of classical antiquity he has brought with him, and the less he will be disadvantaged by the non-Christian content of the classics.

But the unavoidable deficit in appropriate preparation for the academic study of N.T. exegesis might be corrected by prior complete instruction in N.T. grammar, and biblical archaeology, introduction etc. That would, though, in part lead too far, and in part always already in turn presuppose exegesis. So there is nothing for it but to establish the academic presentation of exegesis genetically, so that, under instruction in the correct independent use of the available aids, from which the N.T. language, biblical archaeology etc. are to be learned, the hermeneutic rules in their correct application are brought to consciousness in every given case; but the real certainty only arises if the pupil connects the presentation of the teacher with his own exercises. But these must necessarily progress from the more simple to the more difficult, with judicious use of the aids offered.

22. If the necessary knowledge of history is only taken from prolegomena no independent explication can result.

1. Such prolegomena are, together with critical aids, the duty of every editor who wishes to be a mediator. They can themselves, though, only be based on a knowledge of the whole body of literature which belongs to a text and of everything which occurs in later areas about the author of a text. They are therefore themselves dependent upon explication. They are also at the same time intended for the person for whom the primary acquisition [of the historical knowledge] would bear no relation to his actual aim. The precise explicator must, however, gradually draw everything from the sources themselves, and precisely for this reason his operation must progress in this respect from the more easy to the more difficult. The dependence becomes most damaging if one introduces notes into the prolegomena which can only be drawn from the work itself which is to be explicated.

2. In relation to the N.T. one has made a separate discipline, the Introduction, out of this previous knowledge. This is not an authentic organic component of theological science, but it is practically useful, partly for the beginner, partly for the master, because it is now easier to bring together here all the relevant investigation at *one* point. But the explicator must always also make a contribution, in order to augment this mass of results and to correct it.

Addition. From the differing ways of drawing up and using this previous knowledge in a fragmentary manner, different but also one-sided schools of interpretation form, which easily become affected in an unjustifiable manner.

23. Even within a single text the particular can only be understood from out of the whole, and a cursory reading to get an overview of the whole must therefore precede the more precise explication.

1. This seems to be a circle, but for this provisional understanding the knowledge of the particular that results from the general knowledge of the language is sufficient.

2. Tables of contents given by the author himself are too dry to achieve the aim on the side of technical interpretation as well, and synopses of the kind editors are in the habit of adding to prolegomena bring one under the influence of their interpretations.

3. The intention is to find the leading ideas according to which the other ideas must be assessed, and correspondingly on the technical side to find the main direction via which the particular can be found more easily. Indispensable both on the technical and on the grammatical side, which can easily be shown by the differing kinds of misunderstanding.

4. In relation to what is insignificant one can more readily omit it and in relation to what is difficult it seems to help less, but is all the more indispensable. The fact that the general overview is of little help is actually a characteristic feature of difficult writers.

Addition. General methodological rule: a) Beginning with general overview; b) Simultaneous being-engaged in both directions, the grammatical and psychological; c) Only if both coincide exactly in a single place can one proceed; d) Necessity of going back if they do not agree until one has found the mistake in the calculation.

If explication of the particulars is now to begin then both sides of the interpretation must admittedly always be bound together, but we must separate them in the theory, and treat each of them separately, yet strive in each to get to the point where the other becomes dispensable, or rather where its result appears simultaneously in the first. Grammatical interpretation goes first.

([Note by Lücke] Schleiermacher himself briefly summarises the lecture of 1832 on §14–23 as follows:)

Before the beginning of the hermeneutic process one must know the relationship in which one is to apply both sides (see §12). Then one must establish the same relationship between oneself and the author as between him and his original addressees. Thus knowledge of the whole sphere of life and of the relationship of both parts to it. If this has not completely taken place difficulties arise which we wish to avoid. Commentaries predict this and want to resolve the difficulties. Whoever uses them surrenders authority and only sustains independent understanding if he subjects this authority once more to his own judgement. – If this utterance is immediately directed to me it must also be presupposed that the utterer thinks of me as I am conscious to myself of being. But as even everyday conversation often shows that this is not the case, we must proceed sceptically. The canon is: The confirmation of the understanding which results at the beginning is to be expected from what follows. From this follows that one does not understand the beginning before the end, thus also that one must still have the beginning at the end, and this means in every complex which goes beyond the usual capacity of memory that the utterance must become writing.[27]

The canon now takes on this form: In order to understand the first thing precisely one must have already taken up the whole. Not, of course, to the extent that it is the same as the totality of particulars, but as a skeleton, an outline of how one can grasp it while ignoring the particular. We get this same canon if we begin with the version which involves reconstructing the process of the author. For in every larger complex the author as well saw the whole before he progressed to the particular.[28]

In order now to proceed as uninterruptedly as possible we must consider what is to be avoided thereby, namely misunderstanding. A proposition can be quantitatively misunderstood if the whole is not more precisely (correctly) grasped, e.g. if I take as the main thought what is only a secondary thought, – qualitatively if e.g. irony is taken as being meant seriously, and vice versa. The proposition as a unit is also the smallest thing that can be understood or misunderstood. Misunderstanding is the confusion of one location of the linguistic value[m] of a word or a form with another. The opposition between qualitative and quantitative strictly speaking goes through everything in language, both the formal and the material elements, even the concept of God is subordinated to it (compare the polytheistic and the Christian concept).

The genesis of misunderstanding is twofold, through (conscious) *not-understanding*, or *immediately*. In the first case it is more likely to be the fault of the author (deviation from the normal use of language or use without analogy), the second is probably always the fault of the explicator (§17).

---

[27] In the lecture this becomes clearer by the fact that one sees how the hermeneutic task is led over from oral discourse, conversation, – as the original location of understanding – to the understanding of writing.

[28] In the lecture this canon is determined more exactly in its application in such a way that the prior understanding of the whole is all the more necessary the more the given complex of thoughts has an independent context.

The canon of complete understanding is then formulated as follows: there is complete understanding only via the whole, but this is mediated by the complete understanding of the particular.

[m] *Sprachwert.*

We can also express the whole task in this negative manner: – to avoid misunderstanding at every point. For nobody can be satisfied with simple nonunderstanding, so complete understanding must be the result if that task is solved correctly.

If the process is now to begin, after the task has been grasped and the preconditions have been fulfilled, then a priority must be established between both sides of the interpretation. This falls on the grammatical side, in part because this has been worked on the most, in part because one can thereby more readily rely on an existent preliminary investigation.

Part One
Grammatical explication

1. First canon: Everything in a given utterance which requires a more precise determination may only be determined from the language area which is common to the author and his original audience.

1. Everything requires more precise determination and only receives it in the context. Every part of the utterance, material and formal, is in itself indeterminate. In relation to every isolated word we only think of a certain cycle of manners of use. It is the same with every linguistic form.

2. Some people call what one thinks in relation to the word in and for itself the meaning,[a] but what one thinks in relation to it in a given context the sense.[b] Others say a word has only a meaning, and no sense, a proposition in and for itself has a sense, but does not yet have significance,[c][1] which is only possessed by a completely closed utterance. Now one could admittedly say that even this would be understood even more completely in the context of the world which belongs to it; but that takes us out of the realm of interpretation. – The terminology just employed is to be preferred to the extent to which a proposition is an indivisible unity, and, as such, the sense is also a unity, the reciprocal being-determined of subject and predicate by one another. But even this is not really in accordance with language, for sense in comparison with significance is entirely the same as

---

[1] *Translator's note*: The translation of these three terms for 'meaning' is largely arbitrary, and, as Schleiermacher himself suggests here, the context is what allows us to make sense of what is meant. Think of the still argued-over problem of translating Frege's *Sinn* and *Bedeutung*. In this passage I will always translate each word by the term employed in this sentence.

[a] *Bedeutung.*　　[b] *Sinn.*　　[c] *Verstand.*

meaning. The truth is that the move from the more indeterminate to the determinate is an endless task in every process of explication. – Where a single sentence constitutes a closed totality for itself alone the difference between *sense* and *significance* seems to disappear, as it does in an epigram and gnomic utterance. The latter is supposed first to be determined by the association of the reader, everyone should make of it what they can. The former is determined by the relation to a single topic.

If one analyses an utterance into its individual parts every part is indeterminate. So every single sentence, torn from all contexts, must be indeterminate. – But there are cases where single sentences are given without context, e.g. the essence of a saying (a gnomic utterance) is precisely that it is a single sentence. The epigram is equally complete. According to that canon this would therefore be an incomprehensible, bad genre. The epigram is something absolutely singular, as a heading; the saying is, though, something general, although very often expressed in the single form of the example. The epigram requires a story in the context of which it arose and it is also only via this context that it is comprehensible. If the knowledge of the events and the persons that produced it has been lost, then the epigram is a puzzle, i.e. it is no longer to be solved via its context. Sayings are statements that are used frequently and in differing manners. The sphere of their application and effectiveness is indeterminate. The saying only becomes determinate when used in a determinate instance. It emerges in a determinate context, but in relation to the large sphere of its application, it becomes indeterminate. As such sayings and epigrams do not refute our general canon.

3. The area of the author himself is the area of his time, of his education, and of his occupation – also of his dialect, where and to the extent to which this difference occurs in educated discourse. But it will not be completely present in every utterance, but only according to the judgement of the readers. How, though, do we find out what sort of readers the author had in mind? Only via the general overview of the whole text. But this determination of the common area is only a beginning and it must be continued during the explication and is only completed when the explication is completed.

4. There are many apparent exceptions to this canon: a) *Archaisms* lie outside the immediate language area of the author, and so also of his readers. They occur in order to make the past present as well, more in writing than in speech, more in poetry than in prose. b) *Technical expressions* even in the most popular genres, e.g. in judicial and consultative speeches, the

latter even if not all listeners understand them. This leads to the observation that an author also does not always have his whole audience in view, but that this fluctuates as well. Whence even this rule is a rule of art whose successful application depends upon an appropriate feeling.

We are not enamoured of the proposition, no rule without an exception, for the rule is then usually formulated too narrowly, or too broadly, or too indeterminately. But we do find that writers often employ expressions which do not belong to the language area of their readers. This is, though, because this common ground is something indeterminate with both more narrow and more broad limits. There are, e.g., archaisms. If the writer has a specific reason for such expressions and the antiquated expression must become clear from the context, then the writer is not making a mistake. There are also technical expressions. Unavoidable in a special area; the reader must make himself familiar with them. But if technical expressions are used in another area without particularly strong motives, then the writer will not be fully understood. For this reason Fr. Richter can make no claim to classical status because of the frequent expressions from special areas.[2] To the variability of language in time belongs the assimilation of new expressions. These arise in the continuing context of thinking and expression. As long as the language is alive new expressions are made. But this has its limits. New stems cannot be brought into existence; new words are only thinkable in derivations and combinations. The necessity for these arises as soon as a new area of thought is opened up. If I did not want in this case to form something new in my own language, then I would have to express myself in a foreign language in which this area has already been dealt with. As soon as the fact escapes us that the author has formed a new aspect of language (*etwas neues Sprachliches*) we do not fully understand him in relation to the language; something does not come into our consciousness which was in the consciousness of the author. The same is true of whole phrases. And for this reason this has to be looked out for in all works which were the first of their genre. Every text which belongs in the beginnings of a new area of thought should be presumed to contain new expressions. One cannot expect that what is new in a writer is always immediately apparent in the text; that in which the new was first manifest can be precisely what has been lost for us. Thus it is in Plato, of whom one knows that he produced new expressions for the sake of new philosophical ideas. A large part of his linguistic productions then passed over into all the Schools. In this way many things seem familiar to us that he was perhaps the first to bring into the language. In Plato the written language is based on oral conversation, where the artificial expressions may first have occurred; this eludes us now because Plato could assume in his writings that what he used that was new was, from his conversation,

---

[2] *Translator's note*: The reference is to Johann-Paul Friedrich Richter (Jean Paul) (1763–1825), novelist and essayist, contemporary of Schleiermacher.

not unfamiliar to his readers. In this way difficulty and uncertainty in interpretation arises in relation to the new. – Misunderstanding is often the fault of attributing a particular meaning to already existing expressions. In that case the fault usually lies with the author, whom we term obscure if he attributes a peculiar value to common designations without this being able to be derived determinately from the context.[3] – The newly formed words are just as little exceptions as are technical words, as they must be taken and understood from the common area of language. But with regard to archaisms and neologisms in language one must make oneself familiar with the history of the language in its different periods. In Homer and the tragedians, e.g., it must be asked whether the difference of their language lies in the genre itself, or in the language itself, or in both. Homer's language reappeared in the Alexandrines. In this case one can ask whether the epic remained silent for so long and then reappeared, or whether the works of the Alexandrines are only imitations of Homer. A different hermeneutic process would have to arise according to the differing answers to this question. – A correct overall view must always be the basis if the individual aspect is to be understood correctly.

5. In the assertion that we must become conscious of the language area as opposed to the other organic parts of the utterance also lies the fact that we understand the author better than he does himself, for in him much of this kind is unconscious that must become conscious in us, both already in general in the first overview, and in particular, as soon as difficulties arise.

6. After the general overview explication can often quietly proceed for a long time without actually being free of art, because everything is oriented to the general image. But as soon as a particular difficulty arises the doubt arises as to whether the fault lies with the author or with us. The former can only be presupposed in terms of how much he already showed himself in the overview to be careless and imprecise or also talentless and confused. In us it can have a double cause, either an earlier misunderstanding which remained unnoticed or an insufficient knowledge of the language, so that the correct use of the word does not occur to us. We can only discuss the former later because of the connection with the doctrine of the parallel passages. Here, therefore, concerning the latter.

7. Dictionaries, which are the natural means of supplementation, regard the various manners of use as a collection of many loosely connected parts.

---

[3] Occasionally Schleiermacher here remarks: If we consider the usual process of this new formation we have cause to feel sorry for the interpreters of our literature, for the arbitrariness in this is so great that neither the logical nor the musical laws are observed. In this way corruptions arise which confuse language and make interpretation uncertain. We can only oppose this by not assimilating and disseminating bad new forms of language.

The aim of reducing the meaning to a primary unity is not carried out, because a dictionary would otherwise really have to be ordered according to the system of the concepts, which is impossible. The multiplicity of meanings is then to be analysed into a series of oppositions. The first is that between *literal* and *metaphorical*. But this opposition dissolves when looked at more closely. In similes there are two parallel series of thoughts. The word stands in its own series and only that should be reckoned with. It therefore keeps its meaning. In metaphors this is only hinted at, and often only One characteristic of the concept is picked out, e.g. *coma arborum*, the foliage, but *coma* remains hair. King of the beasts = lion. The lion does not rule, but 'king' does not therefore mean one who tears others apart according to the law of the stronger. Such an isolated use does not give a meaning, and only the whole phrase can become established. In the last analysis one puts this opposition down to the fact that all abstract meanings were not primary, thus to the metaphorical use of sensuous words. But this is an investigation which lies beyond the hermeneutic area. For if θεὸς [God] is derived from θέο [run] (Plato, *Cratylus* 397) or from θεὶζ [?] (Herodotus 2, 52) this belongs to the prehistory of the language, with which explication has nothing to do. The question is whether the abstract (*geistig*) meanings really belong to a second development which can only have taken place after the completion of the language, and nobody will be able to make that plausible. Undoubtedly there are abstract words which at the same time imply something concrete, but here as well parallelism is at work, because both [i.e. the mental and the physical], as they are there for us, are One in the idea of life. Precisely this is the case for the use of the same words in the realm of space and of time. Both are essentially one, because we can only determine space by time, and vice versa. Form and movement can be reduced to each other and 'creeper' [the plant] is therefore not a metaphorical expression. It is no better with the opposition between primary and secondary meaning. *Hostis*, 'stranger', thus 'enemy'. Originally all strangers were enemies. Afterwards one saw the possibility of being friends with strangers, and instinct decided that in relation to the word one thought more of the separation of opinions than of the separation of space, and thus even native enemies could finally be called *hostes*, but perhaps only because they were banished at the same time. Opposition between *general* meaning and *particular* meaning, the former in various kinds of communication, the latter in a specific area. Often essentially the same, often elliptical, like 'foot', for the length of a foot, and foot in metrics for metre, or 'foot forwards'.

Often as well because every art [involves?] a lower area via misunderstanding of the uneducated mass.[d] Also there are often foreign words which have been distorted and re-formed to the point of appearing as native words. It will be like this with all other oppositions.

8. The original task even for dictionaries which are, though, there purely for the explicator is *to find the true complete unity of the word*. The single occurrence of a word in a given place admittedly belongs to infinitely indeterminate multiplicity, and there is no other transition to this from that unity than a determinate multiplicity under which it is subsumed, and this must in turn necessarily dissolve into oppositions. In the single occurrence, though, the word is not isolated; its determinacy does not emerge from itself but from its surroundings, and we are only permitted to bring the primary unity of the word together with these surroundings so as to find what is right each time. But the complete unity of the word would be its explanation, and this is as little present as the complete explanation of objects. It is not present in dead languages because we have not yet made their whole development transparent, and not in living languages because the development is really still continuing.

9. If a multiplicity of meaning is to be possible with the presence of unity, there must already be a multiplicity in the unity, several main points bound together in a manner which can be shifted within certain limits. The sense for language must seek this, where we become uncertain, we use the dictionary as an aid, in order to orient ourselves via the common resources of knowledge of the language. The various cases which occur there are only supposed to be a sensible selection, one must connect the points for oneself by transitions, in order, as it were, to have the whole curve before oneself and to be able to determine the location that is sought.

If the understanding of a sentence via its surroundings is obstructed, we must look around for the general and the particular aids. The former are dictionaries and their supplement is syntax, the latter commentaries on the text in question or on whole genres of the same. The use of the dictionary begins if the lack of a comprehensive insight into the linguistic value means correct understanding is obstructed. In the correct use of the dictionary it is a question of whether the treatment of the elements of language is right, indeed whether it is mine. If it is not mine then I must think my way into the treatment in the lexicon, because otherwise

---

[d] *Oft auch weil jede Kunst ein niederes Gebiet durch Mißverständniß der ungebildeten Masse*: the sense is not clear.

I cannot assess its judgement on the particular case. This leads to the theory of dictionaries. A dictionary should represent the whole vocabulary, the individual elements of the same and their value. There are two different manners of compiling a dictionary, the alphabetical and the etymological. In the etymological manner the basic idea is to collect the isolated elements not in their isolation but in groups in relation to the linguistic laws of derivation. Otherwise one could also classify them according to the concepts, as Pollux wished. The etymological manner, though, obviously gives a more clear image of the language because it leads back the expressions to *one* point. The alphabetical manner has a completely external basis of determination, the convenience of the users. The scientific use of both types is that one looks for the word and the indication of its root in the alphabetical lexicon, but one looks up the root afterwards in the etymological lexicon, where the whole family is given. – The task of the lexicographer is to find the unity of the meaning of a word in its multiple occurrences and to collate the similar and the dissimilar in groups. In these groupings the process of *opposition* must be connected with that of the *transition into one another*, as in every correct observation of a product of nature. The *opposition* of the meanings belongs more to the linguistic task, the *demonstration* of the *transitions* more to the hermeneutic. The most common opposition is that of literal and metaphorical meaning. For the task of finding the unity one must, in this opposition, stop at the literal meaning. For the metaphorical meaning arises outside the sphere of the element of the word. But how did people come to make a use of a word outside its sphere? The opposition seems to have no reality and to negate the unity of the word. But the unity is not to be regarded as absolute, but as the combination of different elements, and the use is guided in each case by the different occurrence of the elements. The whole relationship of literal and metaphorical meanings depends upon that of analogy between and parallelisation of things. If I mistake the figurative, emphatic aspect of a designation then a quantitative misunderstanding arises. Now the lexical combination of the different manners of use admittedly has its convenience. However, one does not arrive at the understanding of a text without arriving at the unity, for the writer has always mastered this, even if he could not give an account of it. If the unity is compound, then one also only finds it if one combines all the manners of use. The process of opposition is only an intermediate understanding for the hermeneutic task, but, as such, it does serve to recognise the original combination, of which the other manners of use are to be regarded as modifications. – There can be true and false in the opposition between the original and the derived in meanings. In the strict sense the simple root is the original in language and the declensions are derived. But this is inherent in the elements of language. The unity of the original is to be sought in the meanings of one and the same word, the derived meanings are only further manners of use. This is true, but it is not an opposition. But the process of opposition is untrue if all meanings are supposed to be original that are found first in the language and which lead to the historical beginning, so that the word gains a history. However that is only true if we could always separate the original most old occurrences from the later derived occurrences of the words. But now a canon is established which is important for hermeneutics, namely that one opposes the sensuous and abstract meanings and calls the former the original, the latter the derived. Put in this way this canon is, though, incorrect and would lead to complete misunderstanding to the extent to which the utterance is a product of the human capacity for thought. No word which has grown in the language has such oppositions, each is instead at the same time a combination of a multiplicity of relationships and transitions. In living speech and writing there is no word of which one could say that it could be presented as a pure unity. It is only arbitrarily manufactured expressions which have not grown in the language that do not have any different manner of use. Like technical expressions. Living, naturally growing language begins with perceptions and fixes them. Therein lies the material for the difference of manners of use, because there are always many relationships in perception. If one now wanted to say that there was no original designation of the abstract, that this was always derived, then this would be a materialist view of language. If one understands by sensuous that which arises via external perception, and by abstract via inner perception, then this is one-sided, for all original perception is inner perception. But it is true that nothing *abstract*[4] is originally in language, but it is rather the *concrete* which is originally in language.

If an isolated expression in a sentence is not clear via the original connection in which it appears, then this can be because the totality of the linguistic value of the expression is not known to the listener or reader. At this point the use of the aids offered by the lexicon begins as a complementary procedure. One must be in command of the unity of the linguistic value to arrive at the multiplicity of manners of use. This can, though, never completely succeed if one fixes the use by oppositions. For this reason the oppositions which the lexicon makes must be negated and the word must be considered in its unity as something which can change in differing directions.

The question arises: to what extent does an essential moment of hermeneutics lie in the history of the language?

Let us say that we have great periods of time before us in which a language has been alive and that we can go back from every point, only not to the beginnings –

---

[4] *Translator's note*: In this passage I have used 'abstract' both for '*geistig*', which has no negative connotations, and, in this case, for '*abstrakt*', which clearly does. In the first case the sense is given by the contrast between the 'abstract'/'mental', in the sense of that which is not derived solely from the objects of the physical world, and the 'physical', where the vital point is that Schleiermacher is concerned to avoid an uncrossable divide between the two. In the second case he means that there can be no language without a world, so language is not abstracted from that world but concretely affected by the relations between things in that world, relations which, of course, require the activity of the 'mental' and its articulation in language to be determinate.

for they are never given to us anywhere in time – and we compare the manners of use of a word by the earliest and latest users – now have the former, using the word in a fully conscious manner, also thought all the meanings which we find in the later use of the word? No one would be able to either assert or prove this. Instead, in a language which dominates many generations, knowledge must arise which could not have been in the consciousness of the earliest users. These unavoidably affect the language. But as completely new elements cannot arise in the already existent language, new manners of use arise which were not in the consciousness of the earlier users. Thus the word βασιλεὺζ [King] among the Greeks. – If we now wish to understand precisely we must know the degree of liveliness with which the utterer produced his expressions, and what they really contained for him when looked at in this internal manner. For only in this way do we find the process of his thought. Although this seems to belong on the psychological side, it must be brought over onto this side, as it is above all a matter of knowing what linguistic content is present to the person using the word, whether an old or a new use. Both are different. For an expression that I am conscious of as new has a completely different accent, emphasis, colouring, than one I use as a well-worn sign. To this belongs knowledge of the whole language and its history and of the writer's relationship to it. But who could dare completely to accomplish this task! In the meantime one does not ever have to want to completely accomplish this task, but in most cases only to accomplish it to a certain extent. But precisely where we do not strive for complete thoroughness we often overlook what we should not overlook. Where there is not the maximum effort there is also less certainty and more difficulty. In the meanwhile there are cases where we are only concerned with particular details and where we, as it were, renounce the complete liveliness of mind by concentrating on individual points. In such cases of self-limitation caution is necessary, though, so that we do not overlook what is important, because otherwise we get into difficulties. But where we seek complete understanding it is necessary to have the complete vocabulary in mind. It is also part of this completeness of understanding that we make a provisional survey of the whole. But this provisional hermeneutic process is not possible and necessary in every case. The more we, for example in reading the newspaper, do not look at the manner of narration itself, but rather only aim for the narrated fact, thus really for what lies beyond hermeneutics, the less we need that provisional process.

10. The same is the case with the formal element; the rules of grammar are, just like the meanings, in the dictionary. Whence the fact that in relation to particles grammar also becomes part of the dictionary. The formal is even more difficult.

11. The use of both aids (lexicon and grammar) is once again the use of a writer, and for this reason all the rules [concerning interpretation of a

writer – in this case of the lexicon or grammar] are in addition valid once again in this case. Both comprehend only a certain period of knowledge of the language and also usually begin from a particular viewpoint. The whole use of both by an academic must also in turn serve to correct and enrich them via better understanding; thus each (particular hermeneutic) case must contribute something to this.

All elements of language, formal and material, have the same value for complete understanding. The former express the connections. If one learns the material elements from the lexicon, one learns the formal elements by the grammar, in particular the syntax. The same is valid of these formal elements (particles) as of the material ones, namely that each of them is a unity, but even this is not to be recognised via opposition, but rather in the form of gradual transition. Only in grammar one is more reliant on the etymological process because here the forms are presented in determinate relationships.

2. Application of the first canon to the N.T.

1. If the special hermeneutics of the N.T. is to be constructed scientifically at each point (of general hermeneutics) attention must be paid to what is thereby posited as a matter of course or excluded in relation to a particular object.[5] –

2. The N.T. language must be subsumed under the totality of the Greek language. The Books themselves are not translated, not even Matthew and the Letter to the Hebrews. But even the authors did not think straightforwardly in Hebrew and only wrote or dictated in Greek. For they could always assume there were better translators among their readers. Instead they, like all rational beings (in particular cases at least, for the first conception which was never carried out does not belong here) also thought in the language in which they wrote.

3. The N.T. language belongs, though, in the period of decline. One can reckon this period as already beginning with Alexander. Some writers of this period approach the [language of the] Golden age or seek to produce it. But our N.T. authors take their language more from the area of common life, and do not have this tendency. But even the former are to be consulted where they simply let themselves go in the style of their time. Whence correct analogies from Polybius and Josephus. Analogies noted from Attic

---

[5] The rest of what is said here concerning the conditions of special hermeneutics in general is omitted because everything which belongs here has been more completely and more clearly dealt with in the Introduction.

writers like Thucydides, Xenophon have a negative use, and it is a good exercise to compare them. This is because one often thinks of the differing areas as too closed-off and thinks certain things could not occur in Classical Greek, and could only occur in Hellenic or Macedonian, and this is corrected by the comparison.

4. The influence of Aramaic is only to be determined via the general observation of the way in which one acquires a foreign language. Proximity to the people and a tendency to universal intercourse are close to each other everywhere, including in the realm of language. Frequently the latter disappears as a minimum. Where the latter dominates too much then the proximity to the people is certainly in decline. But the ability to acquire many languages proficiently by comparing one's mother tongue and the foreign language with the general image of language is a talent. This talent has never been significant among the Jews. That ease, though, which has now gone so far as the disappearance of their mother tongue, was already present among them at that time [i.e. of the composition of the N.T.]. But in the acquisition via common intercourse without grammar and literature mistakes creep in which are not found in those who are academically trained, and this is the difference between the N.T. and Philo and Josephus. These mistakes are twofold in our case. In the *first*, as a result of the contrast between the richness and the paucity of formal elements the N.T. writers do not know how to use the richness of Greek. *Also*, because foreign words are reduced to words in the mother tongue in the process of acquisition, an illusion easily arises that those which have corresponded in several cases will also correspond to each other in every case, and from this presupposition then arises wrong usage in writing. In both points the LXX is very much in agreement with the N.T. and is therefore almost the most fertile means of explanation. But to regard it as the source of N.T. language, from which it supposedly formed itself, is too much. *First of all*, the N.T. writers, in the same way as they are very different in the degree of their acquisition of Greek and in their being limited by the shortcomings we have seen, also had a very different connection to the LXX. *Also*, a further source can be established for them all, namely common social intercourse.

5. Another thing is the investigation of how far the N.T. is still particularly influenced by the LXX because of the religious content. Here it is particularly the more recent writings, the Apocrypha, which come into consideration, and the answering of this question has the greatest influence on the whole view of Christian theology, namely on the principles of interpretation,

to the extent to which interpretation itself is the basis of dogmatics. – The N.T. writers do not introduce any new words for their religious concepts and therefore speak via the linguistic usage of the Greek O.T. and the Apocrypha. The question is, then, did they, despite this, have different religious ideas and therefore other manners of using the words? Or did they also have only the same manners of use? In the latter case there would be nothing new in Christian theology, and therefore, as everything religious which is not just for the present fixes itself in reflection, there would also be nothing in the Christian religion. But the question cannot be decided in an immediately hermeneutic manner and therefore shows itself as a matter of conviction. In the process each person accuses the other of deriving their principles from preconceived opinions; for there can only be correct opinion about the Bible through interpretation. There is admittedly a basis of resolving the problem in the hermeneutic process. On the one hand a thorough comparison of the N.T. and the LXX would have to show whether manners of use occur in the one which are completely alien to the other. But in that case the excuse would always remain that the language area was greater than these remains of the area. On the other hand the assertion based on feeling about whether the N.T. appears in its own right as a development of new ideas would have to help one out. But this assertion can only gain credit via a universal philological and philosophical education. Only someone who proves that they have also successfully carried out similar investigations elsewhere and that they have not been influenced against their own better judgement can become decisive here.

6. Even if in our opinion there is admittedly only a subordinate anomalous influence of the Hebrew origin on N.T. language, it must be asked how much account of this must be taken in the interpretation. There are two one-sided maxims here. One is to remain satisfied with the one linguistic element [i.e. Greek or Hebrew] alone until difficulties arise, and then to solve these via the other linguistic element. But the first procedure thereby becomes devoid of art and not at all suitable for linking the second to it. One can then also just as easily try to explain via the other moment something which has its real basis of explanation somewhere completely different, and one must again rely for knowledge of the other solely on isolated observations. But in accordance with our provisional rule that art must play a role from the very beginning, one should seek to form a general sense of the relationship of both moments which is abstracted from all

particular difficulties by provisional reading and by comparison with LXX, Philo, Josephus, Diodorus, Polybius.

But it is undeniable that the influence of Hebrew in the really religious terms is particularly great. For in what was originally Hellenic – particularly to the extent that it was known to the N.T. writers – the religious aspect which was to be newly developed (not only) found no point of contact, but even what was similar was rejected via its connection to polytheism.

7. For this reason the mixing together of the anomalous is present in the most varied of ways and is, on the other hand, different in each individual writer. The main rule therefore always remains to form a whole for every word from the Greek and the Hellenic dictionaries, and for every form from the Greek grammar and from the comparative Hellenic grammar, and only to apply the canon in relation to this whole. – Advice to the beginner often even to consult the double dictionary where one finds no difficulty, in order to pre-empt any getting used to not proceeding artistically.

A language can only need a special hermeneutics to the extent that it does not yet have a grammar. If the grammar of a language has already been proficiently dealt with, then no special hermeneutics is necessary from this side either, the general rules are then only applied according to the nature of the grammatical combination. Languages in which the relationship of the elements are regular and which are essentially the same [languages] do not need any special hermeneutics in relation to each other. But if the opposite is the case then there must be both a special grammar and a special hermeneutics. The N.T. language is, though, initially Greek. Now this is a language whose grammar has been proficiently dealt with. But the N.T. language has a particular relationship to Greek.

[*Translator's summary of omitted passage*: The history of the Greek language is divided into a period of flourishing and a period of decay: the N.T. is located in the latter, where the multiplicity of dialects has disappeared. The distinction of prose and poetry is very clear in Greek. N.T. belongs wholly to the latter, in its vernacular form. This may cause problems in relation to use of grammars, which concentrate more on literary sources, and therefore fail to consider much that is part of everyday language. N.T. language has a more extensive linguistic basis than is usually realised, because of the mixture of languages in the period of its composition. It also comes to affect everyday Greek language via the dissemination of Christian ideas. To understand N.T. language one must consider the issue of bilingualism. One learns an old language by acquiring the grammar before the 'living' use of the language itself. If we use this language there is a difference whether we use it directly in everyday life or try to project ourselves back into past life, as we do in relation to a classical language. The former use is analogous to what takes place with N.T. language, where the language is affected by everyday use, in the way that 'Germanisms' will arise in the use of a foreign language in everyday discourse. The Jewish people lived in areas where there was a mixture of languages, involving both Greek and Latin, so even apart from the N.T. their language had polyglot elements.]

Now where do we find assistance for the understanding of the N.T.? First we ask where is the location of what is analogous to N.T. language outside the N.T.? In order to find the Aramaic inspiration of the N.T. idiom we must take account of the Aramaic language. If we make a minor concession we can say that the dialect which was spoken at that time in those areas and with which the falsification of Greek began was admittedly no longer Old Testament Hebrew, but related to it in such a way that this is an insignificant difference for the influence on Greek. Without being initiated into the reading of the O.T. in the original language it is impossible to recognise the Hebraisms correctly. But the Alexandrine translation of the O.T. belongs directly in the language area of the N.T. Here a wealth of Hebraisms are to be expected, because when someone translates works from their mother tongue into another tongue which is foreign to them, they can scarcely cover up all traces of the original language, especially when they have the obligation of fidelity which was particularly determined by the sacredness of the O.T. Here is a language area which, in comparison with that of the N.T., is to be regarded as a more pure area. Initially the Apocrypha of the O.T. belong here, which were originally written in Greek, but in the Hebraic manner and spirit, the historical as well as the gnomic. These belong in terms of their whole structure, even in individual expressions and forms, to the O.T. type. The originally Greek writings of born Jews, like Josephus and Philo, which are without particular relationship to the O.T. also belong here. They learned Greek partly in school, partly from use in everyday life; whence in their writings a battle between the purely Greek and the common Greek of common life with hebrewising components. Even apart from this Aramaic mixture the Greek of the N.T. belongs in terms of its time to the Macedonian language period, which is different from the classical character. But it falls directly into the time of the Roman rule. In the writings of this time latinisms are accordingly to be expected in legal, administrative, military expressions. But in all this we are not certain to find determinate analogies to everything which occurs in the N.T. The question arises: was Christianity something new or not? One part of our theologians claims to know that Christianity arose naturally from Judaism, and that it is only to be regarded as a modification of Judaism. But the dominant opinion takes it as something new, whether in the form of divine revelation or in some other way. However, to the extent that it is something new in the broader or more narrow sense, difficulties must be able to result in the N.T. in relation to language which cannot be solved in the language area mentioned so far, where the new did not yet exist. Every spiritual revolution forms language because thoughts and real relationships arise which, precisely because they are new, cannot be designated by language as it was. They would admittedly not be able to be expressed at all if there were no points of connection in the previous language. But without knowledge of the new we would not understand the language in this respect. The impartiality of the explicator demands that he does not rashly decide the question, but only does so via the study of the N.T. itself in this respect.

[*Translator's summary of omitted passage*: It is still not clear to what extent N.T. language is to be explained by other already existing linguistic areas and modes of thought, such as neo-Platonism. The extent of the Hebrew influence cannot be ascertained solely in terms of Greek sources. There is therefore a continual need for a dual lexical process, involving concordances etc. The differing syntactic structures of Greek and Hebrew cause further difficulties, which mean that attention to context is vital. The novelty of Christianity plays a significant role in the language of the N.T. as opposed to that of the O.T. The relation between the Greek and Latin influence complicates this for German readers, where the Latin influence is greater: 'But here it is always the case, according to the principle of Protestantism, for everyone that concerns themself with the explanation of the N.T., that they should go to work as impartially and as free from doctrinal authority as possible and be concerned always to see and to investigate for themself.' There is a twofold process involved in establishing the extent to which Christianity 'forms language': the philologist should only be concerned with the determination of the particular new meanings of the N.T., not with the conceptual novelty of Christianity itself, whereas the theologian will be concerned mainly with the latter.]

3. Second Canon. The sense of every word in a given location must be determined according to its being-together with those that surround it.

1. The first canon (1.) is more exclusive. This second canon seems to be determining, a leap which must be justified, or rather it is not a leap. For first of all one comes from the first canon to the second, to the extent that each individual word has a specific linguistic area. For what one does not believe one can expect in this area one also does not call in for the explanation either. But, in turn, more or less the whole text belongs to the context and the surroundings of every individual passage. Secondly, one comes just as much from the second canon to the first. For if the immediate connection of subject, predicate and epithets does not suffice for understanding

one must have recourse to similar passages, and then in favourable circumstances just as much outside the work as outside the writer, but always only within the same language area.

2. For this reason the difference between the first and the second canon as well – that the former is exclusive and the latter determining – is more apparent than true: rather in all particular cases the latter is also only exclusive. Every epithet only excludes many manners of use, and determination arises only from the totality of all exclusions. In so far as this canon now also includes in its further extent the whole theory of parallels, the whole of grammatical interpretation is contained in the two together.

3. Here the determination of the formal and the material element is now to be dealt with, both, from the immediate context and from parallels, are oriented towards qualitative as well as quantitative understanding. One can make each of these oppositions into the main basis of division and each will always have something in its favour. But the first is always the most natural because it is a constant double orientation which goes through the whole process.

4. The extension of the canon which lies in the using of parallel passages as an aid is only apparent, and the use of parallels is limited by the canon. For a parallel passage is only one which, in relation to the difficulty encountered, can be thought of as identical with the sentence itself, thus in the unity of the context.

5. If both elements are now main parts, it is useful to begin with determination of the formal element because our understanding of the particular follows the provisional understanding of the whole and the sentence is only singled out as a unity via the formal element.

4. In the determination of the formal *element we distinguish that which connects the sentences and that which connects the elements of the sentences. Here it is a question of the kind of connection, the degree of connection and the range of what is connected.*

1. In doing this one has to go back to the simple clause. For the connection of individual clauses in the period, and the connection of the periods with each other is completely the same, whereas the connection of the parts of the simple clause is definitely different. To the first [i.e. the period and the connection of periods] belongs the conjunction with its rules and what takes its place, similarly, to the other [i.e. the simple clause], belongs the preposition.

45

2. There are, as always, and thus also in discourse, only two kinds of connections, the organic and the mechanical, i.e. internal fusion and external stringing together. But the opposition is not strict, instead the one seems often to turn into the other. A causal or adversative particle often seems only to be one which strings things together; for it has lost or made redundant its real content. But often one which strings together also seems to become internally connective, and then it has become intensified or emphatic. In this way qualitative difference (in the manner of connection) turns into quantitative (in the degree of combination); but this is often only appearance, and one must after all always go back to the original meaning. But the appearance often only arises if one does not think the range or the object of connection correctly. Therefore decisions about one moment of connection may never be made without taking all the other questions into account as well.

3. Organic connection can admittedly be more firm or more loose, but one may never assume that the connecting particles have completely lost their meaning. One assumes this if what is immediately connected does not seem to belong together. But first of all the final clause[e] before the particle can be an addition,[f] and the connection can refer to the preceding main clause.[g] In the same way the first clause after the connection can be a preface and the connection can refer to the following main thought. Admittedly such subordinate clauses should be turned into parentheses in order to make the area of every connection apparent. But every kind of writing only tolerates this to a certain, very differing extent, and the easier and more unconnected the kind of writing, the more the author must rely on the reader. Secondly, the connection can also often not even refer to the last main thought, but rather to the whole sequence, because whole sections also cannot be connected in any other way. In certain structured texts it happens that one repeats the result of a section while making a transition and transforms the connection into a whole clause which at the same time contains the main content of the following section; and ponderous forms tolerate certain connections[h] and repetitions, though this as well should not be taken too far. But in the more light forms the reader must himself pay attention, and this is why a general overview before the understanding of the parts is doubly necessary.

There are also subjective connections, namely those via which the reason is given why what came before was said. Because such connections do not

---

[e] *Satz.*   [f] *Zusatz.*   [g] *Hauptsatz.*   [h] *Anknüpfungen.*

46

differ in their form from objective connections one can easily believe this is a diminution of the meaning of the linking particles, and thus a mere transition.

4. That mere connection can also, so to speak, be emphatically intensified, is already evident from the fact that all our organically linking particles are originally only time- and space-particles. So the present merely linking particles can still be intensified individually. The canon for this results from the fact that mere connection may not be presupposed in the whole. It predominates in descriptions and narratives, but even there not in a pure form, because the writer would otherwise be just a mere organ [of language]. Where this does not take place, then, it [mere connection] can only be subordinate, i.e. contained in organic linking, or inferred from it, or preparing it. But where there is no other organic connection it must remain latent in connections that are merely strung together.

The[6] general formula for the difficult cases of connection of clauses is this: If clauses of unequal content are connected, then the connection is not an immediate one, and one must go back to a clause of equal content.

5. *Application to the N.T.*

1. Given that, even if what one writes is also thought in the (foreign) language, the plan is actually often written in the mother tongue, and the connection of thoughts already lies in the first plan, then one should, in the light of this, be particularly aware of the mixing of Greek and Hebrew in the N.T. writers.

2. This mixing has an even greater influence because both languages are very different in the forms of connection. The N.T. writers could not appropriate the richness of the Greek language in this respect in a non-scholarly manner, as non-scholarly usage pays the least attention to this and assimilates less of the value of the forms of connection via cursory listening. This insufficiency also then makes one hesitant in the use of the forms that are really already familiar. Greek signs which corresponded in several cases to a Hebrew sign were then all the more easily taken for synonymous.

3. For this reason it is necessary to form a whole from the Greek meanings of a sign and the Hebrew meanings which correspond to them, and to judge from this in the manner prescribed.

---

[6] From the lecture of 1826.

4. The lighter kind of writing allows the most free scope for the use of this element (the linking) because the clauses themselves are the least artificially intertwined.

5. Great difference between the N.T. authors in this respect. Paul, for example, constructs in the most Greek way, John in the least.

6. Of greatest importance in relation to the incompleteness of the aids is paying attention even where there is no difficulty, otherwise one never develops a feeling for what one can permit oneself. This is why mistakes are so often made here.

6. The accomplishment of the task of determining the element which connects clauses takes place via general co-operation.

1. In going back to the general content the main ideas are initially what counts, in the consideration of the immediately connected clauses, their subjects and predicates, thus the material element.

2. In the most immediate context what counts is the combined formal element, namely the rules explain the particles and vice versa.

3. In what follows one has still to look for co-ordinated or subordinate forms of connection.

4. The application must make the correct sense; the last determination must always begin with unprejudiced reconstruction.

7. Unconnected clauses can only occur if a clause, whether after causal connection or after stringing together, is posited as One with the previous clause.

1. The first is the case if a clause is immediately taken out of the previous clause, so that the main point was already contained in the previous clause, the second is the case if things which are exactly co-ordinated are placed next to each other. Both cases are not rare.

Addition.[7] The determination of unconnected clauses in a coherent sequence of thoughts takes place with the appropriate modification because of the lacking formal sign of connection according to canon 6.

Modern languages have unconnected clauses far more often than ancient languages. We write for the eye, the ancients wrote for the ear. In this case what was unconnected had to occur much more rarely and the connective particles more frequently.

2. All epithets can sink down in certain cases as far as an enclitic insignificance, and the connection which is implied thereby is the loosest connection.

---

[7] From the lecture of 1826.

3. In the case of a lack of critical consciousness the connection can be thought in an indeterminate manner by the author himself.

4. In the case of the N.T. authors everything comes together to create the looseness of the periods, both in the didactic writings, where the causal connection dominates, and in the historical writings, where narrative connection dominates, namely bad training and usage based on ignorance. This is why both are so difficult. One often does not know how far a didactic sequence goes, or how far a historical whole extends. Only Paul and John stand out, the former in the didactic, the latter in the historical. The interest in determining more exactly than the author did himself depends upon the dogmatic interest and upon that of historical criticism. Whence the fact that everything which is dogmatically or critically difficult depends upon interpretation.

As[8] the punctuation was not originally there among the ancients, we must imagine the texts of antiquity completely without it, otherwise one is greatly influenced by the person who put in the punctuation as an explicator, and one becomes dependent on him and prejudiced. Systems of punctuation fluctuate anyway and are incomplete, both old and new. One should therefore get used to determining the connection of the clauses purely from within the inner relationships.

8. The most difficult thing in relation to the connection in the proposition[9] is the preposition and the immediate relation of dependence.

1. In this case it is the same whether the proposition consists of subject and predicate or also at the same time of the copula. The immediate relation of the two can never be mistaken, and even their immediate extensions by adjectives and adverbs grow together via the form into a whole with them. But the preposition links more precise determinations of the verb, namely of its direction, of its object, etc., to that whole. The genitive, the *Status constructus* etc. is a more precise determination of the subject. The sense of the preposition is easily determined via subject and object. But then the decision via the material element comes in.

In[10] relation to the material elements of the simple proposition the question arises whether the proposition is bipartite (subject and predicate) or tripartite (where the copula is added). The first view is the dynamic view, the second the atomistic,

---

[8] From the lecture of 1826.

[9] *Translator's note:* I translate this as 'proposition' here, rather than as 'clause', as elsewhere in this section, because what is said extends to the wider philosophical issue concerning the nature of the proposition which goes back to Aristotle. What is said can, of course, also apply to the clause.

[10] From the lecture of 1826.

because one believes the connection is something else which puts itself next to the parts. It is striking that this latter view is still so generally dominant. If one answered the question, 'what, for example, about the proposition the tree blossoms?', from this side, by saying that it is really tripartite, namely thus: 'the tree is blooming', then that is not at all in accordance with language; it would follow that there is only one single verb, the verb 'to be'. But this is obviously false. The primary thing in languages themselves is the dynamic view of the proposition.

2. In the N.T. the hebrewising tendency is here just as predominant as in the combination of the clauses and one must always have in mind the Hebrew form which corresponds to the Greek.

9. There are cases where one can trace the difficulty just as much to the material as to the formal element.
For example the hiphilic meaning of the verbs and the like can be regarded as a conjugation (formal element) and as its own word (material element) and this is the case for all derived forms of the verb, so that the opposition is also not pure but comes about via transition. In such cases one must see which treatment gives one a more pure and a more rich whole from which one can construct.

10. Subject and predicate mutually condition each other, but not completely.
The most precise mutual conditioning is the idiom,[i] which has the most narrow and most established sphere in the technical realm. The opposite point is on the one side the idea,[j] in which a rare predicate is attributed to a subject outside the usual sphere, and on the other side the gnomic utterance [saying] which also has no more precise means of determination but precisely for this reason remains indeterminate in itself and is determined in each application.

11. Both, subject and predicate, are more precisely determined in themselves and thus also mutually by their adjectives.
1. Adjectives and adverbs point to a specific direction and rule out many things. The connections via prepositions are also still more precise determinations of the verb, as one can see from the fact that the preposition also becomes of its own accord a component of the verb.

2. However this is not sufficient, instead the really positive element can only be given by being involved in the reconstruction of the whole sequence of thoughts.

[i] *Phrase.* [j] *Einfall.*

12. For the N.T. the task is of great importance and difficulty because of the new and unique concepts.

13. If the immediate determination is not sufficient, mediated determination must come in via identity and opposition. Similarity and difference are to be reduced to this.

14. Opposition is everywhere, but it is most present in dialectical composition. In relation to the N.T. Paul comes particularly into consideration here.

15. The rules for the discovery of opposition are the same for the identical and the opposed.
1. For there can be no judgement about the opposed except in relation to a higher identity, and in the same way one recognises identity only via a shared opposition.
2. In both cases it is equally a question of the certainty that we are putting the relationship of two clauses in the same way as the author put it himself.

16. A sentence in which the same subject or the same predicate predominates without interruption is still to be regarded as belonging to the immediate context (identity).

17. If that which returns after an interruption belongs to the main context of an utterance, but not that which interrupts, then identity is most probable.

18. If what returns is a subsidiary thought and what interrupts is the main thought then one can only be convinced of the identity according to the sameness in the context and according to the identity of type in the formulation of the thought itself.

19. With regard to the main thought one can go beyond a text itself to those of the same author which can be regarded as One with the first text, and thus also to texts of others which follow from the identity of the school and of the perspective.

20. In relation to the subsidiary thought it is, when observing § 18, more a question of the identity of the language area and the kind of writing than of the person and their perspective.
To what extent can subsidiary thoughts be explained via other passages where there is the same main thought? Qualitatively but not quantitatively.

21. The more one relies on others in the search (15.), the more one must be in a position to check their judgement.

22. In the application to the N.T. the philological perspective, which isolates every text of every writer, and the dogmatic perspective, which regards the N.T. as One work of One writer, are opposed.

23. Both come closer together if one ponders the fact that with regard to the religious content the identity of the school, and with regard to the subsidiary thoughts the identity of the language area, become relevant.

24. From the dogmatic perspective the canon remains false that: One should assume metaphorical usage only in the most exceptional case.[11] This canon presupposes a particular personality of the Holy Spirit as a writer.

25. The philological perspective fails to live up to its own principle if it rejects mutual dependence along with individual formation.

26. The dogmatic perspective goes further than it needs to if it rejects individual formation along with dependence, and thus destroys itself.
It destroys itself namely because it must attribute to the Holy Spirit the undeniable change of mood and modifications of perspective.

Addition.[12] This would also be in contradiction with the Pauline theory of the relationship of the One and same Spirit to the various talents in the individual members of the congregation, 1. Cor. 12.

27. The question still remains, which of the two should be put above the other, and the philological perspective itself must decide this question in favour of dependence.
In part the individuality of the N.T. writers is initially a product of their relationship to Christ, in part, as far as Paul and John, who are the more individual by nature, are concerned, one of them completely changed, so that he would be better explained via other N.T. writers than via his own pre-Christian writings; the other obviously came young to Christ and only developed his individuality as a Christian.

[11] This is to be understood from: Ernesti Instit. interpret. ed. Ammon, pp. 114, 115. 'Vulgare est praeceptum, quod jubet *non facile* (*or*, non sine evidenti causa aut necessitate) *discedere a proprietate significationis*' [The maxim is commonplace whereby it is not easy (*or* not without evident cause or necessity) to depart from the literalness of meaning].
[12] From the lecture of 1826.

28. If the philological perspective denies this, it destroys Christianity.
For if the dependence on Christ is nothing in comparison with personal individuality and the national failings, then Christ Himself is nothing.

29. If the dogmatic (perspective) extends the canon of the analogy of belief beyond these limits, it destroys the Scripture.
For a *locus communis* [commonplace] from the clear passages of the Scripture cannot be used to explain the obscure passages without the Scripture being explained via dogmatic consciousness, which destroys its authority and therefore conflicts with the principles of the dogmatic perspective itself. For the setting up of such *loci communes* is a dogmatic operation in which one must, besides abstracting from the individuality of the person which is being doubted, also abstract from the indubitable particularity of the occasion.

Every passage is a combination of things that are common to other passages and things particular to this passage and cannot therefore be correctly explained via what is common alone. The things in common cannot be correctly established until all passages are explained, and the fluctuating opposition of clear and obscure passages can be explained by the fact that originally only one passage is clear.[13]

As[14] the belonging together and harmony of the thoughts of the N.T. the analogy of belief is admittedly a true concept.

30. The analogy of belief can therefore only emerge from correct explication, and the canon, as a truly hermeneutic canon, can only be: There is a false explanation somewhere if nothing in common emerges in an agreed form from all the passages which belong together.
One can therefore only say that the probability of incorrect explanation then lies with that passage which alone resists the discovery of something in common of this kind.

31. The unity and difference of the N.T. can be compared with the unity and difference of the Socratic school.

---

[13] Schleiermacher means, according to the lecture of 1826, that if one calls what gives a determinate sense clear, then in every given difficult context for the gradual genesis of understanding only One thing is originally clear.
[14] From the lecture of 1826.

Socrates[15] the master also writes nothing himself. His views are only transmitted in the texts of his pupils. These admittedly form themselves in an individual manner after his death, but the Socratic flavour remained in all of them. No one doubts the identity and individuality of the Socratics. And the same is the case for the relationship of the disciples to Christ. But the relatedness is greater in the N.T. writers than among the Socratics because the power of unity which came from Christ was greater and, even among the Apostles who were significantly individual, like Paul, was so powerful that in their doctrines they referred exclusively to Christ. Even the fact that, for example as a proselytiser, Paul had effects in a different and in a wider sphere than Christ did not essentially weaken the predominance of unity which came from Christ. For even if the idea of proselytisation first became clear among the Apostles primarily via Paul, the fact remains that in this Paul was not conscious of any other power than that of Christ, and if the idea had not been part of the doctrine of Jesus, the other Christians would not have acknowledged him as a Christian, let alone as an Apostle. Among the Socratics, on the other hand, we find that they often concerned themselves with objects which Socrates never touched, and in this their individuality and difference emerged more freely.

32. Philological explanation must precede the use of the N.T. as a whole.[k]
Without[16] the latter (dogmatic explication) the theological task is not completely accomplished, but without the preceding philological explanation, which tries to understand every thought and every expression via its context, one cannot have a good conscience in relation to dogmatic explication.

33. The principles of parallelism are different for both because of the possibility of the same content being present in completely different use of language.

34. It is essential to separate completely the two procedures (the philological and the dogmatic) and the explicator must have a clear consciousness about which one he is engaged in.

35. If the explication which takes place on the assumption of prior knowledge of the language is to be carried out in the same way as the explication by means of which the knowledge of the language comes into being, then a determinate language area must be marked out by the use of the parallel passages in the sphere of a word.
In fact everything which is cited beneath determinate meanings in the lexicons as an authority must be a collection of parallel passages.

---

[15] From the lecture of 1826.   [16] From the lecture of 1826.

[k] *den zusammenstellenden Gebrauch des N.T.*: the sense is not wholly clear.

The[17] knowledge of the language arises via hermeneutic operations. The first thing is to have as complete indices as possible on the individual writers, thus – use of parallels. From this we then gain indices for the language, for specific areas, for the philosophical, rhetorical, mathematical area, etc. In this it is largely a matter of presenting in context those expressions which occur mainly in the key passages, the customary expressions of every object and their dissolution into general linguistic usage. In this way the true dictionary arises from both operations; it must give the main location for every word, and, beginning from there, present the dissemination of the usage in being applied to related areas, as historically, chronologically as possible. In the same way as the use of parallels, often in the broadest sense, is necessary, so that one goes over in a comparative manner to related languages, to the root language, explication also always requires the use of parallels in the narrower and the broader sense. The knowledge of the language which the explication presupposes is still incomplete. It is only sufficient to begin the artistic explication. But precisely for this reason artistic grammatical explication must in turn have effects on the extension and completion of the knowledge of the language.

36. Via this (35.) the old rule that if there are still traces to be found in the text itself one should not seek the means of explanation outside the text becomes very restricted.

1. For if words do now in fact occur with the same meaning outside the text, then one would in fact take up such passages into the dictionary. The difference between more easy and more difficult passages cannot be cited against this, but it is admittedly this difference that was the basis of that rule.

2. It would be very restricted in relation to the main ideas in the N.T. because the religious transformation did not affect everything, instead many ideas remained the way they were for the people at the time, in part also because ideas of the time were cited in opposition to Christian ideas.

3. In relation to subsidiary ideas it is obvious that other N.T. writers are not more closely related to one N.T. writer than other non-N.T. writers who share the sphere of thoughts, level of education, and language area with him.

4. The rule is worth even less in relation to the N.T. if by the term Scripture one also understands the Old Testament as well. For this contains much with regard to the main ideas that is mistaken and had already become alien to the whole N.T. era, and with regard to the main ideas it belongs to a time of which only a little was transferred into the N.T. era.

[17] From the lecture of 1826.

55

37. As the sense is not in the individual elements but only in their being-together, the most immediate parallels are those which present the same being-together.
It is always a kind of arbitrariness to declare a word to be the more obscure word, for it can just as easily be the other word, e.g. John 7, 39, where one would be wasting one's effort if one wanted to look around at random among the various meanings of πνεῦμα ἅγιον [Holy Spirit], instead the correct parallel is Acts of the Apostles 19, 12, and one can really say the difficulty lies in the εἶναι [to be], which is not to be taken strictly here, but means 'present in the appearance', 'be communicated'.

38. One must always pay as much attention to quantitative as to qualitative understanding.
Therefore, do not only begin with it in relation to difficult passages, but rather in relation to easier passages, in the formal and material element of language, in words and whole sentences.

39. The minimum of quantitative understanding is redundancy, the maximum is emphasis.
1. Redundancy is when a part contributes nothing to the whole. But this never takes place in an absolute manner. Emphasis is: first, if the word is to be taken in the greatest range, in which it usually does not occur, then, as well, if all subsidiary ideas that it can arouse are also intended. The latter is something endless.

2. But because the end-points are not really given, one assumes an average, as what is usual, and what is below it moves toward redundancy, what is above it toward emphasis.

40. Everything which is more or less redundant, as it must after all have a basis, must have emerged either with regard to the musical in language or from a mechanical attraction, and one must be able to prove one of the two if one wants to regard something as redundant.
1. Mechanical attraction can only take place if the connection of two parts of an utterance has become a set phrase and an idiom.

2. For musical reasons something redundant can only be present in those genres where this element is more prominent, and in those passages where the logical plays less of a role, the latter being the case when the form of opposition is completely lacking.

3. Parts of the subject or of the predicate can be redundant in this way if it has dissolved into multiplicity. This can also be the case for secondary

determinations of either subject or predicate if they do not have a determinate opposition opposite them.

41. What is supposed to be emphatic must make itself recognisable by a more accentuated position and other indications.

1. One cannot unconsciously go beyond the usual measure of significance, it [emphasis] must always want to be noticed, because the emphatic use of a word is always an abbreviation, putting something into a word which could otherwise stand next to it. If the first [putting the word in an emphatic position] therefore cannot take place with appropriate clarity, then everyone naturally chooses the other indications.

2. There must always be another part of an utterance in relation to which another part is emphatic, and this must make itself clear via the combination.

42. The maxim of taking as much as possible tautologically[18] is just as false as the maxim of taking as much as possible emphatically.

1. The first of these is the more recent. It is thought to be sufficiently justified in the N.T. by the predominant form of parallelism and by the – for the most part – lesser logical stringency; but this is unfounded, and in the light of the propositions above one must no longer have recourse to it. People thought they were particularly justified by every easy appearance of synonymy.

2. The second is the older, and is connected with the view that the Holy Spirit is the author and that it would not do anything in vain, whence no redundancy, no tautology, and therefore initially everything related is emphatic, but then anything at all as well, for there is something too much in every word if it is not completely exhausted in every location. But given that the person of the writer was never absent for the original listeners and readers and they could only judge speech and writing in terms of the usual presuppositions, then the excuse that the Holy Spirit had the whole of Christianity which believes in inspiration – which can only judge it according to the proposed maxim – in its eye is of no use, as this Christianity could only arise via the correct understanding which communicated itself to the first Christians; so this maxim is quite reprehensible.

3. As the truth now lies in the middle, no other rule of judgement can be given than that one should always have an eye on both deviations, and

---

[18] *Translator's note*: the crucial sense of 'tautology' here is the idea of saying the same thing twice, albeit using different words to do so.

should ask oneself which could be applied with the least abnormality. Here in particular the stressing of figurative expressions comes up, as, seen emphatically, every metaphor is an abridgement of a simile, and in the same way one can always also render a simile itself emphatic. Whether what one still wants in a simile also lies in the same area in which the simile is located must also be judged solely according to the rules proposed. For otherwise one just does get applications and imputations. On the other hand one must also remember how close metaphor is to idiom: for then no emphasis is to be expected. Emphasis dominates the most in strictly dialectical and in witty discourse.

43. The degree to which redundancy or emphasis is to be assumed does not just depend on the genre of the utterance but also on the stage of development of the object.

If an object has been appropriately worked on in conceptual manner then one can begin with the mean [between redundancy and emphasis] and it only depends upon the genre of discourse when or where one has to expect more emphasis or more redundancy. But if the object is still new and the language for it has not yet formed then an uncertainty arises as to whether elements chosen also achieve the aim, and where in the particulars the language is based on something determinate a tendency arises to secure what has not yet been sufficiently secured by another expression. This is the source of accumulation which is then sometimes taken for tautology, sometimes for emphasis. The fact of the matter is, though, that one must not regard them as one and the same, but also not as opposed to each other, but rather as One, and develop the idea from them taken together. In the N.T. this is least the case in Paul, because his terminology rested on a mass of oral instruction, in John it is most the case. A result of false emphasis was then that all single expressions, [like?] renewal, illumination, reincarnation were taken up into the dogmatic system of concepts, from which arose a confusing, unscientific superfluity. A result of false tautology was that a minimum of content was attributed to the expressions, and the concept itself was renounced.

44. The quantitative understanding of clauses leads back to that of the elements and that of the means of connection.

1. Clauses have a relationship to each other and one to the unity of the discourse. In the latter everything depends upon the opposition between

main and secondary ideas, in the former everything depends upon the opposition between *co-ordinated* and *subordinated*. Everything is a main idea that is said for its own sake, everything is a secondary idea which is only said in order to clarify, even though the latter can often be far more detailed than the former. Main ideas to be recognised by the concepts which occur in them. As secondary ideas involve redundancy, and have no place in the ideal of strictly scientific discourse, the relationship between main and secondary ideas is to be judged in the same way as that of redundancy and emphasis.

2. Whether clauses are co-ordinated or subordinated must become clear from the particles and the ways of connecting; but the content is something extra to this. The more the forms of connection are fixed in a language and a genre of discourse, the less one first needs to ask about the content of the clauses, and, vice versa, the clearer the context, the less an anomaly in the use of the forms of connection matters.

3. In loose forms, as those of the N.T. in fact are, it is difficult to distinguish main and secondary ideas via the language area, because this opposition itself is not strongly established, but instead one is turned into the other via a minor change of subject. Then the other must help out, and as one recognises the relationship of one clause to another, one must also find out the relationship to the whole by means of the same.

Addition. The incorrect classification of dogmatic passages is to be explained by this, and is really based on the maxim that in the N.T. texts everything dogmatic is immediately supposed to be a main idea. But this maxim is untenable.

Concluding Remarks

The topics we have just dealt with have drawn our attention mainly to technical interpretation. Not that the maxim that each side should really be self-sufficient is wrong in itself; but it presupposes a knowledge of the language which is so complete that it is not possible without completed explication.

As I must now use the knowledge of the language of other people if there is a lack in my knowledge of the language, but can only use this itself with a deficient knowledge of the language, in every such case technical explication must be a complement. And it is the same the other way round: I can only use others' knowledge of the author via my deficient knowledge of them themselves, so grammatical explication must serve as a complement.

[*Lücke*: Schleiermacher himself notes here in the margin of his notebook that he changed the lecture in 1828 from § 4 onwards by putting the material element first. Even more significant is the change already from § 3 onwards in 1832. But the marginalia for both the lecture of 1828 and 1832 do not provide a coherent clear outline or even a directory. Comparison of transcribed notebooks shows that the oral presentation after 1828, which was more and more independent of the written plan, sometimes shortened and omitted, at other times extended and incorporated new material, in ever changing order. In these circumstances it was impossible to retain the editorial method used so far. In order not to lose anything essential and of importance, it seemed advisable first of all to give the lecture as Schleiermacher conceived it in 1819 complete, with clarifications and discussions interpolated here and there from the lecture of 1826, but then to follow this, from the transcribed notebooks, with the last, most complete lecture of 1832 in a summary which, as far as possible, is complete. This is what now follows.]

If, after applying the first canon to the N.T. (§§1 and 2), we orient ourselves further in grammatical interpretation, the most favourable case is where, after appropriate preparation, of which the overview of the whole is a part, we can, while continuing to read the details directly, determine the individual elements of a sentence from its contexts in such a way that there is no doubt that we have grasped the sentence in the way its author thought it. But if this is not the case then we must seek to bring to mind the whole linguistic value of the elements bound together in a sentence. For this we use the lexicon. One must, though, bring to mind the linguistic value of all elements in the sentence, and not just of the one that causes difficulty, because it can often happen that we only have difficulty with one through lack of knowledge of another element. For this reason one must investigate everything. There are admittedly exceptions here, if one has, from previous use and practice in the language elsewhere, got the certain feeling that one is unfamiliar with only the one element. But one should thereby check oneself very carefully in order not to get into an embarrassing situation which would have been easy to avoid via a more precise procedure.

If we have appropriately brought to mind all the linguistic values then it is a question of correctly determining the local value of every word in the context of the utterance. But there is a limit to be sought here. This lies in the fact that the becoming-one of noun and verb is the sentence, in which the former is subject, the latter predicate, which mutually determine each other. The limit becomes extended if we think of the sentence as extended with a certain degree of evenness, so that every element still has something determining with it. In this way we have elements via which we can get closer to the task. The fact is that not only is the noun determined by the verb, but also by what is attributed to it, or the influence which the verb has on the noun receives a certain direction by what is attributed to the noun. However, this only takes place in this way in simple sentences. But often a subject is for several verbs. Then all verbs are determining and must relate in the same sense to the noun, if it is not obvious that the various linguistic values are being played with. But the determination does not just begin with the whole sequence of verbs, but at the same time from all the adjectives which have been added to the verbs and nouns. Here the question now arises how we recognise that an element which is disputed in terms of its local value is meant differently in one place with which we are concerned from in another. – This differs according to the structure of the thoughts. If the content of a sequence of thoughts is given in advance by a heading then one can conclude that the concept designated therein is the main concept, and one has every reason to believe that the word which designates the same thing will occur everywhere in the same sense, even in the case that the concept can be divided. For the designation would always remain that of the whole, and it would be illogical if, without it being expressly noted, the expression were used in a partial sense. If we, therefore, have an overview of the whole via a heading or provisional read-through we can determine the limit within which the main thoughts and the linguistic elements expressing it must occur in one and the same sense. Such an overview can, namely, not be achieved without noting whether an expression occurs in different places in different significances. But this canon of identity is only valid for the expressions which are essential constituents of the utterance. For in the case of inessential expressions there is nothing which could have prevented the utterer using an expression differently in different places, as long as it was in accordance with the general linguistic value. But this is only a relative opposition. For what seems in itself inessential in the structure of thoughts can, in its particular location, be essential in the development of the structure. We must therefore seek another opposition.

As soon as a structure of thoughts in ordered discourse is of more than absolutely minimal length we not only get a difference between main and secondary thoughts along with the linguistic elements which pertain to each but also an opposition between those elements of language and thoughts which are parts of the whole and those which are not really parts of the whole at all but are merely means of presentation. If e.g. a thought is made clear and graphic in a coherent utterance by a comparison, the comparison is only a means of presentation and in fact alien to the object, and it only comes in in order, as an alien element, to give part of the whole more determinacy and clarity. This can often be something isolated, but it can also often run through the whole presentation. Here we have a real inner difference in the utterance, not just a question of more and less. In the case of such figurative, comparatively employed expressions we have, in comparison with the construction of the whole from its essential elements, no clear indication at all, because comparisons, figurative expressions can be used now in one manner, now in another.–

Now how does the canon of finding the local value relate to the first canon (1.)? The latter is only negative, excluding or preventing the determination of the local value being sought in a language area which is not common to the author and the readers. The general language area is, though, more precisely determined in every utterance or text, and our second canon relates to this more precise determinacy in the context and is therefore the positive canon.

It is now a question of the extent, of the extension of this positive canon. As soon as one goes beyond the barrier of the simple and complex sentence, in order to determine the local word-value, the use of parallel passages begins. Initially these are passages of the same text, in which the expression is used in a similar manner. But only if the conditions for determining the local value are the same in both passages and the first canon is not infringed, so that the parallel therefore lies in the same language area, is the parallel an explanatory aid. On this condition I can also take parallels from other texts of the same author, indeed from texts of other authors.

Another extension of the canon comes into play if the writer himself explains a sentence in the same structure of thoughts via an opposition. The easier this is to grasp, the more unambiguous, the more explanatory it is. Such oppositions are often more effective for hermeneutic determination than analogies, as opposition is much more decisive than analogy and mere difference. We are then in the area of the object itself; by positing one thing and excluding another, we determine and understand the former via the latter more acutely and more exactly. There is in this, therefore, an important hermeneutic aid. If opposition and analogy can be combined in the same language area and in the same or a similar structure of thoughts, then the explanation is even more significant. But this hermeneutic aid is only valid initially in relation to expressions which have their essential location in the context of the whole and which belong to parts of the object. However, if it is the case that obscurities arise when the writer wishes to explain his object via things outside it, then the only thing left to do is for me to look for a passage where something is talked about *ex professo* [explicitly] which is only touched on in passing in a questionable passage, or where the same thing is used in an analogous fashion. But then one must determine more clearly the relationship between what is explained here and what is explained there.

If we pursue the canon that has been established further we must, in order to proceed organically, first and foremost *distinguish main and secondary thoughts* in relation to the elements of an utterance which can be controversial. If we could always hold onto this classification everywhere in the same way, then we would also always have an assured link for our provisional procedure, via which we gained a general overview. But here a difference comes into play. The more logical an utterance is, the more the opposition of main and secondary thoughts comes to the fore, and the more the structure already results from a general overview. If we now move with this to complete understanding, then it can often be the case that it is advisable to leave the difficulties in the secondary thoughts to one side for the time being and above all to get hold of the main thought and to construct the understanding of the secondary thoughts by beginning with the main thought. Where this logical analysis can take place hermeneutic understanding is easy. But that is not always the case. We have hermeneutic tasks where no use can be made of that operation. It is lyric poetry which most eludes logical analysis. In lyric poetry there is such a free movement of thoughts that it is difficult to distinguish what is main and what is secondary thought, and what is mere means of presentation. The final reason for this is that in lyric poetry, where it is a question of expressing the movement of immediate self-consciousness, the thought itself is really only a means of presentation. But if all thoughts are only means of presentation the relative opposition between main and secondary thought disappears. In the same way this opposition disappears, only in the opposite manner, when all thoughts are main thoughts, i.e. in strictly scientific systematic presentation. Here a thought is the immediate form of the whole, and everything particular is an integrating part of the whole. In this way we have the two end points for our canon, where it seems to have the least value. But they are the most suited to making clear the aptness of the theory beginning with the opposed points.

The hermeneutic task is particularly difficult in relation to lyric poetry. The movement of thoughts of the lyric poet is completely free, but the reader is not always a lyrical reader, and to this extent he is incapable of reconstructing the lyrical poem from out of his own consciousness. The hermeneutic canon that has been established here is based on the assumption of a bound[1] train of thought, and is therefore not immediately applicable to lyric poetry, because here unboundedness prevails. How are we now to proceed? The provisional overview of a lyric product admittedly does not give us a difference between main and secondary thoughts, but it does

---

[1] *Translator's note*: the opposition between what is '*gebunden*', 'bound', in the sense of subject to rules and constraints, and what is not thus 'bound' is central to the whole of Schleiermacher's thought. I translate the word literally (and artificially) because any other English word has connotations which do not exactly correspond to the meaning.

emphasise many things which we are certain about. But this is initially what appears as the negation of the bound train of thought, i.e. what presents itself as a leap and as a turning point. This, though, leads back again to what is bound, from which even the most free movement of thought cannot completely free itself. Organic form and the manner of its being linked together are essentially the same in the lyric sentence as in bound presentation. It is just that the linking together is treated more loosely. The linguistic elements are the same, only in different relationships. But because logical opposition and subordination are lacking it is best to go straight into the detail after getting an impression of the whole. But this is the case only from the linguistic side, not from the psychological side. This is different in systematic scientific presentation. Here everything stands in the relationship of subordination or co-ordination of the individual parts of the whole. We get a general impression of this relationship via the overview and then it is just a question of determining in detail the relationship of sub- and co-ordination more precisely. But that does not involve any further difficulty if we grasp the structure of the text correctly as the author had it in mind. However a difficulty can lie in precisely this. Revolutions in the area of natural science and ethics have produced new systems and rejected old ones. If one now comes suddenly and without reflection from the presentation of an earlier scientific system, after one has grasped it, to another, new system, one must, after constructing the language, leave the details still indeterminate, until one has grasped the whole. If one wished immediately to compare details in the new system with details in the preceding system, one would misunderstand, for the relationship of the details is different in every whole. If there are transitions, points of contact between the old and the new, then the process is easier, but it remains essentially the same, for the change is based on facts which are either completely new or which display completely new relationships. In the process, even if what is new is initially communicated in the previous language, new expressions are produced. The task always essentially consists in both producing the hermeneutic construction and seeing the whole all at once.

Between the two aforementioned end- and limit-points, where we can more generally designate the first as poetry, the second as prose, lie all the different kinds of composition and the modifications of the hermeneutic process determined by them. The general hermeneutic difference between poetry and prose is that in the former the particular wishes to have its specific value as such, in the latter the particular has it only in the whole, in relation to the main thought. Of the kinds of composition which lie in between, among the poetic kinds the dramatic comes closest to prose, and in it everything wants to be understood as One and so to a certain extent all at once. The real centre on the poetic side is epic poetry. Here there is always a combination of several thoughts, but each one is there individually. There we have the domain of the main thought, but as soon as that thought presents itself individually the domain of secondary thoughts arises, but around this is a general poetic life, and there the thoughts are, in the more narrow sense, means of presentation. In the same way, in prose there is a form which is closest to lyric poetry, the epistolary form. Here there is a free stringing together of thoughts which have no further link than the self-consciousness of the subject which is aroused now in this manner, now in another. The real domain of the epistolary form is in the relationship of mutual acquaintance. Where that does not exist the letter goes out of its domain. Historical presentation forms the centre as far as prose is concerned. Here the main thoughts are parts of the presentation, which are essential to the fact which is to be presented. Sentences which present themselves while the fact is being presented are secondary thoughts and means of presentation. The didactic can come close to the strictly systematic, but if the presentation becomes rhetorical it permits a wealth of secondary thoughts and means of presentation.

However, the question which was initially at issue here was to what extent, where such differences and gradations take place, the hermeneutic process must be different according to the canon that has been established. Now here the following rule comes in according to what has been said so far: It is to be assumed of everything which belongs to the main thought of a structure of thoughts that it is used in the same meaning as long as the same context continues to exist. But this is not valid for that which is only a means of presentation. This can have differing local value in differing passages. Parentheses do not cancel out the context and its identity. They are precisely just interruptions, after which the context which is not yet closed re-establishes itself. Whence even among the ancients the fact that the beginning and the end of the parentheses lose themselves, so to speak, and are not noticeable. Only where there is a real conclusion which is intended by the author is the context broken off and the domain is thereby limited in which the determination of an indeterminate expression is first to be sought. But if there is not sufficient indication in such a closed context for the determination of a questionable local value, one can, if the same structure of thought is anywhere to be found, even if it is in another writer but in the same language area, use this as a supplement. One has, though, to be careful, in using such supplements or means of explanation, to take account of the degree of relatedness, for the greater or lesser justification and the greater or lesser certainty involved in their use is dependent on this. If the difficulty lies not in the main thought but in the secondary thought, then the determination of the local value of the expression must be sought where the secondary thought appears as a main thought, but, in order to be certain, not in a single passage but in several. This rule is based on the fact that the more an expression is a secondary thought the less one is to assume that it is taken in its complete determinacy. This has a psychological reason. In the writing of a text the writer is accompanied by ideas which impose themselves upon him more or less forcefully along with the main thought. This accompaniment of ideas is determined by the individuality of the writer and so the way in which secondary thoughts come into the context also depends upon this. The more this individuality is known the easier it gets to establish the local value of an expression as a secondary thought from its familiar overall value. An author may give his main thoughts clearly and distinctly, but he may not be precise with the secondary thoughts because the accompanying ideas in his everyday life do not reach complete determinacy and remain hints; in this way he also cannot and does not want to give the expression a greater determinacy than the idea has. In many writers the secondary thoughts are objectively related to the main thought. This is the case in authors who are used to proceeding logically. Indeed, the more logically someone thinks and writes, the more the secondary thoughts recede. But the more illogically, the more easily the most alien and the most distant things can be expected if there is only a small amount of analogy. In relation to logical writers one is therefore compelled to grasp the secondary thoughts in relation to the main thoughts more precisely, whereas in relation to the others [the illogical writers] one has less cause to be very precise about secondary thoughts the more alien they are. But from all this it follows that here the hermeneutic operation encroaches on the psychological side. – If the manner in which a linguistic element is used in a secondary thought has something constant, which is mainly the case for customary expressions, there is correspondingly less difficulty and all the more certainty. The less an object is already fixed in general thinking, the less customary expressions are to be expected. But in this one has to pay attention to the fact that the more general a customary expression has become, the more it loses interest, and the more easily one neglects it. In this way customary forms age and lose their value. If a writer is practised in such out of date customary forms he becomes old-fashioned. Here a different value therefore emerges and the following rules in relation to it: The more often a secondary thought and its expression occur in certain combinations, the greater is the certainty and ease of understanding; but the more this grows the value of the expressions decreases. For this reason a correct evaluation of the value is necessary each time. – The rule given above for the finding of local values of the secondary thoughts, namely to compare where they occur as main thoughts, where they have their real location, is only applicable when the secondary thoughts emerge with a certain clarity and with ease, but not where they are on the border of clear consciousness and start to wander into confusion. In this last case an indirect procedure is necessary. One must ask, namely, in what direction has the secondary thought that is adduced been able to contribute to the effect of the whole? If one has found that, one then can apply the rule above and say the author has taken the secondary thought with its expression out of this or that parallel structure and used it in the particular sense.

This leads to a more precise consideration of the relationships of the concepts and their designations, which are so important for the hermeneutic operation. We distinguish linguistic and logical relatedness. The former has a dual nature, first that between root words and derived words, and then the collateral relationship between the derived words of the same root. If the root is certain and the form of derivation known, the procedure is that of a calculation; for we have in the root that which is common to all, the unity, and in the forms of derivation we have the law of the differences. If the root of a given family cannot be found, but derived words of another root word are given whose usage I know to be similar to the one in question, then I can also use these as an explanatory relationship. Admittedly this seems to presuppose a specific relationship. If I do not find an analogy for the use of a root word in the language area where it is to be sought, and if the root word is not used like the word derived from it, then one is to assume an archaism in relation to the difference of time, a provincialism in relation to location, or an idiom. The use of collateral relationships is much broader.

In logical relationships we must go back to the opposition between general and particular ideas. Words which designate concepts which are derived from the same higher concept and are co-ordinated with each other are related. This presupposes a way of constituting ideas via opposition from out of something in common. In this way, if one goes back to the basic principle of opposition, the explanation arises from things which are opposed. If an expression, which I can only consider in its location to be a general idea, is obscure to me, i.e. does not lead to all the ideas which are co-ordinated with it and are derived with it from One higher concept, then I can only reach understanding if I have an eye on all the ideas which arose via division and opposition, for with them I then have what has been divided itself. The structure of all parts becomes what has been divided itself and will have to contain the complete formula for the basic division. But one often gets into difficulties with this. If the explanation of a general expression is lacking, then this is the same as if there were a hermeneutic task for individual cases. – One is, e.g., not yet agreed about a certain border between animal and vegetable. If the word animal occurs in a writer precisely in the border region between animal and vegetable, then the word is obscure without a specific general explanation. If this explanation is lacking and I am to look for it, I can only find it if I have everything in a logical structure before me which exhausts the expression. The result of this is that not everything can be achieved via what is opposed, namely, like in the case cited, if the border, the principle of opposition, is not completely determined. This leads to the question of whether another relationship also occurs, apart from that via opposition. Certainly! There are relationships which are determined by differences (distinctions) which are not oppositions, which are not relationships of exclusion. There is, e.g., no pure opposition between animal and plant, and if we have to say that both are forms of life that are connected by an immediate transition, then we will indeed perceive many differences which admittedly lead to determinate oppositions, but they will be purely quantitative. So there are areas where qualitative opposition among ideas dominates and those where transitions (quantitative) opposition dominates. In the area of colours, e.g., we do have certain oppositions, but they are dominated by transition; even if we have certain expressions for what falls in the middle, there are always colours which, located on the border, can be attributed both to one and to another area. The more immediate the transition, the greater is the relatedness. This kind of relatedness is more difficult to deal with than that which arises through pure opposition. There the consideration comes into play that, in the same way as there are different ways of seeing, there is also a difference in the idea of one and the same object. Where such a difference occurs it must always be taken into account in the explanation of an expression by relatedness. This connects to our principle that everything individual can only be understood via the whole. All ideas which are linked by oppositions in a structure form a whole; but the same is true for every structure of transitions. If a single thing is to be explained via the connection with another writer, one must be certain in advance that the other has the same way of seeing, the same way of imagining.

If we look at the various characters of the linguistic elements in this respect, we will find, looking at the question as a whole, that the noun is the region in which opposition dominates, the verb the region where transitions dominate. For the noun includes all determinate forms of being which occur to me, be they produced by nature or by art, in itself. The former are, though, by far the largest part of this region. Verbs, designating activities, are already thereby directed towards transitions, thus towards differences which are not oppositions. Here only in general the rule [is valid] that much greater caution is necessary in the explanation of a word via mere difference than via pure opposition, for here we have to do with what is objectively determined, which is connected to the fact that the designation of opposition is much more firmly established in the language.

But the relationship above of the differing regions of noun and verb is only valid in general, for we find that sometimes verbs are derived from nouns, and sometimes nouns from verbs. If these are the two main directions in the development of the imagination, then it follows that explication is more certain where the language in its main form entirely exhausts the idea; then the language itself will be the indication of one and the other [noun and verb]; but to the extent to which it fluctuates explication must also fluctuate. In Hebrew, e.g., where the assumption is universal that all root words are verbs and all nouns derived, explication is made much easier precisely because of this simple orientation of the language in this aspect. But where both directions are in the constitution of the language, the determinate indication in the language itself is also lacking, and a great wealth of means of explanation must be given in order to proceed with certainty. If one now has all the expressions which together form a whole, but which are different because of modifications which can always be attributed to a certain opposition, one can then order them in a certain manner and determine their value to each other, and if one can then also say that in the language area with which one is concerned all the expressions occur and that the writer uses them all, then one can determine the local value via the writer himself. But if the manner of writing is of another kind then the sphere of the moments of explanation given in the text itself is more narrow and one must go beyond it.

Now as far as the thoughts are concerned which are only means of presentation in a given structure, one must first bring into view everything which is generally designated by the expression *comparison*. This implies that an idea from another area is used in order to highlight one which lies in the particular structure. As such it is alien to the structure, not there for its own sake, but only in relation to what is compared. One can think this in the most narrow and the most broad manner. Every developed allegory is such a means of presentation, although it is itself a whole structure of ideas. It belongs there, but so does everything that we call parallel, simile, indeed, going even further, everything explanatory, thus also the example, to the extent that, as something particular, it is not there for itself but only to explain the general. In turn the general can, among historians, be a maxim, a means of presentation, via which the specific perspective is indicated from which the particular thing that is being narrated is to be viewed. If one wanted to collate such maxims in order to characterise the historian one would be mistaken.

The most narrow of such means of presentation is the figurative expression where the content of the linguistic element is something alien if we take it in the immediate linguistic value. But often the utterer does not even want such an expression to be thought in its literal linguistic value. Such expressions often fix themselves in the language so that their literal value is no longer thought at all.

This is the complete range of means of presentation, the general type is the comparison, the two end points are developed allegory and simple figurative expression.

If such an expression is not immediately clear in the context, and is instead ambiguous then a hermeneutic task arises in which we have to distinguish several cases.

First, as far as the case in which the literal linguistic value of such figurative expressions should not be thought is concerned, it is immediately clear that the canon above for the determination of secondary thoughts (namely from passages where they appear as main thoughts) cannot be applied here. For if the literal linguistic value is not to be thought then I cannot explain the figurative value by it. But there are, of course, customary figurative expressions. Certain objects have certain complexes of figurative expressions through which they can be presented in a certain respect. These touch on the literal expressions, but are so distant from their particular linguistic value that they cannot be understood from here in their relationship to what they are supposed to explain. One speaks, e.g., in relation to a painting of the 'tone', which is taken from music, and of 'motifs', which is taken from poetry, and this is reciprocal. Where such a relationship occurs the basis of explanation is in what is identical, since precisely this is the cause. But that is precisely the area where the hermeneutic operation is most difficult. Music, painting, poetry are related as arts. If I speak of colour in poetry, of tone in painting, the expression for the different arts is the same. But the linguistic usage has established itself differently, for it, tone is only an element of music, not of painting. The expression therefore had to undergo an extension before it could be transferred to an unfamiliar area. Such expressions may often be used without the thought really having become clear. But where such transferrals take place the comparison must rest on a relationship that can be demonstrated, because otherwise the figurative expressions would be completely arbitrary and we would not be able to understand them. In order to be able to survey the whole area from here we distinguish two points. First, there are such precise relationships in differing structures of ideas that the relationship offers itself of its own accord in order to serve as a means of presentation for the other. Second, there are, however, comparisons which at first sight appear arbitrary, which therefore only rest on chance relations, not essential relatedness. This last kind will never achieve such general validity, but it is not necessarily reprehensible. One should just avoid excess! If this kind occurs economically and is then made easier for the reader it has an effect and the utterance becomes succinct. But it can often happen that we take a comparison which rests on inner relatedness for one of the opposite kind, because we are not familiar with the inner relationship. In this way hermeneutic confusions arise which rest on false appraisal. Here the necessity of the psychological element comes in. One must know the writer, the way he goes about things, and the way his thoughts are produced, in order to know if he is comfortable or not in using what is arbitrary. In the latter case one will always presuppose inner relatedness as the basis of comparison. In arbitrary comparisons, which can become customary, something or other in common must be presupposed as the basis of the combination; there will be, even if there is no inner relatedness, at least a parallel, which can, however, concern something merely incidental. The main task is to find the point of comparison and thus to construct the comparison itself. Depending on whether what is used for the explanation from a structure of thoughts is distant or near, the task will be difficult or easy. It is a question of being sufficiently familiar with the literal content of a figurative expression for the *punctum saliens* [salient point] of the comparison to result from it. The usual lexical aids are not sufficient for this. The lexica can only demonstrate the figurative use of the individual elements of language in technical expressions and in those customary expressions which have gone over to some extent into everyday usage. One must turn to the aids where one finds the object itself explained in its whole context: from this one must complete the knowledge of the context in such a way that the point of comparison cannot escape us. In general, for understanding expressions which are merely means of presentation, knowledge of the language alone is not sufficient, and it must be connected to the most substantial knowledge of the real. We distinguish the two cases: The more a comparison, based on inner relatedness, comes close to the customary expressions which are rooted in the language, the easier understanding is. But the more the opposite is the case, the more arbitrary combination there is, the more difficult is understanding. However, even arbitrary combinations must, if they are to have truth, rest on an objective analogy and be traceable to this. Here one must distinguish whether such a comparison is being used in order to constitute the context, or merely as an ornament. The first case is obviously the more difficult, especially if the analogy is hidden, as, e.g., in Hamann.

Customary comparisons rest on parallels which are given in the construction of thought as it has gone over into the language. One of the most usual, which has almost gone over into literal usage, is the parallel between space and time. Here the reduction is natural and easy. More significant is that material changes, relations are explained by abstract relations, and vice versa. The latter is more predominant. It is easy to attach the opinion to this that there were not really any abstract expressions in language. This can admittedly not be conceded in such a general way, but for a certain stage of development it is inevitable that the abstract be explained comparatively by the sensuous. The opposite is rarer, but Klopstock, e.g., made use of this in an excellent manner. But such parallels rest on the solid basic parallelism between the realm of ethics and the realm of physics. In the last analysis all real comparisons, even if often in a subordinate manner, go back to this. This is their universal basis. But they are each particularly determined by the manner of thought of the era, of the nation, and of the particular region to which the writer belongs, finally by the difference of individual perspective. One must therefore put oneself into this perspective in order to understand a given comparison. So much with respect to our hermeneutic canon in relation to the *material* element of language.

If we now apply this to the N.T. . . .

[*Translator's summary of omitted passage*: The N.T., with the exception of Revelations, involves two main forms: historical and didactic. Didactic form involves letters, which allow considerable freedom of combination and which are sometimes more like speeches, at others more like confidential communications. In the latter the question of context is more complex – here Schleiermacher makes similar points to ones above concerning the need to have a general overview to avoid the danger of false analogy between expressions in different contexts. In historical texts the difficulty of establishing the context is made greater by the fact that the text may be constructed from fragments from different periods. This is most true of Matthew and Luke, less of Mark, and not at all true of John. In Matthew 13 similes concerning βασιλεία τ. θεοῦ [rule of God] seem to be all from different periods. With regard to parallels the question arises as to what extent the N.T. is a whole, and how the differing writers relate to each other. Inspiration is not the central issue here, for reasons given earlier. The obvious form of unity is of texts by one author, but even here the author can change his ideas over time, so the recurrence of an expression is no guide. This leads again to the canon that the part can only be understood via the whole. The N.T. has texts by the same author composed at different times, but what of collections of texts about the same subject by different authors? Even disputations, which are an example of this, involve something 'identical': 'One is not in dispute if nothing in common is presupposed.' If the authors knew nothing of each other at all one must collect all the recurring main concepts and see how they relate to the secondary aspects, which will show whether they really involve the same conceptions. This latter case is the one for the N.T., and this is the method to be applied, and it must be done with great care. The question is complicated by disputes about the identity of the authors of N.T. texts: the Epistle to the Hebrews will be interpreted differently, depending on whether it is assumed to be by Paul or not. One must assume a degree of identity of the doctrines and convictions in the N.T. Otherwise Christianity would be self-contradictory. But the contradictions between the texts mean one must not stay at the level of the words employed but of the main thoughts and their interconnections.][2]

As far as the determination of the formal element is concerned,[3] one must go back again to the clause as the combination of noun and verb. The simplest

---

[2] Everything from the beginning of the *Concluding Remarks* to here is a clarification of the propositions from § 10 ['*Subject and predicate mutually condition each other, but not completely*'] onwards.
[3] From here on cf. § 4 above.

form of this is where the noun is in the nominative and the verb attaches itself to it. Depending on whether the verb is determined differently in terms of person and tense, the relationship to the noun and therefore the content of the clause is different. This is not a separate element of language, but the universal condition in language, under which alone the more precise determinacy of the clause is possible. If the clause consists of several elements the parts of the clause will thereby be linked to each other without the clause ceasing to be a simple clause. If something is added to the noun, by which a relationship to other elements is to be designated, the preposition comes in, or, if it is lacking, the structure of the other nouns. But both can be together as well. As long, though, as we have an organic connection between a noun and a verb, however much they are determined, the clause remains simple.[4]

The connection of the clauses with one another can be a *stringing together* or an *organic* connection.[5] If two clauses are organically connected, so that a whole results and one immediately gets the sense in relation to one of them that it is only part of a whole, then a period arises, whose main form is that of initial and final clause. The strung together clauses stand in the relationship of co-ordination. Even if one clause is a longer period and the other a simple clause, they are after all only co-ordinated parts of a whole. Languages differ in this respect. There are those which are not capable of any building of periods or in which the capacity to do so is minimal, and there are, on the other hand, those which are capable of it to a great extent etc. But that the opposition between organic (periodic) connection and connection which is stringing together is only relative is clear from the fact that if, e.g., a very coherent period is to be translated from Latin into a language which does not have such a capacity, there is nothing for it but to analyse as appropriately as possible what is organically connected in Latin into wholes which are as small as that language permits. In this way the period has lost its organic unity, but it is to a certain extent possible to enable readers to think the same relationship of the parts as was intended in the organic period. If the opposition were absolute this would be unthinkable. Otherwise there would have to be completely different worlds.[a] If we are still conscious, despite all the difference of languages, of the identity of our worlds and laws of thought, then mere stringing together in language

[4] Cf. § 8.
[5] Cf. § 4.

[a] *Weltverhältnisse.*

also cannot exclude organic connection as its absolute opposite. Indeed we have this relative opposition in one and the same language. What one person presents in large organic periods, the other likes to split up, he prefers to string together.

If it is to be thought possible that a form which merely strings together should produce the same effect as one which connects organically, we must assume that the individual connecting elements of language from time to time also only have value for the way they can string together. Both movements correspond to each other in language so that the one cannot be thought without the other. There is admittedly a significant difference between languages of lesser and greater capacity. But as both opposed movements lie in the nature of language both must also occur in all languages, including in those of great capacity.

The difference in value between the two kinds of connection is admittedly a qualitative one. The kind of connection which merely strings together does not make an organic unity, but the kind which connects organically does not make any new unity, it just makes something part of something else. This makes them [the kinds of connection] exclude each other, therefore a qualitative difference in value takes place. But both kinds of connection can represent each other. If a linking element represents an organic connection then an emphasis arises. This is then a quantitative difference. The same takes place if an organically linking element is only used to string together, thus where its value is diminished.

Elementary knowledge of the language already has the effect that one does not mix up linguistic elements which merely string together with those that connect organically. But uncertainty can arise as to whether an element which one knows to be by nature organically connective is merely being used to string together in a particular passage. In order to obviate this difficulty, indeed to avoid it, one must follow the inner context of the thoughts exactly, and infer the understanding of the sequence of a new clause from this.[6] If we consider the linguistic elements which connect the elements within the single clause, then even here uncertainties and differences of understanding can come in.

Languages are very different in this respect. Some are rich in inflections of the nouns, others have no inflections and express the relationships of one to the other by particular elements of language, others, finally, admittedly

---

[6] Cf, § 6.

have such inflections, but they have a certain paucity of them. A language which just has the genitive inflection already achieves much with this, because all connections which are to some extent immediate can be expressed thereby. But in all other cases the language must have recourse to other linguistic elements. But even languages with the greatest wealth of inflections do not completely lack particular linguistic elements which designate the connections within the same clause. Where both come together both must also always be linked together, the preposition must not be separated from its case. In many languages this separate element (preposition) has different meanings, depending upon whether one or another inflection is connected with it. It is not enough just to know this. As long as the unity of those meanings is not found, the difference appears arbitrary, and understanding is not completed. Our aids are in this respect still very underdeveloped.

The same is the case with linguistic elements by which clauses are connected to each other. In many languages the verb has an inflection for expressing the relationship of a clause to another (subjunctive), and a primitive form which involves the assumption that the clause is an independent clause. If those forms (*modi*) are abundant, then the language can in the same measure do without particles. If a language also does not have many of these, then it is generally unable to bear large combinations of clauses. Where particular connecting linguistic elements (conjunctions) and *modi* come together both must be taken together. Yet each has its unity for itself, like the preposition and the case. But it is precisely here that great difficulty often lies for explication, namely in the fact that the unity of the linguistic elements is not immediately apparent. This is more difficult among the formal elements than among the material elements. The differences in the different languages often make direct translations very difficult. The certainty that one has correctly understood and has made the connection which the author wanted can often come only later, when one has grasped the context of the whole. The important aid is here once more the preceding overview. This furnishes all the more certainty the more the connection of thoughts is organic. The connection is, though, all the more organic the more the train of thought is logical or dialectical. In descriptions and narratives, on the other hand, stringing together predominates. The more the free play of thoughts dominates, the greater the uncertainty of connection, indeed cases occur where complete certainty is impossible.

The stringing together can be contingent and be between completely contingent statements, which, by the way, can in turn have organic connections within themselves. For example, if a statement is to be explained by examples, and example is strung together with example. In the total context connections which merely string together have a subordinate value. If organic connection occurs within the latter this connection has a minimal influence on the total context.

It is often very difficult correctly to determine the range and the relationship between the connections. If an utterance also consists of clauses which are as simple as possible, then they will have unequal value for the total context, some will be main thoughts, others secondary thoughts. If a formal element of connection happens to be present, the question is whether it strings together or connects organically, whether it links single clauses or larger paragraphs. These must be distinguished. Mixing them up brings confusion and misunderstanding. Here the determination of the material element (in relation to the content) and the formal element meet in the process of the general overview. If one knows from this overview that secondary thoughts occur, then one also knows that the formal element expresses the connection of the individual clauses; but if one finds main thoughts which are co-ordinated with each other, then one also knows that individual paragraphs are connected with each other.

In the connections themselves the following inner differences emerge. The connected clauses can be equal or unequal, i.e. they can be related in the same way to something in common or not. *Both and* designates the relationship of equality, *Not only but also* designates intensification. The writer often, by just stringing together, leaves to the reader the more precise determination of the relationship. If one then sees that the author wants the relationship to be grasped in one way or another the individual linguistic elements take on an emphatic value. But for this there must then be a particular indication in the utterance. An intensification can, on the other hand, also be used without one really being there. – But it can also happen that the writer presents two things for the context of the utterance in exactly the same way, but that he is thinking of an intensification which he thinks will occur to the reader of its own accord. This is then subjective connection which only lies in the activity of thinking, whereas objective connection relates to a state of affairs.[b] Since no linguistic elements exist which can expressly designate this difference, difficulties and the danger of confusion arise.

[b] *Sachverhältnis.*

The duality of positive and negative connection is peculiar to linguistic elements which connect organically. The positive presents itself most generally in the causal relation, the negative in the relationship of opposition. Both, which are of opposite value to each other, cannot and should not be confused. But each can be subjective and objective for itself. Subjective, namely, if the utterer, e.g. in the causal form, explains why he said what came before or why he expressed it in that particular manner. There are no different linguistic elements for the difference of subjective and objective causal relationships. Admittedly the two can often be easily distinguished, but confusion is often also easily possible.

Organic connection can be so loose that in the end it turns into mere stringing together, in which case the linguistic elements take on a reduced value. One cannot say that the elements had both kinds of value. That would mean confusing language so much that every correct organisation of thoughts would come to an end. One may only say that, because both kinds of connection are not strictly opposed, transitions take place. But precisely from this, from the different conception of the formal element, far more difficulties arise than from the differing conception of the material element. The real source of help here is again the overview of the complete context in which material and formal element determine each other.

We find *unconnected clauses* almost everywhere, albeit to differing extents according to the differing languages.[7]

Unconnected clauses can either begin something new or not. In the first case one uses paragraphs, headings, which in material terms designate the content, in formal terms designate the particular section. In the second case the lack of connection can be based on the fact that the preceding clause relates to those which follow it as an announcement of what is to come and as an overview. This can be indicated by formulations like *as follows* and the like. – Unconnected clauses that are not anything new can be *thought of* as strung together or as organically connected. This is often easy to decide if the material elements give an indication. But to the extent to which the value cannot be grasped via the material element, which is then the dominant element, the explication is difficult. Here grammatical explication moves into psychological explication. It is a question of the type, of the genre of composition. Every genre has its own rules in this respect, and in the same genre there are, in turn, individual differences, where one follows

---

[7] Cf. § 7.

objective connection more, the other permits more subjective connection. The subjective connections come down to the fact that the writer makes more of his sequence of thoughts arise before the reader. But it is precisely this which one genre of discourse allows more, the other less; one demands it the other rejects it. But in all genres there is always free space for the individuality of the writer. In the same way it depends upon the language and the use of language of the writer how often and in what manner he strings together or links organically in an objective or subjective way. On this side the whole process rests on the correct conception of the formal linguistic elements, how these determine the total context.

As far as the application of what has been said to the N.T.[8] is concerned, then it is clear from what has been said so far that everything depends upon grasping the unity of the whole correctly every time.

[*Translator's summary of omitted passage*: The N.T. poses great problems as far as this unity is concerned: the historical texts cannot be said to form a unity, and are compiled of texts which had their own unity. However, the boundaries of these texts are no longer clear. There are two kinds of stringing together: of narratives and of events. To clarify their difference, though, one already requires the intended explication itself, e.g. in relation to the first three Gospels. The assumption that these are compilations shows in the lack of temporal and geographical indications in the texts. These problems do not apply in the same way in the case of John. There is a need to distinguish didactic passages in the Gospels and the really didactic texts, namely the letters. There is a continuing problem of establishing which parts are meant to belong to larger wholes (organic) and which do not (strung together): this affects the whole approach to interpretation of the letters. The circular aspect of interpretation cannot be avoided here: depending on which initial assumption is made, the procedure for interpretation will differ. How does one make the initial assumption without deriving it from the text to be interpreted? This depends on the overview, but this cannot finally solve the problem. A major problem is also the fact that the text is a result of the combination of Greek and Hebrew, which (as described above) have differing attributes. How, then, was it that the hermeneutic difficulties involved in the N.T. were recognised so late? The dogmatic interest meant that the N.T. was regarded differently from other texts. Parallels were often made simply for dogmatic purposes, to clarify particularly difficult statements, which meant other relationships were ignored. The decline of dogmatic interest is, as such, a great advantage in hermeneutic terms. The contemporary combination of hermeneutics with historical criticism is particularly important here, as is the concern with the nature of the language of the individual writers of the N.T. –

[8] Cf. § 5.

Here Schleiermacher essentially repeats remarks from the preceding text about the assimilation of Greek in Palestine. – The basic thought is that Greek allows more organic connection than Hebrew, but that this difference is not rigid.]

The presupposition of an earlier era, that, because the Scripture emerged from the Holy Spirit, one was not allowed to assume that there was any imperfection in the N.T. manner of writing, has, because it is itself false, also led to false maxims which unfortunately often occur even now and have an effect. These false maxims show up particularly in two points, *first*, in relation to the qualitative, the relationship of the literal to the figurative, *second*, in relation to the quantitative, the relationship of the emphatic to the insignificant, the tautological, the redundant. We do not arrive at such maxims from our principle; but they have earned the right to closer examination because of their currency.

The first maxim, which includes all elements of language, both *material* and *formal*, in a completely general manner, is that in the N.T. figurative use is never permissible as long as it is at all possible to employ the literal uses. Those passages exclude themselves in which the figurative use is specifically indicated, thus, e.g., in all obviously metaphorical and parabolic passages. The cases that are being thought of are those where the literal and the figurative are equally possible. The literal use should always be preferred in these cases. This rests on the presupposition that where both literal and figurative use was possible the N.T. authors always chose the first. The ancients already set great store by this κυριολεξία [use of literal, figurative expressions]. But the necessity for κυριολεξία is not everywhere the same. It is, e.g., necessary in the making of an agreement, where it is a question of the greatest possible clarity of expression. But what right has one to expect κυριολεξία of N.T. writers? *First* it is assumed that one only uses the figurative if the literal use in the language is not just lacking but is not present. But the omnipresence of language is supposed to lie in the inspiration of the Holy Scripture, i.e. the continual presence of the correct and literal expression among the writers of Holy Scripture, thus infallibility in this respect. *Then*, however, it is also said that the N.T. writers are precisely just as much intended to give a precise representation of divine truth as a contract is intended to indicate in an exact manner the obligations of both parties, so that the same rule must be valid for both; whence nothing but literal expressions are necessary if the Scripture is not to fulfil its purpose in an incomplete manner. – One can even admit this in a

certain sense without that theory. But we must still establish certain boundaries; we will have to say that *to such an extent* and *in such* passages that rule
should apply when it is a question of the representation of such truths. But
precisely with regard to the particular nature of the N.T. that can be
reduced to next to nothing. If we look, e.g., at the way in which the words
δίκαιοσ [just], δικαιοσύνη [justice] and δικαιοῦσθαι [justify] are used,
then we see that they designate particular ideas of the relationship of man
to God as it arose in Christianity; at the same time we find that they have a
polemical relationship to O.T. usage. – If the relationship of man to God is
grasped in a particular way in Christianity, how should this be expressed?
If κυρίωσ [having power over] was strictly to take place, new words had to
be invented for new ideas. That was not possible. They could therefore
only be represented in an indirect manner, i.e. already existent expressions
had to be taken, but used differently, potentialised. The Apostle modified
the secondary relationships, changed the more precise determinations of
those expressions, and transformed their basic thought in this way. For
every Jewish reader this was a figurative use of the expressions: he had to
say the Apostle uses δικαιοσύνη in a different sense from the way we do.
In this way it is precisely in the presentation of the main truths that figurative use is found. If that maxim is applied in the usual manner then the
correct explication is missed and much damage is done. The dogmatic
value of the N. and the O. T. is obviously different. Much that related to
the political and the theocratic relationship in the O.T. had to be completely
modified when it was taken up again in the N.T. – Furthermore it must be
remarked against that maxim that the N.T. Scripture is not the original
doctrine, but has oral doctrine as its basis. In this way two possibilities arise.
Either the written text is an explanation, a further development, or it is a
fixing of already familiar truths. In both cases the κυριολεξία does not
need to dominate as decisively as in the first original announcement. As
such the maxim has no value and no basis at all for the N.T.; but the question whether something is used literally or figuratively can only be
explained in the N.T., in exactly the same way as it can in every other writer,
by the context. In accordance with the above, inspiration cannot cancel out
this principle which alone is correct.

The *other* maxim relates to the difference of the quantitative value of the
expressions. There are, as the oldest philologists and logicians already said,
expressions which allow a More and a Less. It is here not a question of
verbs and adjectives which involve difference of degree, but of quantitative

differences of local values which are determined by the context. Language also has, along with the logical value of the word, a musical value, this is the rhythmic and the euphonic. If something is added in a period because of the rhythm then this does not, of course, have the same logical value as something else which is necessary in the context of thoughts: logically it comes closer to redundancy. It is the same with the euphonic in relation to single sounds. The single sound is not in itself a dissonance, but it can become one in being together with other sounds. If I find an expression in a sentence where another synonymous expression immediately occurs to me the question arises as to why the writer preferred precisely this expression. If the context now indicates that precisely this expression was necessary then it has here its highest value, because the difference of the other, synonymous expression is included in it. In this case the expression has a particular stress, it is *emphatic*. But if the writer only chose the expression for rhythmic or euphonic interest then it has a lesser value, i.e. an indeterminate general value, because the difference of the synonymous expression is not included, and it is logically indifferent whether one or the other expression is present: this is then the opposite of the emphatic. This opposition is given and determined by the dual nature of language. Many kinds of style demand more of the musical than others. But even in the most strict genre of discourse the musical influence will never be completely lacking. Now the maxim has been proposed that one should understand everything in the N.T. as emphatically as possible. Why? Because the N.T. books were supposed to have no other aim and character than to present the pure divine truth. But the N.T. obviously contains passages in which the rhetorical, others in which the musical element plays a not insignificant role. Therefore the maxim is false. One cannot say that the emphatic is peculiar to the N.T. It can also be found elsewhere. In every composition there are differences which point to either the emphatic or the redundant. The point from which one must begin here is the identity between thinking and speaking. But this identity allows a lot of room for manoeuvre. A greater or lesser amount of linguistic material can be consumed for one and the same thought. Admittedly there must, strictly speaking, also be more thoughts where there are more words, because every word is an expression. But we can think of cases in which everything must be thought in a more limited linguistic material that only seems able to be expressed via a more extensive linguistic material. If, where there is less material, the context makes it possible for the reader to add what is lacking in his mind, the same thing is achieved as it would be if more material were being used. In this way different methods can be thought of in different cases, i.e. cases where the canon of the emphatic is applicable and where it is not. In the N.T. the older explicators had the maxim indicated above, to take as much as possible emphatically, the more recent, on the other hand, to take as little as possible. But both maxims are obviously only the expression of opposed one-sidednesses and are therefore both of no use. It is enough to point to the Pauline letters, in which rhetorical passages, particularly final passages of paragraphs, often occur, in which a certain fullness of language predominates and many words are almost tautological. Here is, therefore, the opposite of the emphatic. But we also find ὀξύμωρα [paradoxes] in Paul, and, which is related to this, a certain play with the meanings of the same expression. Such passages also have a certain rhythmic character, but that is subordinate, and the demand therefore arises to take the expressions seriously. If one applies the canon of the former passages to the latter, or vice versa, one mistakes the meaning of the writer. If one now looks at the opposite of this kind of passages where the thoughts are not continually being developed – for even ὀξύμωρα are only points of rest in the middle of the discourse – at those where a certain development of thoughts continues, then we also find an opposed character here. Namely in Hebrew we find, instead both of the periodic and of the difference between prose and poetry, a particular type or parallelism, in which there is a certain swaying of thoughts, so that in a certain Arsis and Thesis[9] the same thought is expressed with a slight modification. The dialectical difference disappears, the clauses have a different colouring, but in no way the character of dialectical clarity. Where we find this type in the N.T., namely in the gnomic and in the *hymnic*, the Hebrew linguistic character predominates, and it would be mistaken to distinguish the differences in a decisive manner. On the other hand this canon may not be applied to clauses which progress dialectically; rather the opposed canon must be applied. Both rules have their realm of application in the N.T., one must appropriately distinguish each of them.

The quantitative difference also occurs in the N.T., particularly in the formal linguistic elements, namely in the use of particles. Adversative particles

---

[9] *Translator's note*: Frank here appends the useful note: '*Arsis* (Greek = raising; literally: the lifting of the foot while beating time or in the rhythm of a dance), the weak rhythmic element, the periodic pausing or the intermittence of the beat, as opposed to the *Thesis*, the (taken literally) treading of the foot to accentuate the positive part of the bar'.

are used in non-opposed clauses, organically linking particles are used merely to string together, and so on. The same is the case the other way round. If the value of the particles is diminished in the first case, it is increased in the other case. In the N.T. this partly rests on the lack of acquisition of Greek and on the influence of Hebrew thought. The task is to distinguish the different cases appropriately. One-sided use of each of the maxims would lead to the greatest confusion. In applying the general rules N.T. hermeneutics has only to take account of the particular, whose basis is the relationship of Greek to Hebrew in the N.T.

The correct use of the aids for the explication of the N.T. depends upon the correct consideration of the maxims described. Not only commentaries, but also lexica, and grammars are worked out according to those maxims and are then, of course, to be used with great care. In one's own procedure the canon should be: as long as one does not necessarily have to take account of the Hebrew and of the particularly Christian element in the formation of the N.T. language one should just stick to the general hermeneutic rules. In doing so one should then look at the particular manner of composition and the character of the writer: whether the writer proceeds in a manner devoid of art or not, and whether he sticks to the language of common life. One should, as far as the N.T. is concerned, be careful not to make a marked difference between historical and didactic texts, for there are no historical books in which there is nothing at all that is didactic.

This leads back to the whole question of the object of representation. One asks: are there certain objects or complexes of concepts in the N.T. to which one or the other maxim is exclusively to be applied? If we have just spoken of the different composition of the individual passages, where one or other of the maxims should preferably be applied, then the question arises whether the different composition of the passages coincides with the difference of the objects? – Where there is a development of concepts in the N.T. dogmatic or moral objects will be the content. Because the N.T. is mainly concerned with these. Even if something rhetorical occurs this is not outside that sphere, but if a concept is developed with dialectical clarity, a passage with rhetorical richness can follow. Form is therefore the main determining aspect in relation to the application of a maxim. False application rests in part on the tendency to find religious ideas in the N.T. in the form in which they later developed. It is part of the idea of the canon of the Holy Scripture that in theological negotiations one goes back to the N.T.

But it is just as natural that different ways of using N.T. expressions in theological negotiations arise from this, depending on how the development progresses and how it is different. The normal use of language in everyday life exercises an involuntary power on the exegete. One thinks the N.T. ideas every time in connection with the particular theological negotiations of the time. From this, however, artificial explications arise, with which one wishes to justify the *dicta probandia* [sayings to be appraised] in the sense of the particular theological negotiations of the time. The rule must therefore be established that in the exegetical process the particular theological use of language of the time must be regarded as non-existent. One can best prevent this [false application] by the method touched on above of putting together all expressions of the N.T. which are necessary in a certain respect and which form the core of canonical significance in all the combinations in which they occur in the N.T.

Here the language forming power of Christianity in the N.T. is to be taken into account. Christian usage is, so to speak, camped on Jewish usage. The N.T. writers could observe a double procedure in the formation of Christian expressions on the basis of Jewish usage: either remain with the existent Jewish usage and connect what was new with it, or oppose new usages to the earlier Jewish usages. The first procedure is historical, where taking up[10] dominates, the other is dialectical, where opposition dominates. What is characteristic here does not lie in the person who speaks or writes. Everyone could now observe the one process, now the other, according to the circumstances. The difference of the procedure reveals itself in the form of its occurrence. The explicator has to pay attention to this. For example the Jewish expression δικαιοσύνη is used in the Sermon on the Mount in the first manner, in order to take it up into the language, but in the Pauline letters it is used in a dialectical manner, polemically. In Jewish piety sacrifice had great significance. But it is the Christian view that all sacrifice is cancelled out by Christ. This could now be presented either by extending the concept of sacrifice by taking it up into the language, or by negating it and saying that there is now a relationship between man and God in which sacrifice has lost its influence. The former procedure dominates in the N.T., the other is only a result of it. – If one now puts the main concepts at issue here together in all respects, one must also be able to

---

[10] *Translator's note*: I have earlier translated *anknüpfen* and its derivations simply on the basis of the sense of 'connect': the word literally means 'tie on'. It is, though, also used when one 'takes up' what someone has just said in a conversation, as in '*Da möchte ich anknüpfen*', which is the sense here.

recognise how the N.T. uses every idea according to one method or the other. In the last analysis everything rests on a synthesis of all different occurrences. It is a major difficulty in this respect for the explication of the N.T. that historical criticism is not yet completed and still contains so much that is controversial.

In the didactic writings this is less significant. In general they have the same linguistic usage. It is less a question of the personal identity of the author and even the difference of time has no great influence, as they are separated by a generation at most, in which no significant progress or changes can take place. Only Paul has his own domain, but here the amount of text is sufficient to find all the necessary analogies; the others form a whole without there being any particular hermeneutic significance in their differences. And their linguistic usage was under the influence of Paul, because he first of all educated Hellenic congregations, thus also fixed Greek usage in the doctrine. In doing so he held on so strongly to the mother congregation in Jerusalem that it thereby became possible for the other Apostles to accept his approach.

The historical writers[c] create greater difficulties because of the controversial nature and the uncertainty of the manner of their coming into being and their unity. Understanding of the quantitative is only certain if the critical task has been accomplished first. But the explication is supposed precisely to play a role in deciding what, according to criticism, is uncertain and controversial, because the external evidence is lacking. The hermeneutic procedure must take account of this and therefore be very careful in the determination of the results. Explication has to look at two things here, *first* at the relationship of the individual narratives, *then* at the relationship of the individual didactic elements. As far as the *latter* is concerned, namely the speeches, one notices that they do not correspond to the particular circumstances, in as much as they are either too short, or, in the longer speeches or the ones that are too long, that the particular things therein often do not cohere sufficiently to form a unity. Now such a speech is either only an extract of the one that was really made, but still a whole, or not a whole, but collated by the reporter from differing speeches. Explication must pay attention to this and examine every connection hermeneutically to see if it is original or linked arbitrarily, clause by clause, line by line. Here everything depends on exact observation of the connecting elements. – As

---

[c] *Schriftsteller*, though it would seem here to make more sense to say *Schriften*, 'texts'.

far as the relationship of the historical elements is concerned it is obvious that we only have particulars, not a continuous whole, because otherwise the whole life of Christ would shrink to a very great extent. Now we must decide whether there is an exact connection between the particulars or not and we must investigate whether the lack of connection is noted or not. In the Gospel it is noted where there is a gap or a connection, where the continuum begins and ceases. In the first three Gospels this is not the case. There one must then pay attention to the composition of the connecting forms. But their value, whether the same or different, can only be established by comparison. In this one must begin where the narrative yields something definite and judge the controversial passages according to this. In this way hermeneutics comes to the aid of historical criticism. Admittedly the latter ought to be completed beforehand, then the procedure would be purely hermeneutic. And it could be if the external evidence about the origin and original composition of the Scriptures were adequate. But as this is not the case the hermeneutic and critical procedure must be connected so that they can complete each other. But precisely here it is evident that the grammatical and psychological element of the explication are inseparable.

It was admittedly maintained above that each side had to be able to be carried out and completed for itself in such a way that the other became superfluous. And this is in fact the true goal, the ideal. The test as to whether the task is completely accomplished is admittedly that the one procedure yields the same as the other. But in reality great differences often occur in this respect. We can think that we understand a text linguistically in such a way that we thereby have a measure for the psychological peculiarity of the writer. But that presupposes that all difficulties on that side have been solved or that none are present. In the same way, if I have precise knowledge of the psychological peculiarity of a writer I can also understand the linguistic side without difficulty, although this is more difficult and itself always presupposes linguistic knowledge. But, looked at more exactly, the linguistic side for its part also presupposes the psychological. It is impossible not to always connect both sides, one would otherwise have to renounce the connection between language and thought and completely abstain from further reading. The linguistic task can to a certain extent be isolated if one deals with particulars purely lexically or grammatically. But as soon as one wants to understand a whole, to read in a coherent manner, the isolation of the linguistic side is impossible. Carrying out grammatical explication separately is a mere fiction.

In the Letter to the Romans one can take it as acknowledged that psychological explication has not yet completed its work. There are still many passages whose context is disputed. If we have determined the total value of every expression and its differences by the collation of the main elements of the letter in all their occurrences, we can then decide whether, e.g., many of the difficult questions are posed by the Apostle himself or are alien to him. In the first case the local value of the expressions which occur there would have to agree with all other passages, in the other case they would have to be different, so that the questions appear as objections of the opponents. In this investigation the grammatical and the psychological side complement each other.

We make a relative opposition between more easy and more difficult connections of thoughts. The subjective difficulty can go so far that one says: I cannot think that anyone would combine things in that way. Until the impossibility of another combination has been proved, one is not satisfied. But if the grammatical explication is complete and certain one is thereby compelled to accept that such a combination exists. In this way the grammatical explication determines the psychological. But in the same way the case of a grammatical puzzle can occur, so that someone says, I cannot believe that a word has the value which it in fact appears to have until the impossibility of finding another value is demonstrated. Here psychological construction is decisive and, if it is complete and certain, compels one to acknowledge the local value that was doubted.

Part Two[1]
Psychological[2] explication

1. The common beginning for this side of explication and for grammatical application is the general overview which grasps the unity of the work and the main characteristics of the composition. But the unity of the work, the theme, is here regarded as the principle which moves the writer, and the basic characteristics of the composition as his individual nature which reveals itself in that movement. The unity of the work in grammatical explication is the construction of the language area and there the basic characteristics of the composition are constructions of the manner of connection. Here the unity is the object, that by which the author is moved to the utterance. The objective differences, e.g. whether the treatment is popular or scientific, are already included in this. But the author now orders the object in his individual manner, which is reflected in his order itself. In the same way, given that everyone always has secondary ideas and these as well are determined by their individuality, individuality is recognised via the exclusion of related ideas and the adoption of alien ideas.

[1] This part is less worked out in the unpublished manuscripts than the first part. It lacks the specific application of the general hermeneutic principles to the N.T. Here as well it seems most advisable first to give the whole of the lecture which Schleiermacher conceived last, and then to have the lecture of 1832 follow in extracts, using the marginalia Schleiermacher made in his notebook.

[2] In his unpublished manuscripts Schleiermacher calls this part *technical interpretation*, although in the Introduction he regularly called the other side of explication the *psychological*. But in his lecture of 1832 he calls this part *psychological*, but distinguishes within this a dual task, the *purely psychological* and the *technical*. The marginalia of 1832 agrees with this. We have all the more reason to follow this division and designation because it not only belongs to Schleiermacher's final conception but also, as the development will show, to a really more profound justification and exposition of this side of hermeneutics.

By recognising the author in this way I recognise him as he collaborates in the language: for in part he produces something new in it, because every connection of a subject and a predicate which has not yet been made is something new, in part he preserves what he repeats and reproduces. In the same way, by knowing the language area, I know the language to the extent that the author is its product and is in its power. Both are therefore the same, only looked at from a different side.

2. The final objective of psychological (technical) explication is also nothing but the developed beginning, namely, to look at the whole of the act in its parts and in each part to look in turn at the material as that which moves and the form as the nature which is moved by the material.

For if I have seen through everything particular then there is nothing left to understand. It is also obvious that the relative opposition of the understanding of the particular and the understanding of the whole is mediated via the fact that every part allows the same treatment as the whole. But the objective is only achieved in continuity. Even if much is to be understood just grammatically, it is not to be understood in its necessity, which one only becomes aware of if one never lets the genesis out of one's sight.

3. The whole objective is to be termed complete understanding of style.

We are used to understanding by style only the treatment of the language. But thought and language everywhere combine with each other, and the particular manner of grasping the object combines with the ordering and thus also with the treatment of the language.

As man is always located in a multiplicity of ideas everything arose via adoption and exclusion. But if this or anything else did not emerge from personal individuality, but was instead superficially learned or habituated or done for effect, then this is mannered, and what is mannered is always bad style.

4. That objective is only to be achieved by approximation.

We are, despite all the progress that has been made, still a long way away from this. The dispute over Homer would otherwise not be possible. On the three tragedians. The incompleteness of their differentiation.

Individual intuition[a] is not only never exhausted but also always capable of correction. One can also see this by the fact that the best test is undoubtedly imitation. But as this is so rarely successful and higher criticism is still susceptible to confusions, we must still be fairly far from our objective.

5. Before the beginning of psychological (technical) explication the manner must be given in which the object was given to the author and in which the language was given to him, as well as what one can know from elsewhere about his particular manner.
In the first of these one must include the state which the particular genre to which the work belongs was in before his time; to the second what was usual in this particular and most closely adjoining area. Therefore no precise understanding of this kind without knowledge of the contemporary related literature and of what was given to the author as an earlier example of the style. This kind of coherent study cannot be replaced by anything else in relation to this side of explication.

The third of these is admittedly very laborious, but as it is not easily [available] except third hand and therefore is mixed up with [the] judgement [of others], which can only be assessed via an explication of the same kind, so one must be able to do without it.[3] Descriptions of the life of the authors were originally, no doubt with this intention, added to their works, but this relationship is usually overlooked. Appropriate prolegomena should, though, draw attention to the most essential part of the two other points.

From this prior knowledge a provisional idea arises during the first overview of where individuality is primarily to be sought.

6. For the whole procedure there are, from the beginning, two methods, the divinatory and the comparative, which, though, because they refer back to each other, also may not be separated from each other.
The *divinatory* method is the one in which one, so to speak,[4] transforms oneself into the other person and tries to understand the individual element directly. The *comparative* method first of all posits the person to be

---

[3] *Translator's note*: I have added the words in square brackets as the meaning of the German, which is not immediately evident, has to be conjectured from the context. This, of course, corresponds with Schleiermacher's own approach.

[4] *Translator's note*: As Frank points out, this vital qualification is regularly omitted when this passage is quoted, even though it is definitely in Schleiermacher's hand-written manuscript.

[a] *Anschauung*.

understood as something universal and then finds the individual aspect by comparison with other things included under the same universal. The former is the female strength in knowledge of people, the latter the male. Both refer back to each other, for the first initially depends on the fact that every person, besides being an individual themself, has a receptivity for all other people. But this itself seems only to rest on the fact that everyone carries a minimum of everyone else within themself, and divination is consequently excited by comparison with oneself.

But how does the comparative method come to posit the object under a universal? Obviously either once more by comparison, and then there would be an infinite regress, or by divination.

Both may not be separated from each other. For divination only receives its certainty via confirmatory comparison, because without this it can always be incredible.[b] But the comparative method does not provide any unity. The universal and the particular must penetrate each other and this always only happens via divination.

7. The idea of the work, which must first come to light as the will which is the basis of the execution, can only be understood via the two moments, of the material and of the sphere of its effect.

The material alone does not determine any kind of execution. It is, as a rule, admittedly easy enough to establish, even if it is not directly indicated, but at the same time it can also, when indicated, lead to a false view. On the other hand, what one can term the purpose of the work in a narrower sense is located on the other side, is often something completely external and only has a limited influence on individual passages, and it can anyway usually be explained via the character of a few people for whom the work is intended. But if one knows for whom the object is supposed to be worked on, and what that work is supposed to bring about in them, then at the same time the execution is thereby determined, and one knows everything one needs to know.

[At this point Frank usefully includes, as I now do, the following separate presentation, written by Schleiermacher in note form, of *Part Two. Of Technical Interpretation*, which Lücke did not include. Frank follows the date, suggested by Hermann Patsch, of 1826-7. However, Wolfgang Virmond (Virmond 1985) has convincingly shown that the text almost certainly dates from 1805, and is

---

[b] *fantastisch*: Kimmerle reads '*fanatisch*', 'fanatical'.

part of Schleiermacher's *first* lectures on hermeneutics in Halle. The fact that Schleiermacher used this manuscript to lecture in 1819, and even worked on it for his last lectures on hermeneutics in 1832-3, suggests a fundamental continuity in his conception, even though the emphasis sometimes shifted with regard to 'technical' and 'psychological' interpretation.]

Of Technical Interpretation (probably 1805)[5]
(*Marginalia*: I)
Introduction. Parallel with grammatical interpretation.

Grammatical. Understanding the utterance and compound aspects of the language. Technical. Understanding as representation of thoughts. Composed by a person. Thus also from out of the person.

Grammatical. The person with their activity disappears and appears only as the organ of the language. Technical. The language with its determining power disappears and appears only as the organ of the person, in the service of their individuality, as in the former case their personality in the service of the language.

Grammatical. Not possible without technical. Technical. Not possible without grammatical. For how should I know the person except via their discourse, especially in relationship to this discourse?

Grammatical. Nonetheless the ideal of the task looked at one-sidedly: understanding in complete abstraction from the technical. Thus technical as well. The ideal: understanding in complete abstraction from the grammatical.

(Explanation.) Namely in such a way that 1) if one knows the writer one already expects a certain manner even independently of the language: he could have written in another language 2) that one understands connection and content, which are the real object of grammatical interpretation, solely via the law of combination of man.

Grammatical. Understanding is only achieved via the connection of all contexts. Technical. The reconstruction of the combination is only completed with the accompanying progress into the detail, only in situ.

Grammatical splits itself into two opposed tasks; so does technical. The unity of the person is to be found and the expressions of this unity should be known in a determinate manner.

Grammatically. One [task] is, as unity, a general view, the other, as multiplicity, a partial limitation. In the same way technically. The unity [is] the general view of the literary totality of a person, the multiplicity [is] the limited applications of the same to particular cases.

Grammatical. Each presupposes the other. Technical, the same is the case. For whence should one derive the general view but from the combination of the

---

[5] *Translator's note*: The text is in note form with many abbreviations: I have not attempted to reproduce these, and have simply tried to translate the main sense.

opposed partial views. One must therefore have understood these, and whence can one understand their content but via the general unity.

Grammatical. The object is not the language as a general concept, also not as an aggregate of applied particulars, but rather as individual nature. Technical. Object is the capacity of combination and expression not as a general concept, as logical laws, also not as an empirical aggregate, but as individual nature.

Explanation. 1) In the language as a general concept nothing is left but the necessary forms for subject, predicate and syntax. These are not positive means of explanation, but only negative, because what contradicts them cannot be understood at all. In the same way for the capacity of thought as a general concept: the logical laws; what contradicts them cannot be regarded as the capacity of thought, but the capacity of thought cannot at all be understood merely in its own terms. 2) Observations of language as an empirical aggregate are not means of explanation, but products, which can always be added to by new explanations. In the same way for the technical. Observations about the capacity for combination or psychological laws. They are at best indications that are intended to draw attention to what contradicts them as something particular and individual.

Grammatical. The individual nature of the language is a representation of a specific modification of the capacity for intuition.[6] Technical. Character as individual nature is in the same way a specific modification of the capacity for thought. Organic with natural beings. Every plant is a harmonically developed particular modification of the process represented.[7]

(*Marginalia*: II)

Grammatical. The individuality of the language of a nation is connected with the individuality of all its other shared works. But we are not concerned with this context and its shared centre. In the same way for the technical. The individuality of combination and presentation is connected with every other expression of individuality, and the more exactly one knows a person the more one finds the analogy. But we are not concerned with this context and its centre, but only with the individuality of presentation = style. Explanation of what one needs in all arts and just as much in style.

Grammatical. The elements of a language as presentations of a specifically modified capacity for intuition cannot be constructed *a priori*, but only recognised via comparison of a great number of individual cases. In the same way on the technical side, one cannot construct the differing individualities *a priori*.

---

[6] *Translator's note: 'des Anschauungsvermögens'*: earlier in the passage I have translated *Anschauung* with words like 'view': here it seems more to have the Kantian sense of 'intuition', of the whole way the world is 'given to us' (this sense is also present to a lesser degree in the earlier cases).

[7] *Translator's note*: The sense of this obscure passage would seem to derive from Schleiermacher's familiarity with Schelling's *Naturphilosophie*, in which the mental and the physical are different aspects of a same underlying 'absolute identity', which are to be understood by their analogies to each other, so that 'Nature is to be visible mind, mind invisible nature' (Schelling I/2 p. 56).

Grammatically, one cannot summarise individuality in a concept, it wants rather to be intuited.[8] In the same way technically. There can be no concept of a style.

Grammatically, the complete understanding of the language would only be the understanding of the centre. Technically the style is, in the same way, only understood by the most complete understanding of the character. But in both cases this is inaccessible and can only be reached by approximation.

Grammatically the mutual presupposing of the opposed operations did not cancel out the possibility, but just determined it more precisely, in the same way technically. There are more simple isolated expressions (more simple, i.e. for which one does not first need a technical interpretation, but which are just grammatically comprehensible), via these one obtains the first general intuition of individuality. This makes more difficult expressions comprehensible which in turn complete the intuition, and so on into infinity.

On the other hand one might say that what can be understood grammatically could not be good at also making individuality visible. But it [individuality] can be understood grammatically, though its necessity cannot be comprehended; but it could be different grammatically in many ways with just as much justification. For this reason such passages have their basis of determination after all in individuality, which therefore can also be to a certain extent recognised more exactly by practice. If one says: grammatical interpretation itself needs technical interpretation, this is only valid for the first temporary grasping of the context in the mind, which precedes all understanding of something individual and particular as such. This makes the operation possible and elevates it to being something artistic.

If individuality is admitted, one might object that it is not located in the individual. 1) Not every writer has it – admittedly not. But then whole classes constitute an individuality, and the individuals behave just as organs or as isolated expressions. 2) It lies more in the object, in the form of art rather than in the writer, historical style is different from philosophical style. Note. The task, which in itself the most important,[c] is after all to know every form of art via the style of the writer, and one trusts oneself to do that if one knows the writer thoroughly. One can even know fairly well how, e.g., Plato would have written if he had written history. The individuality of style therefore exists even when there is a difference of forms.

(*Marginalia*: III)

The same thing becomes clear from the following. If someone develops certain peculiarities through various forms against the character of those forms, we do not take this for the true individuality of style, but rather disapprove of it under the name of mannerism. Individuality of style is supposed therefore to be able to be

---

[8] *Translator's note*: 'intuited' in the sense that what one grasps is not reducible to the conceptual means one has of describing it, precisely because it is unique.

[c] *die an sich meist*: the sense is not clear.

modified via forms but yet remain the same. Furthermore, if someone transfers what belonged to an alien individuality into their own product which is completely analogous in terms of form, then we recognise it as alien via its conspicuous affectedness, which would not be possible if the individuality belonged to the form. This is the origin of all floweriness, *flos orationis* [rhetorical ornament].

One might perhaps prove that the ancients thought personal individuality had to coincide with a specific form, because no one ever dared to go beyond One form. On the other hand, it is not just that one can put forward the modern era in which the opposite is demanded and in which one presupposes that it is a subordinate talent that expresses itself only through One form, but the basis of this opposition can also be established. The basis is that what pertained to the nation was more prominent among the ancients; that is why they were attached to the forms in which this was laid down and to the perfection of the mechanical aspect in this, which demands a practice of exclusion.[d] For us, on the other hand, individuality should stand out more and be seen. For this reason one wishes to draw it out via varied manifestations and gives up on mechanical perfection.

For this reason individual unity remains the main issue, the other things must be found along with it.

On the finding of the unity of the style

Law. Every writer has their own style. Exceptions: those who have no individuality at all. But they, all taken together, form a common style.

Specification. As this unity cannot now be grasped as a concept, but only as an intuition, it is generally only the limit-points which can initially be determined. These are: individuality of composition, of the large structure as the first, and peculiarity of the treatment of the language for the finding of individuality as the last. *Explanation.* 1. That the former must be the first already results from the nature of the hermeneutic operation, which must begin with the overview of the whole. But this first thing is usually completely overlooked and the beginning is made with the last. Judgements about the personal use of language are, though, completely unreliable if they have not resulted from analogy with the composition, and also generally go into far too much detail. 2. These two end-points simultaneously include the whole. There is nothing in style but composition and treatment of language. 3. These two elements are also not to be regarded as complete opposites. For the thoughts, which are really elements of the composition, are also parts of the means of presentation, real language. Conversely, the language is often an essential element of composition.

(*Marginalia*: IV)

---

[d] *eine ausschließende Übung*: in the sense of excluding individuality.

Method. Twofold. By comparison with others and by observation in and for itself. The first is regarded as better, but one really does not need it in physiognomy and the like. It necessarily breaks up the whole once again, in order to seek the corresponding parts elsewhere and is therefore invalid. (*Marginalia*: N.B. The beginning should have been made with the method which observes in and for itself.) One can only use them as aids for one's attentiveness, in order to find that which best enables one to recognise individuality. But even for this what is far better than comparison with another individual is comparison with the whole from which individuality has singled out such and such in a particular manner by virtue of its principle. (*Marginalia*: Attention to rejection [of linguistic and formal possibilities] also plays a role here.) Therefore, for the constitution of the language, comparison with the whole area of the language, for the composition, comparison with the totality of the object.

1. Discovering the individuality in the composition

In general the procedure is as follows: The unity of the whole is grasped and then one sees how the individual parts relate to it overall. The former shows the idea of the author as a basis, the latter his particular way of taking hold of it and presenting it. The idea of the author vouches for his significance, not his individuality, but the way in which he presents the idea does vouch for his individuality. For this depends upon the particular organisation of his capacity for intuition. Once one has obtained the first general view, then one goes into more detail with it. The degree of harmony of the detail with the general view determines the completeness of the author as far as his significance is concerned. The manner in which it is carried out confirms or corrects the first intuition of individuality, and so on into the more precise aspects.

First task. Finding the inner unity or the theme of a work

Note 1. One usually calls this the purpose, wrongly. The purpose distances itself all the more from the idea the more arbitrariness there is in the production. The purpose can, compared with the idea, be something very subordinate, and yet, precisely when one sees things from the viewpoint of the purpose, the idea can seem to relate to it solely as its means. 2. One usually assumes the most direct route to get to it to be the author's own indication at the beginning or the end. Wrongly. Many texts indicate something which is far below the real theme in importance as their object. It is also the case that the purpose is far more often presented than the idea. Examples of the first especially in modern literature. Of the last also in ancient literature. Epic announcements contain only the purpose, not the idea.

Solution. 1. Compare the opposed points beginning and end. (Note. The first overview begins, therefore, in as elementary a fashion as possible.) Progressing relationship = character of historical and rhetorical composition. Identity-relationship = character of the intuitive composition. Cyclical relationship = character of the dialectical composition. (*Marginalia*: V) *Provisos.* 1.) Be careful to distinguish what relates to the purpose at both ends, and what relates to the idea. 2.) Be careful to distinguish the right beginning and the right end. a) The beginning of the whole is at the same time the beginning of its first part, the end of the whole at the same time the end of its last part. Example. The end of John['s Gospel] could easily relate just to its last section, only the identity with the beginning shows that it relates to the whole. b) Be careful to distinguish the limits of the whole. Truly mad ideas have come via this into poetics: that the Iliad was regarded as being originally a whole, the Pentateuch, Joshua as well. In the same way a book can, although it is otherwise a unity, consist of many wholes, which one must separate from each other.

2. If beginning and end provide nothing or not enough for the unity, then compare the emphasised passages. Ones which are emphasised in the same way must have the same relationship to the idea and therefore the idea must emerge from them. (Note. One sees again how grammatical interpretation is presupposed here. For this must teach how to distinguish the emphasised passages; also the other task of technical interpretation, namely the determination of the individual use of language. For everyone here has their own way of emphasising.)

Corollary. 1. There can also be compositions in which nothing is emphasised. But then the same thing is the case negatively, because in each presupposition one finds there has to be emphasis of some kind or other. This absence takes place a) in everything which comes close to epic structure, but where, as in immediate sensuous intuition, nothing may stand out; b) in a certain noble simplicity, especially in practical representations; c) in dry wit and irony. 2. There can also occasionally be passages that are intentionally wrongly emphasised, as in pastiche. We are given German dictionaries. They are least capable of finding this in this way. But individual emphasis can be of particular help in indicating material seriousness.[e]

3. One now goes further into the detail and the subdivisions of the individual parts, in order to pursue the emphasis until one comes to that which, as it were, stands still, which forms the bare surroundings. The more precisely the lessening of the emphasis corresponds to the distance from the idea which has been presupposed, the more the presupposition is confirmed. On the other hand, the more deviations and emphases, that do not harmonise, then the more suspicion of the presupposition. *Corollary.* Therefore, despite this, no other presupposition is to be made. This presupposes an incompleteness on the part of the writer,

---

[e] *den materiellen Ernst*: the sense is not wholly clear, though it has to do with identifying the tone of a passage.

whereby his idea did not always remain equally clear to him, and he let himself be distracted by other things; accordingly one must continually pay attention to this incompleteness.

Second Task. To find the individuality of the composition. *Explanation.* Only this is the true subjective aspect. A writer can develop his individuality via several different ideas. Two different writers will arrive at completely different individualities in relation to one and the same idea.

Solution. 1. There are two ways: immediate intuition and comparison with others. Neither of these can stand on their own. Immediate intuition does not get to what is mediated; comparison never gets to true individuality. One must unite them with each other via the relationship to the totality of the possible. 2. Seek this totality of the possible, which can only result from intelligent comparison of the particulars. 3. See how the main parts of what is to be explained come together from this totality. The law of this coming together which is manifest in the whole and in the particulars is individuality.

Explanation. 1. What is provisionally to be found is the totality of what was available to this writer. One must therefore restrict oneself to the limits of the sort of people and of the era. (Where the writer has creatively brought about what is to be found, it is found of its own accord.) Individuality of a nation and of an era is the basis of personal individuality. E.g. One may not say in relation to ancient dramatists that our characteristic compositions were available to them, or the sentimentality of the lyric poets [was available]. (Note. The writer is therefore only to be understood via his age.) 2. One finds this totality a) via comparison of what is of the same period and of the same type, b) using analogy from what is of a different type and of a different era, according to the general laws of combination. For example, if we only had One Hebrew historian, we could still find the totality from the lyric poets. 3. The process now turns in differing degrees in advance to the opposed sides, often more for comparison with the particular, often more for immediate intuition. In what circumstances [does] each of these [take place]?

Result. Individuality as a unity cannot be reproduced; something which cannot be described always remains in it, which can only be designated as harmony. The main points of view are, though, the following. 1. The particular way in which the writer develops his idea, material literary cast of mind is recognised via the overall selection and ordering. 2. The tendency to strictness or gracefulness in composition, formal literary cast of mind, is recognised via the relationship of what is there merely to fill out [the text] to the whole, via the overall relationship of the details in the parts.[f] Note. Most people consider this to be the character of the individuality of the era. This is only founded to the extent to which either inadequacy is the cause of strictness, or extravagance and weakness is the cause of gracefulness.

---

[f] *durch das Verhältnis des Ausfüllenden zum Großen durch die Massenverhältnisse des Details*: the sense is not at all clear, and I have been fairly free with the translation.

Examples of simultaneous large differences. 3. The deviation from one's own objective train of thoughts via the influence of the idea of the state of mind or train of thought of the readers, or the popularity of the composition. Note. Many people consider this to be the character of the genre: but it is found as an element in all genres. Admittedly one must also pay attention to it to the extent to which the object gives occasion, or not, to think of a specific audience. Division into works and occasional writings is the best view of this point. The same thing is to be found wholly in the detail as well. But they are not subordinate kinds. Plato and Lessing were very much occasional writers (in German literature there was a time when it was considered presumptuous to be supposed to be anything else) now every rascal wants to write a work. The tendency towards one or the other is therefore part of one's character.

Application to the N.T. [end of interpolated manuscript]

The[9] task of psychological explication in its own terms is generally to understand every given structure of thoughts as a moment of the life of a particular person. What means do we have to achieve this task?

We must go back to the relationship of a speaker and a listener. If thinking and the connection of thoughts is one and the same in each, then, if the language is the same, understanding results of its own accord. But if thought is essentially different in each, it does not result of its own accord, even when the language is the same. If we take each case in absolute terms, the task disappears, for in the first case it does not arise at all, because it completely coincides with the achievement of the task, in the second case it is, it would appear, unachievable. But the opposition never occurs as extremely or as absolutely as this. For in every case there is always a certain difference of thinking between the speaker and the listener, but not one which cannot be overcome. Even in everyday life if, in a case where the language is completely the same and completely transparent, I hear the utterance of another and set myself the task of understanding it, I posit a difference between him and myself. But in every case of wishing to understand another the presupposition is always present that the difference can be overcome. The task is to go more precisely into the nature of and the reasons for the differences between the speaker and the one who understands. This is difficult.

But first we must still draw attention to another difference, namely to the difference between the indeterminate, fluid train of thoughts and the

---

[9] From the lecture of 1832.

completed structure of thoughts. In the first there is, as in a river, an indeterminate transition from one thought to another, without necessary connection. In the second, in completed utterance, there is a determinate aim to which everything relates, one thought determines the other with necessity, and if the aim is achieved the sequence has an end. In the first case the individual, the purely psychological predominates, in the second the consciousness of a specific progress towards a goal predominates, the result is intentional, methodical, technical. The hermeneutic task accordingly splits on this side into the *purely psychological* and the *technical*.

Every person is, from time to time, albeit only inwardly, in the sort of state of mind which is regarded as empty in terms of its real life-content. If such states gain the upper hand then the life-content of the subject is diminished. One calls such a person absent-minded, they are, we say, lost in their thoughts, i.e. in the kind of thoughts which in fact are basically empty. As long as such a state is an inward state it is, of course, not an object for our theory. But what about our habitual colloquial conversation? If it is not some kind of business, such that a specific object is discussed and an intention arises, then it is just that ideas are exchanged, often without immediate relation to each other, so that what one person says has no necessary influence on the emergence of thoughts in the other person, one speaks more *next to* than *to* each other. But even such a free, loose conversation is already the object of explication and, particularly in relation to our task, a very intricate one. The more someone speaks from within themself and the basis of their combination lies purely within themself, the more the question arises as to how they arrived at what they say. It does happen that one thinks one knows how the other person will respond to what one has said to them. It is something significant if someone has the ability to understand the succession of the ideas of another as a fact of that person's individuality. Looked at in literary terms this admittedly has no value, because the purely free play of thoughts does not easily become literary. But what is analogous in the literary realm is the letter written purely in friendship. Such letters by notable men make up a not insignificant part of our literature. As deeds[g] of their mind in personal relationships they have great influence on the understanding of the rest of their literary products. The free productions of thought of greater objective content belong here, e.g. descriptions of journeys and similar things that lack the form of art, in

---

[g] *Tatsachen.*

letters. These can be understood equally as a manifestation of the mind of the travellers and of those who are doing the describing. Let us imagine two people travelling together who reproduce their conceptions. These conceptions will be different. If we know the objective nature of the matter the difference will thereby be reasonably clear for us. But we often only get to know the object from differing descriptions: then it is difficult to distinguish the objective and the subjective therein. Furthermore, descriptions of what happened in memoirs, diaries, and the like, in which the reproduction of one's own conception in a manner free of art dominates, belong here. Here judgement and objective perception can get very mixed together, so that the distinction of the objective and the subjective elements becomes difficult. The task is then to regard the reproduction of the conception as a fact in the mind of the author.

It is completely different if the combination comes under the potentiality of a specific goal. In that case there is a different link of the progression, a constant quantity, a specific relation of every point to the proposed goal in comparison with every preceding point. If the goal is different, the manner of the combination is different. Here there is a method of combination and there is artistic production. Opposite the artless writer of memoirs on that side, e.g., stands on this side the artistic writer of history. The hermeneutic process is naturally different in the latter case from the former. I cannot make demands on the writer of memoirs that I make on the writer of history.

There is no genre of communication through discourse in which this difference does not exist. Everywhere, even in the realm of science, there is a free play of thoughts which to a certain extent precedes artistic production in a preparatory manner. One would be very wrong to banish that free play from the literary domain. Historical research would, e.g., be incomplete without the artless writers of memorabilia. Indeed this is even the case in the domain of science in the more narrow sense. In a philosophical work of art, the more strictly scientific it is, the less I can recognise the genesis of the thoughts of the author. The genesis is hidden. The author did not find what stands at the top of the system immediately, it is instead the product of a large number of sequences of thoughts. In order to understand such a work in terms of its genesis as a fact in the mind of its author something else must be given, namely a work of free communication. Without this the task can only be accomplished via a large number of analogies. So it is difficult to get to know Aristotle psychologically from his works, because we lack a work of the free play of thoughts by him. Plato is already easier to get to know in this respect because his works have the form of free presentation. This is admittedly only a mask, but one can see through it more easily than in Aristotle. The same is even the case for mathematics. For a long time the *Elements* of Euclid were regarded as a textbook of geometry, until others said that his purpose was to demonstrate the inclusion of the regular bodies in the sphere, that he thereby began with the Elements, but progressed in such a way that he always had that point in mind. It would only be possible to decide about this subjective side of Euclid if we had a work of the other kind by him.

The difference of the production of thoughts is not just conditioned by the object and by the individuality of the utterer, but also by the difference of the forms of art. Pindar, for example, sang of the expedition of the Argonauts, this is something quite different from the epic poems about the same material. Indeed Pindar himself would have presented it quite differently in epic form from the way he presented it in lyric form. The explication therefore must pay attention to the laws of the differing kinds of production included in the concept of the work of art. Otherwise it misses the different characters and interests.

The relative opposition of the purely psychological and the technical can be grasped more distinctly in terms of the first being more concerned with the emergence of thoughts from the totality of the life-moments of the individual, the second being more a leading-back to a determinate wish to think and present, from which sequences develop. The two sides come closest together if a wish to present, a resolution is only registered and its occasional coming into play is waited for. But the difference lies in the fact that the technical is the understanding of the meditation and of the composition, the psychological is the understanding of the ideas,[h] among which the basic thoughts are also to be included, from which whole sequences develop, and is the understanding of the secondary thoughts.

Two moments belong to psychological interpretation. It becomes more easy and more certain the more analogy there is between the manner of combination of the author and of the explicator, and the more precise the knowledge of the material of the thoughts of the author is. Both moments can complement each other in a certain manner. The more precisely I know the material of the thoughts of the other, the more easily will I overcome

---

[h] *Einfälle.*

the difference between his and my own manner of thought, and vice versa. If I think of the one condition as completely fulfilled, the other must thereby be fulfilled at the same time.

If we now look in the same way at the technical side in general, we must begin with the presupposition that some state of thinking, a sequence of thoughts develops from an activity of life. To the extent that a sequence of thoughts arises from an activity of life it is implicitly already completely posited at its inception, i.e. the whole sequence is only a development of that moment of emergence; the individual parts of the sequence are already determined by the deed via which the movement of thoughts arises, and if I understand this sequence then I also understand the deed. But then everything drops out which has no basis in the individuality of the thinker; I only find what has developed from the free deed itself. At this point the technical necessarily comes in. For as soon as someone wants to bring something to consciousness with a free decision, a free deed, which are here the same, then he is immediately compelled to follow a method. But this will differ depending on whether the person asks himself in his self-determination: how can I manage thoroughly to research the object, or asks: how do I move what I have thought through in a certain direction and how do I represent it for certain people? The former is the method of *meditation*, the latter the method of *composition*. Both are always two different things and to be distinguished, not just in particular examples but in every case where the concept of composition is involved. Meditation can only from time to time hold onto the decision in a passive manner, so that it is only occasionally effective, and then the composition, the linking of the particulars into a whole, is postulated as a second act. But this situation is basically always present. For even if the form is already given in the first decision (think of someone making the decision to make a poem of a certain kind) and this form already involves a lot of exclusion and positive elements, in the composing particulars will still arise in such a manner that they must provisionally be put to one side. So the hermeneutic task is therefore precisely to understand both acts in their difference.

This distinction between meditation and composition can make it doubtful whether the main division into the psychological and the technical side of the task can be held to in the further examination, or whether the subdivision in the order of the composition should be considered. Thus in this case, first the finding of the decision, i.e. of the unity and real direction of the work (psychological), then understanding of the composition as the *objective* realisation of the work; then meditation as genetic realisation of the same (both technical); then secondary thoughts as the continual influence of the whole of the life in which the author is located. For if we consider the utterance as a completed whole and explain it via its beginning-point then the end-point is thereby given at the same time. The beginning-point can only be understood via the life of the individual, thus psychologically. In this way we come to the technical side. There composition and meditation are then to be considered. These already implicitly lay, though, in the beginning-point. So the task returns to the psychological side. And so it appears as if both sides, the psychological and the technical, could be united. However this is not possible. Each side forms a whole with regard to the rules.

The essence of the difference between both sides lies in the fact that the person is free on the purely psychological side and we must therefore go back to his circumstances as principles of his self-determination, whereas on the other, the technical side, it is the power of the form which governs the author, both in the moment of meditation and of composition. Here the form is already present in the decision on the conception. To the extent that the form is something already existing it is clear that the author is just as much organ of the form considered as a type of spiritual life as a whole as we regard him on the grammatical side as organ of language. This also does not essentially change even when we come across the inventor of a form. There we ask: how did the author come to invent a new form, a new genre? We distinguish a negative and a positive moment. The former is the moment where the seed of a complex of thoughts rejects the existing forms because of a lack of inner agreement. In that case either the material must be given up or a new form must be sought. Once it is sought the positive moment comes into play. A newly invented form is never absolutely new. It already exists somewhere, only not precisely at the point where the author wants to produce it. It either exists in another artistic domain, so that when the author pulls it over to his domain he still appears, despite all novelty, as imitator of the already existing form. Or the form is already present in life, only not yet used in art. In this way ancient drama, when it came into being, took its form from conversation which is everywhere present in life, in the same way as the early type for the artistic form of epic is the story. Even the choir in the dramas finds its type in the meeting of the individual with the people. We must therefore say that even the inventor of new forms of presentation is not purely free in his decision; it is admittedly in his power whether the form should become a permanent form of art or not, but even in the formation of the new he is in the power of the analogues which already exist.

By now holding onto the main difference between the psychological and the technical side we naturally begin with the understanding of the impulse in the individual and move on to the continued influence of the whole of life on the development of the whole, and we can presuppose as already known from literary life what must thereby be mentioned about the composition.

The psychological task in particular

The task involves two aspects, which are very different in relation to the totality of the work, but very similar in relation to the production of its elements. The one aspect is the understanding of the whole basic thought of the work, the other is the comprehension of the individual parts of the work via the life of the author. The former is that from which everything develops, the latter is what is most contingent in a work. But both are to be understood via the personal individuality of the author.

The first task is therefore the unity of the work as a fact in the life of its author. The question is how the author arrived at the thought from which the whole developed, i.e. what relationship does it have to his whole life and how does the moment of emergence relate to all other life-moments of the author?

One might think the task is already solved by the title. But this is deceptive. For the title is not something essential for hermeneutics and was almost always missing in antiquity. In the works of antiquity it is usually of a later origin; it is also often without significance for the unity of the work, e.g. the title *Iliad*.

In the accomplishing of the task one must begin with the following opposition. On the one side, the more a work belongs in terms of its form to the career of the author, the more its genesis is self-evident. The only question left would be how the author came to this particular career. But this is of no interest at all in relation to the single work in question. The opposed case is the one in which the task is difficult to the extent to which the activity from which the work emerges appears contingent in the life of the author. In this case the whole life of the author would have to be available for the task to be accomplished. We distinguish here the question: *in what circumstances did the author come to his decision, from the question what does this decision mean in him, or what particular value does it have in relation to the totality of his life?*

The first question relates to what is external and only leads to an explanation of what is external. Indeed there is in it something which easily leads away from the correct path. In the emergence of a writer's decision there are always contingencies. The same thing which in one case is inherent in cast of mind and life can also come into existence in completely different circumstances. One can very easily get into trading in anecdotes if one looks around here and combines what one finds.

If one thinks of a prolific author and puts his works together for oneself, the correct way of considering them will aim to prove a certain necessity in them, prove the inner progress in their temporal sequence, how he rose, reached his peak, and then sank again. Without such a view of the temporal sequence in the works one does not understand any writer. It is also admittedly important if allusions to the circumstances of the time etc. occur that one should understand the allusions via the circumstances of the time. But the external circumstances in themselves never give a sufficient explanation of the decision.

In general the following rule can be established in relation to this: The more a work has emerged from the inner being of the writer, the more insignificant the external circumstances are for the hermeneutic task; if, on the other hand, the author was compelled to the work by external matters, it is all the more necessary to know the external reasons.

Much more important is the *second* question: what does the true, inner seed of the work, the decision in the life of the author mean?

Only in relation to true works of art is the question the same as the question of the relationship between matter and form. But on this side the hermeneutic task has an incomparably greater domain. Think of the case in which several people work on and represent the same historical material: how differently will they represent it? The one writes a chronicle, the other gives a history which is pragmatically coherent. The one has a primarily critical tendency, the other wants to make visible the ethical motives of the events. Without knowledge of the particular tendency, of the particular aim, one does not understand the construction of the work.

But the tendency, the aim of a work can be understood in very differing ways. The difference will not necessarily be immediately obviated by the hermeneutic rules; everyone will use them in their own way, according to their own viewpoint.

Now there are admittedly cases in which the author announces his most personal tendency. But even this is peculiar. If one carries on reading with the said tendency in mind and passages occur without a trace of that tendency, then one will doubt whether the author really had that tendency. So the accomplishing of the task will be made very difficult. The most difficult thing, though, is when one has works before one which intervene in business life. Here there can be cases in which the tendency is deliberately hidden. If one has exact knowledge of the attitude and manner of thought as well as of the circumstances of the author and if a particular circumstance occurs in his works, then the accomplishing of the task is thereby made more easy. But there are cases where the question of the tendency of the author cannot be answered at all. If the question is at the apex of the whole hermeneutic procedure, then the procedure really is threatened, even on the grammatical side, if that question cannot be answered. There are works which remain hermeneutic puzzles, where we lack everything needed for answering that question. But there is something which can reduce the trouble. There is, as was stated at the very beginning, an opposition between the unity of the whole and the individual parts of the work, so that the task could be set in a twofold manner, namely to understand the unity of the whole via the individual parts and the value of the individual parts via the unity of the whole. If the unity of the whole is not known, then I also cannot understand the individual parts via it, so I must then take the other path of recognising the unity of the whole via the most complete understanding possible of the particular. But this is itself very difficult, whence there is no certain path to the accomplishing of the task. It is just that what is puzzling is thereby restricted in a certain manner. The main thing, though, is the method according to which the whole and its unity is to be understood via the particulars. This happens by means of the composition, but, in order not to confuse the two sides of the interpretation, the psychological and the technical, it happens in such a way that only as much of the composition is presupposed as can already be understood at this point of the explication. If, in analogy to a work of art, everything particular fits into the unity of the material and the form then, by recognising this, I have accomplished the task. If on the other hand not all the particulars fit into the unity of the material and the form, and do so in such a way that what is left has something in common, then the hidden unity, the secret aim of the author lies precisely in this. It is, of course, very difficult to recognise this aim with certainty. One can illustrate this for oneself by the hypothesis of the anti-Christian tendency of the work of Gibbon. Every such aim disturbs the natural uninhibitedness of the writer in the composition. Whence a secret intention in works which are located purely in the domain of art and science is less to be expected than in works which belong to business life. If something of this kind occurs in works of art and science then the artistic and scientific value is thereby significantly reduced. Business life is a very limited area for literary production. But there are quite often conflicts between the purely scientific and artistic direction on the one side and the direction towards the shaping of life on the other. The diplomatic can find its way into the work here. This primarily happens in times and conditions where there are factions in the domain of art and science who intervene in life, or where the life of the life of the state is in opposition to scientific and artistic life. A complete knowledge of the life–circumstances and conditions of the author is therefore necessary in order to know whether such secret intentions are to be sought in his work or not.

The preliminaries to the study of a work must indicate whether such a unity, in which the whole is to explained via the particular and vice versa, is to be presupposed in it. But the real tendency is thereby only given in general. The task is then, however, to pursue the tendency through all details of the work.

If, in order to accomplish this task, we attend very carefully to the seminal decision[i] of the author, then the question first of all arises as to what sort of a quantitative part of his life such a decision is.

The seminal decision can have a threefold value in the author himself. We have the maximum value in the real life's work, if that decision is one which fills the whole of his life. The minimum value is the occasional work which is not connected with any part of the career, but is purely coincidental. Between them lies a third possibility, studies, as preliminaries to a work which also usually begin with an occasion. Each such product is not the work itself, not a part of it, but also does not belong to the occasional because it has a relation to that work. These are the three quantitative degrees of the seminal decision, and it is easy to see that they are of the greatest importance for the hermeneutic operation. If the hermeneutic procedure lacks knowledge and lacks a correct view of the differing value of the seminal decision from which a text emerges, then misunderstandings are inevitable. One cannot explicate an uncompleted work as a real

---

[i] *Keimentschluß.*

life's work. In the former case, for example, unevennesses in the treatment are to be expected. The more organised a work, so that everything is precisely connected with the whole and with the fundamental unity, the less unevennesses will be noticeable. In the former case the hermeneutic procedure must be different from in the latter.

How do we come to the point where we can determine whether a work is one or the other? We must know the whole activity of the author. Let us think that one and the same writer has made a real work and also made studies for the work, but the former has got lost and only the latter are still extant. If I do not know that then it will be hard to come to a correct judgement about the author. One will say that the work is incomplete, one-sidedly worked on. That, though, is a false judgement and the understanding of the text as an action[j] is thereby essentially altered. Or another will judge that there is no harmony at all in that product and that one can infer from this that the author did not have the same interest in working on the whole genre and only worked on individual parts. But this judgement would be just as false. Both judgements are detrimental to the hermeneutic treatment, but both rest on the lack of knowledge of the whole activity of the author. If we take the opposition between works and occasional products, then it is clear that the author must express himself much more clearly in the former than in the latter. For the latter are based on simple impulses and are elements which exist for themselves. There is a certain self-denial in them and the activity of the author determines itself more via his relationship to the person from whom the impulse came. He must also orient himself in terms of the taste of the circle in which his product emerged. The material will find its explanation via a specific circle of the whole life to which it refers, not via the author himself. Something that is an occasional piece could also have become a work, but then it would have become a completely different work. There is one example of high artistic value where that difference is hard to recognise, namely the Pindaric odes. On the one hand they appear as occasional pieces, on the other they are completed works of art, and in this way what seemed opposed here appears in mutual interpenetration. The puzzle is solved if one says that the poet has made those occasional pieces into his career, i.e. the poet wants to manifest himself precisely in this particular area of life to which the poem refers, and he therefore also compels the occasional piece, as such, to become a work

---

[j] *Tatsache*: literally 'fact', but the stress is on the '*Tat*', the 'deed'.

of art. Such a phenomenon is rare but for hermeneutics it must be correctly assessed in its quantitative value.

If we take both differences, between occasional writing and work, together, and assume that every work could have a unity which is higher than the pure relationship of matter to form, then the success of the hermeneutic task completely depends on this unity being correctly found. Both kinds ['occasional' and 'work'] have a different value according to the difference of the value of the writer. In the case of an unimportant writer one does not concern oneself with what he wanted with the work. But in what does the difference between an important and an unimportant writer consist? The latter is a writer where it is least a question of understanding the work as an action in his life, where instead this side completely disappears in relation to the grammatical. There are, as stated above, cases where the writer seeks to hide the unity of his work. In such a case those parts will be mainly the ones which cannot be understood via the mutual relationship of matter and form. Let us now compare this with the difference we have just remarked upon and ask: what belongs to the maximum and what to the minimum? If we think there is nothing individual in a work that cannot be understood via the relationship of matter and form, then this would in a certain sense be the most complete work of art, but, because it is only a work of art, it would be very imperfect as the work of the individual. If it could really be completely comprehended via the relationship of matter and form, then, if the form were given, the whole activity of the author would relate to the fact that he chose the material and the form that belonged to it. But this cannot occur in this way because there are no forms that are so absolutely determinate that if the material is given everything is a matter of course. But the more determinate material and form, the less anything individual, anything characteristic can occur. If we are to think that a work has a certain degree of perfection without any influence of the individuality of its author, the area to which it belongs would have to be mechanised. In established forms one approaches such a mechanised area. The more determinate are the laws of a form, the more empty of individuality is the product. In this way individual life is opposed to that which is mechanised. But the relationship is different in differing texts. The individual aspect never completely recedes.

Here we get into difficulty in relation to what was asserted in the theory of art. Think of the case of ancient tragedy. Here the form is determinate in a certain way and to a certain degree. If several poets have to work on the same material at the same time then their plans will be very similar. The bigger the difference is between them, the more greater or lesser imperfection will be on one side or the other. But what is the basis of the difference? If we infer the whole thing from an act of will of the authors, what did one author want and what did the other want? The relationships of material and form are thereby only external. If one wanted to say that the one or the other had a particular political or moral aim then the theory of art would object that injury was thereby done to the pure character of the work of art, a work of art should not have a particular aim. If this theory is right then one would only be allowed to say that a particular direction could be the basis, but not a particular aim. This is, though, only the case to the extent to which the work to be explicated is a pure work of art, for there nothing is left over, everything is resolved in material and form. If the value of a text is to be that of a pure work of art, then nothing else may be posited in the seminal decision than pure self-manifestation in the mutual correspondence of form and content. But in this way the question arises for hermeneutics as to whether a work wishes to be regarded as a work of art, or not. Is this now determined by the form or not? If art has formed itself in a certain way in a particular linguistic and national domain, then one must be able to determine with certainty via the form whether a work wants to be treated in this way or not. But where has this ever been so completely determined? Even if one thinks it in the most complete manner possible in the context of the life, there will still be cases in which the real art form is misused for particular purposes. This is, though, easy to notice. The artist has perhaps hidden his real purpose, but the work of art will contain details, and they will not be scattered details or irrelevancies, which form a whole and constitute the real tendency. But here we come to a large area which in this respect is in a certain sense ambiguous. There is namely everywhere, in all areas, including outside the real area of art, a certain tendency towards art, whereby the question becomes ambiguous and the answer difficult. The writing of history, for example, has a purely scientific origin, but it has a great proximity to the domain of art. But nobody recounts events without their own way of looking at and judging the matter in question. This is their aim, but something unavoidable; but to the extent to which that is the case, it is unconscious and as such without influence on the composition. It is quite different if someone uses the writing of history as the means of recommending or withholding certain principles and maxims. That is a specific aim which does not lie in the natural relationship of matter and form. But the more a particular aim of the representation dominates in such a way that it must hide itself, the more the form is to be regarded as an artistic domain for itself. There is therefore not just an opposition between praxis and art, but also between science and art. Scientific representation also has its purpose in itself, but it is a different purpose from self-manifestation in art, namely the communication of something objective, of knowledge. To the extent to which the scientific representation approaches artistic form another composition also arises. The more a scientific object allows such a proximity the more the question arises in the explication as to whether the writer wanted such an approximation. If he wanted it from the beginning, then it will present itself in the whole composition. However, as far as the hidden aim is concerned, it is less conceivable in purely scientific communication than where a proximity to artistic form takes place. In this case the particular aim is not so apparent and needs to be sought. Now there is a certain amount of art in written representation per se. A greater or lesser amount of this influences the whole composition. The same thoughts demand a different representation when the text is also supposed to be artistically pleasing from when only the aim of objective representation dominates. If one misses this difference then one cannot reconstruct the procedure of the writer in an appropriate manner. But even though pure artistic representation for its own sake and the achieving of an objective purpose are extremes, a certain artistically pleasing treatment of language even belongs to the latter, because otherwise the readers are put off. It is just a question of determining the degree of the artistic element.

Everything which is communication by discourse in a certain compass is the object of the art of explication and is either located in a certain business circle or is analogous to science or to art. These cannot possibly be strictly opposed to each other. Even what is practised in a business circle can have an artistic presentation. There are things in common and transitions. But one can posit certain points of view for oneself and distinguish whether a work is to be comprehended more from the one or more from the other point of view.

Certain complexes of thoughts which become the object of explication have a unity which lies in the relationship between object and form. That is the objective unity in all three areas. One can further distinguish in this: the objective unity, to the extent that it lies purely in the material, and the technical unity, in relation to the form. The one must be understood via the other. In addition every complex of thoughts has a unity which goes beyond that unity, the subjective unity, the intention of the will[k] of the author, through which material and form come together. In every work which lies in the area of art no other unity is to be presupposed apart from self-manifestation. Because, as was said above, purely artistic production is altered by every other kind of direction, the task arises of finding it if it is present. In general the question is: how does one find the subjective secondary aims in the various genres and areas of composition? One may never directly presuppose such a secondary aim, for a hint of it would have already to arise from the text itself. Above the case was assumed that in works in the area of art an existent form of art dominated to such an extent that the difference between several works which artistically present the same material became very small. But this was only a fiction used to show how the objective unity could dominate to such an extent that subjective self-manifestation could not adequately emerge. However, if we now assume that a state of the art comes closer to that dominating power of the objective, but at the same time a powerful impulse towards self-manifestation is present in the subjects, then in this case new forms will be sought. An antagonism arises between the artist's being dominated by the form and the producing of the antagonism in the form.[10] If we think that there is a secondary aim in this, then it will exercise a certain power against that domination of the form. And it is precisely in this that one will recognise the self-manifestation of the author. Everything which is not determined by the presentation of the material gives us an image of the author in his manner of thinking. In the same way, if several authors treat the same object with the same tendency and there are elements in which that common tendency does not show itself, then one recognises in this the difference and individuality in the will of the author. There will be elements even in every scientific work from which the measure of the will of the author in the presentation can be assessed. If the scientist has the aim of arousing pleasure by his presentation, then the original intention of the will of the author results from the putting together of the purely didactic form with the elements which do not essentially belong to it. The particular secondary aim

[10] *Translator's note*: this 'producing' can also be read grammatically as referring to the production of the domination of the artist by the form. I think it refers to the antagonism, but the context does not allow any certainty in this case.

[k] *Willensmeinung*: the term probably derives from Georg Friedrich Meier's *Attempt at a Universal Art of Explication* of 1757.

can be hidden or not. In the latter case, e.g., a scientific text will obviously be polemical. In the pure domain of art it is necessary to hide the secondary purpose, in the domain of business life hiding it is only a possibility. In the former the hiding is posited together with the intention of the will from the beginning, and will therefore make itself noticeable even in the presentation of the detail. If, on the other hand, the hiding is only a possibility, then one needs to pay a lot of attention during the hermeneutic operation to finding what is hidden; one would then have an inkling of it in advance via exact knowledge of the writer and his situation. In this case it is important to grasp the main thoughts and the secondary thoughts correctly. The main thoughts are connected in a precise manner to the penetration of material and form, the secondary thoughts are not. But the relationship differs a great deal: the determinacy of the relationship essentially belongs to the unity of the work and determines its character. In order to gain insight into this character one must think of the relationship in its extremes. On the quantitative side of the relationship the opposition between main and secondary thoughts can disappear if the secondary thoughts are either excluded or take up a relatively equal space. If the opposition is eliminated then the work will be more a free combination of thoughts, a free play. On the other hand, if the opposition dominates, the unity of the work will be more specific, more elevated. In the other case the self-manifestation of the author emerges more sharply. In general we can assert the following: Where there is determinate form, that opposition dominates, and vice versa, where the opposition does not dominate there is formlessness or the form is a minimum. The qualitative relationship is designated thereby. If the opposition is not eliminated by a decision, then that is nothing but surrendering oneself to free production from the point where there is the decision onwards. Such an action would be nothing at all if there were not a determining point there, a point of connection. One can illustrate this by free production in conversation; there the point of connection is at least being together. The analogy to this in the area of writing is correspondence, a dialogue which has been separated via the form. Here the opposition between main and secondary thoughts is not at all in the original volition of the writers. Opposite this stands all production in which that opposition dominates.

For hermeneutic theory the question again comes in here as to the relationship of the psychological and the technical.

If we begin with the seminal decision in order to grasp the unity of a work as a deed in the life of its author then the development of the seed is, apart from the free play of thoughts, the object of technical interpretation, in which we have distinguished meditation and composition.

If one thinks of the case of a free letting oneself go in thoughts which are communicated to another, then we must, in order to find the point of connection, know the relationship between both, the author and the reader. In that case the difference now immediately arises between what develops of its own accord from this relationship, and what comes to the writer from outside. One must understand this difference, but it can be a minimum in this case. In the same way one cannot maintain that, e.g., a letter has no form, no composition. In that case the difference between meditation and composition also emerges to the extent that the letter in fact has thought-content. Admittedly this is all to a restricted extent. The opposition between main and secondary thoughts is always developed via the necessity of the form, even if it is not intended from the beginning. This is the most immediate issue, on which all further hermeneutic operations on this side depend. Whatever the form is, from the moment when the decision for a form has arisen the author is the organ of the form, free or bound organ, depending upon whether the form itself is more free or bound.

The unity itself can be thought more strongly or more weakly in the seminal decision. The weakest unity is if the decision is just to let oneself go in the communication of thoughts. In this case the opposition between main and secondary thoughts is completely eliminated. It is strongest and most fruitful for explication if it is most binding for the author and refers to a specific form. Between these two end-points lies the whole mobile sequence of single moments.

Application of what has been discussed so far to the N.T.

[*Translator's summary of omitted passage*: There are difficulties with regard to psychological explication in the N.T., which involves both historical and epistolary forms. The four Gospels (historical) cannot be seen in terms of the seminal decision of the authors because the titles are a later addition. They all deal with the life of Christ, but cannot be termed biographies. They seem to use the same stories as a basis, but differ in their manner of selection, and differ as writers. It is no good looking for the unity of each Gospel via a general overview, because they need to be considered together. The unity is a task for historical criticism: this is a result of the hermeneutic process itself. The main question is whether the Gospels are individual products or collections of existing stories. Some of the Gospels deal with the early part of Jesus' life, others not: is this a question of not knowing about it, or of deliberate omission? The hermeneutic procedure is very different in each case because the unity is conceived of differently. Mark and John do not include the childhood, but the former simply lists events, the latter makes them part of an overall whole. For John this means the omission of the childhood comes about because it does not fit the aim of presenting Christ as the founder of the Church. In the case of Mark this seems not to be relevant, so the omission may be contingent.]

Let us consider the disputed question from another side, namely how a historical product that we call biography must be constructed.

It is not possible to represent a *continuity* of fulfilments of time. If it were possible it could only happen in the form of a *strict chronicle*, for there time divides itself in consecutive sections. If one abstracts from this and posits in the biographical content a difference between what deserves to be communicated precisely because of its content and what does not, then gaps will emerge. Such a product would then have to be regarded as an aggregate of particulars. Continuity is the basis of the description of a life because life is One. Although continuity cannot be immediately represented, and can only be presented in the form of the particular that separates itself off, the relation of the particular to the continuity must yet be present. This relationship does not lie in the identity of the subject, but rather in the course of time. The particulars must be arranged in terms of time so that the reader can recognise the continuity. Mere collations of particulars without that continuity are just materials, elements for a biography. One cannot directly make a biography out of them; it remains, even if one arranges the particular in temporal sequence and provides it with linking phrases, just an aggregate which lacked internal connection in the course of time.

[*Translator's summary of omitted passage*: John presents the life of Christ as a biography, whereas the others give only a collection of particulars with no essential unity. In terms of what was the collection in the others arrived at? This raises difficulties of historical criticism for hermeneutics, because different accounts of the origin will give rise to different hermeneutic solutions. 'The desire, therefore, to resolve the question of the unity of the work purely hermeneutically in each particular case is the first basis which must only be preceded by that of historical criticism.']

As far as the *didactic* scriptures are concerned, their epistolary form allows one the assumption of a complete laxity, thus the least degree of unity and determinacy, so that there is no opposition between main and secondary thoughts. If one takes the thoughts singly, they all appear as secondary thoughts, and one would just have to establish how they emerged at precisely this time and in this way. But the letter form also allows the possibility of an approach to strict form and unity; e.g. in the real business letter. In didactic letters a great multiplicity is conceivable in relation to the unity. The minimum would be the decision freely to let oneself go. But on the other hand, the didactic letter can come very close to strict didactic and rhetorical form. Think of the task of communicating certain knowledge about a particular object to other people. Then there would be an objective unity, and that aim can very well be achieved in letter form. – Furthermore the question now arises as to the difference between the general didactic form and the particular epistolary form; whether and to what extent it is a different thing to instruct one person or several persons in a letter, or in a text which is directed indeterminately at the public. The difference can be very small if the letter form is fictional, e.g. in Euler's letters to a princess. But it is a different thing if knowledge is communicated in a letter form which is determined by a specific personal relationship between writer and recipient. In that case the letter form is something true, a real moment of life of the association between two persons.

If we begin from the opposite point, from the decision just to let oneself go, then consideration of the people for whom one is writing is a *limiting* principle. Free play is inhibited, limited, if it is a question of something which does not appear suited for those to whom I am writing. But the image of those to whom one is writing can be so vivid in the soul of the writer that nothing occurs to him except what lies in that sphere and is fitting. In this case the relationship to others is a *determining*, indeed a leading principle.

If we think that someone has made the decision to let themselves go in free communication to several people then this will emerged at a particular moment. If the writer was in a completely calm state then it needs an impulse to produce such an act of will. It only needs to be a vivid memory or an externally favourable opportunity for the communication. If the state the writer is in is identical with this act of will, then the basis for the determination for the direction of his communications also lies in this state. What was vividly present to him now lies as the developing seed in the act of will and if nothing significantly changes and the act of writing ensues with the greatest possible speed, then the act is the unfolding of that moment. But if we say that a significant change in the state of the writer takes place, then elements of this change will come into the text without the writer necessarily mentioning this change. The will is altered and transfers itself to the present state and drops the previous one. If we think that different states in the act of the writer fill substantial periods of time, then the parts which relate to them will separate, particularly for the reader. Precisely for this reason the writer himself will separate these parts as different sections, and if in doing so he notices the difference of time, then such a communication is epistolary. It is the effect of the changed states and the communication thereof. The letter form remains, only the unity has become a different unity; indeed it can remain in its truth despite all the extension of the thoughts, even if it is given the external dimensions of a book.

We now ask in relation to the didactic content of the N.T. Letters whether the epistolary communication of the didactic content *could* be given the dimensions of a book? No! for in the didactic one cannot put sequences of thought with a different content together as One; instead the analogy with a didactic book is either there, in which case the truth of the letter form is excluded, or the truth of the letter form is there, and then the work can only have a lesser dimension. The dimensions particular to the letter form are, though, determined by the fact that it must be a continuous act for the reader. If the letter goes beyond this, then the letter form does indeed also cease. If a work cannot be read through at a sitting, then there is reason to split it up, but with the splitting up the letter form is also excluded and we have a book in external letter form. Here there are transitions which can be empirically fixed in a fairly precise manner.

Now we still have to take note of the fact that the letter form, if it is not purely subjective, can have a certain proximity to the rhetorical. The didactic wants to communicate knowledge, the rhetorical wants to give rise to a decision that turns into action. If someone wants to give rise to such a decision then the communication will refer to something specific in life, and there can be the same degree of strictness here as in a public speech where one has the person one wants to move before one. This, though, completely negates letting oneself go, because the necessity is there to produce the decision which, for the recipient, can be an action if the decision is carried out by all parts working together. If such a speech wanted to extend to the point where its first beginnings were supposed to be forgotten before one had finished reading it, then it would not need to be written at all. Certain limits are set here, therefore, and everything is to be withheld that cannot contribute to the achieving of the aim. Here we have extremes, but there are many transitions between these extremes.

How do we find the unity in a given case? Where there is nothing but the didactic or the rhetorical in a letter the unity will not be able to be missed. But where such a didactic or rhetorical unity is completely lacking one has to pay attention to how the lack of unity or the diminished unity is modified by the mutual relationships between the sender and the receiver of the letter. The aspect of this form which connects to the latter, the diminished unity, is the more difficult side of the task, which connects to the former, the lack of unity, which is the easier side. In the former there is a duality of the didactic and the rhetorical. If a hidden intention becomes probable because of single isolated points in a communication of this kind, then one suspects a rhetorical purpose is more likely than a didactic one. In relation to the didactic a hidden purpose is only probable if the didactic aim cannot be achieved in a direct manner, but only indirectly and without being noticed. It can, though, happen even more easily that a rhetorical aim hides itself, particularly in communication by letter. Much less in oral communication, because here success is only momentary. Communication by letter is not as influential as oral discourse; the recipient of the letter has time to go back to how he is being influenced, which the listener in oral communication cannot do. The intention must hide itself all the more, the more different the interests are on both sides.

In the N.T. it is unthinkable that the didactic and rhetorical aim of the N.T. should have needed to be hidden in this way. It corresponds to the way things were that the writers wish to instruct and the readers wish to be instructed.

[*Translator's summary of omitted passage*: This common interest obviates the need for hidden rhetorical persuasion. The main task is to distinguish whether the aim is more didactic or more rhetorical, via the general overview. The assumption of a rhetorical unity is inappropriate for the N.T., as a determinate aim is not necessarily present.]

In the determination of form of purely free communication we assumed that the opposition between main and secondary thoughts was not in effect in this case, – not as if that form did not allow this opposition at all, but because it is not constitutive for this kind of writing. There is therefore in this case no thread at all that one could pursue. Our task of finding the unity thereby becomes null and void; but by this one is only saying that a real unity is not present at all. If we construct the original act of will for ourselves, it is the fulfilment of a moment in the writer which already finds him in a certain state. The impulse towards communication enters into a mind which is fulfilled from elsewhere and now the impulse does indeed have a direction, namely towards these particular persons. As such, indeterminate free communication is not unrestricted licence, but everything particular must be grasped in a reasonable manner if the state of the writer and an image of the nature of those to whom the communication is addressed is given. What is not connected to that did not arise from the determinate decision, and in this way a determinate limitation arises, but there is a duplicity therein, so that either all the elements of the communication can be grasped purely from the state of the writer, and the difference as to whether it was intended for this or that particular person is minimal, or it is conversely the case that the state of the writer is more or less indifferent at the moment of the impulse from outside. In the former case the writer is at the same time the object and everything is to be grasped from his circumstances, in the other case the person who is being written to is the object and everything is to be understood via the knowledge one has of him. One can think a point of indifference between these extremes, a change between the moments in which the writer manifests himself and his momentary state, – and those where he disappears into the consciousness that he has of others. The more one or other of these two sides dominates, the easier it is to grasp the context, the more the indifference dominates, the harder, and there everything particular has to be explained in its own terms.

[*Translator's summary of omitted passage*: The task is easier the more didactic the text, because the relationship of writer and audience is clearer. Otherwise we need to know about the state of both the writer and the readers. But we can usually only do this via the letters themselves. The aim of the writers of the N.T. letters in general is clear, though they may have used different methods for different audiences. One must beware mixing the later development of Christianity with the original task of the Apostles. It is also vital to distinguish what was given to the Apostles by Christ and what was already given to them before Christ and was combined with what Christ gave them.]

The entry of another unity into the main development is what one calls a *digression*. There are forms which do not allow anything of this nature, but there are other forms besides epistolary forms in which digressions occur. In every form they are to be judged in terms of the particular manner in which they occur. In letter form they can only be explained in the way that from the second, which has a different unity to the first, namely completely indeterminate unity, something comes into the first. But one should not allow oneself in the general overview to be confused into asking about the determinate object, for when it is linked again it is clear that the main thought is kept in mind. Now this really belongs to the composition itself; it must, however, be mentioned here, because the task of finding the unity is supposed to be accomplished here, but it has to be remarked how intrusive digression is. If we now stay with the free form of the letter, we have above established two things. The writer can write from out of his own state, or from out of the image that he has of the state of others; only the image must not fix him to a single object, otherwise the other form arises. If someone writes from their own state, and in such a way that they speak of themself and their circumstances, then this is the simplest case and no one can then mistake it. The letter writer can be affected from elsewhere, but if this is just solicitude, without their own personality being affected, and if only thoughts emerge which are determined by sympathy, then the whole thing in fact did emerge from the state of the writer. It can appear in this case as if he were speaking from out of the state of the recipient, but it would be wrong if one wanted to follow this appearance in the explication. If nothing more is given to me it is equally possible to find what is right or what is wrong: the decision often rests only upon gentle hints. It is a different matter if one has a precise knowledge of the sphere of life of the writer and the recipient. In that case there can never be any doubt whether someone is excited from somewhere else, or has written only from out of their own state. Yet it is often only the more or less emphatic tone which decides.

[*Translator's summary of omitted passage*: In the N.T. the lack of direct information about the author and the recipient of the Epistles makes interpretation difficult, it having to be surmised from the letters themselves, which leads to an inevitable indeterminacy. The nature of the indeterminacy depends in part upon whether the letter is to an individual or a group, but even knowing this will not allow a complete explanation of the occasion of the letter, because the writer may have been moved to it by something else which does not appear in any way in the letter (e.g. of First Epistle of Paul to the Corinthians). The difficulty and the dangers of the conjectures to which indeterminacy gives rise are illustrated by the long-held assumption that the Epistles were influenced by Gnosticism, but this has been shown to be historically mistaken because Gnosticism only developed later in the form assumed by these conjectures. If difficulties in interpretation arise one must try to establish the idea of his audience the writer had in mind, but this may give rise to a variety of viewpoints. Given the dependence of the future development of Christian doctrine on the Epistles, this ambiguity in interpretation is demoralising. There are, though, letters which have a certain didactic unity, namely to the Romans, the Galateans, and the Hebrews: these can serve as a hermeneutic basis for the other Epistles, even if there can be no final certainty.]

If various presuppositions are possible, then one can only decide in terms of the greater correspondence of the particular with this or that unity. The establishing of rules comes to an end here and the realm of tact begins, which emerges from the particular talent for analytical combination. Here the only rule that is valid is to keep the various possible viewpoints in mind in relation to every particular progression, including in relation to the elements which do not belong together with the main question.

If we now return to the general issue, we come, as a consequence of the order we have established by wanting to put the more psychological side before the technical, to the elements which really presuppose the technical, but which still cannot be understood via the technical.

The first task was correctly to understand the impulse which is the basis of the whole act of writing as a fact/deed in the writer. But we said that there were more and less elements which are not directly connected with the impulse. What is directly connected is to be understood by meditation, thus by a certain consciousness, and gets its appropriate location via the composition. But every text also always has elements which we distinguish as secondary thoughts and these also can only be understood as facts in the thinking process of the writer, but in the sense that the process is independent of the original impulse. How are these elements now to be understood? –

If we consider a conversation this is first of all a completely free state, which is based, not on any specific objective intention, but only on the mutually stimulating exchange of thoughts. But the conversation does easily get fixed on something and that is even striven for by both sides. In this way a common development of thoughts and a particular relationship of the utterances of the one to the other arises, and what results from this does not concern us here. But a conversation also allows breaks. Then the question arises as to how the speaker came to this? The task is to get to know the genesis of such breaks.

It will be fairly generally the case that one anticipates such breaks – admittedly only if one is more familiar with the involuntary manner of combination of the other person. The greater this familiarity, the easier it is to guess the subsidiary thoughts, to recognise the genesis of what gives rise to the break. If we take more precise account of this one sees that the general more logical laws of combination, via which the essential parts of an utterance are determined, have nothing to do with it. We must go back to the psychological and seek to explain what determines precisely the free, or rather involuntary manner of combination. In doing so we must base this on our own observation of ourself. This analogy alone makes it possible to set oneself the task of knowing the genesis of the secondary thoughts. The most natural thing here is to think of oneself in the state of meditation in such a way that a certain tendency towards the distraction of thoughts is present as an inhibition. What is meant is not a wanting to think, but rather a not wanting to be bound in one's ideas that has to be overcome at every moment. This is different in every person but it occurs in everybody. If we do not overcome the tendency to distraction the meditation must cease in the continual change in the course of the ideas. If the changed manner of thinking begins at a certain point then only another meditation arises. But here it is a question of that free play of ideas in which our will is passive, though mental being is still active. The more freely we let ourselves go in this manner, the more the state is analogous to dreaming, and dreaming is that which is simply incomprehensible, precisely because it does not follow any law of content and therefore appears merely contingent.

In order to find a mediation for this whole area of the incomprehensible, we must go back to the state of meditation and ask, how does it relate to our whole being?

Here two things must be distinguished. Every state of thinking is in and for itself a moment, and thus transitory. But on the other hand such a state leaves something persistent behind, deposits something, and the repeatability of the original moment depends on that. If this were not the case every idea would disappear in the moment itself and our whole being would disappear every time in each moment. In the state of meditation the momentary disappears, we retain what became at one moment in another, and thence the whole thing is at the same time an act, and this belonging together, which lies in the continuing decision, overcomes the momentary disappearing and should really completely overcome it. Now there is one more state which is analogous to meditation, this is the state of observation where productivity takes on the form of receptivity. There it is exactly the same thing, the objects change, they disappear, but the ideas gained thereby remain and are not to be forgotten. The act of will binds them and alters their characteristic of momentary disappearance. What has remained behind becomes repeatable if that particular act of will occurs, admittedly in different degrees in relation to time and to the object. We now ask, how do we relate to what has remained behind? We have it and we do not have it. The latter, if we compare it with what immediately fills every moment, the former, to the extent that it can be repeated without being originally produced again. It is reproduced from the first genesis. But this reproduction is attached to a particular act of will if it enters into the realm of meditation or has an immediate relationship to observation. But the reproduction can also ensue without an act of will. In this case we can rarely give a certain account of it, but if we observe ourselves in the state of wanting to be distracted, then everything that occurs and interrupts the meditation can only be such a reproduction of ideas that have already been received. We therefore have to distinguish a sequence of ideas which every time fills each moment and depends on the act of our will, thus meditation or observation in the wider sense, but then, however, we have a mass of ideas without really being in command of them, which are therefore not subordinated to our act of will. If we observe what distracts in the state of meditation then it is the wanting to be of such distracting ideas, thus the direction towards our whole being, to which the specific wanting to be of a moment emerges in opposition. Such an act can only be understood from out of our whole being. If we are in the state of communication, thus of simultaneous meditation and expression, then the same tendency to distraction will be here as well, for the same act of will divides itself into two moments: determinate thinking and communication. But if we have overcome the distraction in the real meditation without communication, then it will not be the same distraction that occurs in the second act, the presentation, but it will also always be a distraction. If, in communicating, we think of those elements which cannot be explained by the dominating act of will, then we are only left with the fact that they derive from free play. But if such ideas are taken up into the communication, then this must happen by an act of will. For if one thinks of someone who has been involved in strict meditation, so that he has complete control of his object, thinks of how he now establishes the order in which he wants to communicate his meditation, thus of how he conceives of the composition, then, once it has come about and he has been as strict in the composition as in the meditation, and there is nothing in his communication that could not be most precisely explained via the original act of will, he has remained in κυριολεξία;[11] if this person now looks over his composition – then two cases can be thought –. He is either satisfied that he has kept strictly to the object, or it will appear meagre to him. This latter judgement is based on a difference in what constitutes the content of free play, for if there were nothing in it that did not have a relationship to the particular meditation, then he would not need to blame himself for rejecting it. The act of will must have had a certain power of attraction for him not to have so lightly let go of it. On the other hand, where strictness is praised, there is a difference in the original act of will itself: one or the other must have been included in his intention, but the specific form of communication refused one and admitted or encouraged the other. Where we find this we can presuppose a condition of free play, and of the whole stock of ideas such that elements were in it which were able to be connected to the object. Looked at in another way, such *conscious* distraction in the original act of will is a positive stimulation of the free play of ideas, in order to draw everything related in as well. In the same way as we distinguish the different elements, which is admittedly only possible after we have accomplished the first task (for if I have not found the unity I also cannot distinguish the essential and contingent elements) and the task arises of grasping their emergence, this task rests on knowledge of the secret stock of ideas and then on the way in which we can infer from ourself and our composition to the author and his composition. If we have complete knowledge of the author, so that we know him as we know ourself, we have a completely different measure from what we have if we do not have that knowledge; in the former case we can set ourself the task of knowing not only what secondary thoughts occurred to the author, but also what did not occur to him, and what he rejected and why he rejected something. We can know this via an analogy established between him and ourself, for which we have the elements in our knowledge of him.

The more such products we have from a writer which are, in terms of their essential content, such a letting-oneself-go, the easier it is to arrive at that knowledge of him. But in this the consciousness of the writer in relation to those for whom he writes comes into consideration first. If there were something in a letter which is outside that particular sphere, then that

---

[11] *Translator's note*: 'literal meaning'.

would have happened[12] by mistake or as a result of thoughtlessness. In that case the momentary state, the momentary condition of the writer comes into account. For every writer, if they have to deal with the same objects in differing circumstances, will perhaps have the same main thoughts, but the secondary thoughts will be very different. Here the case occurs that one only gets the idea of the state in which the writer finds himself from the thoughts that intervene. But here there is much that lies outside the possibility of rules that could be established. In general it is the case that the more someone has observed themselves and others in relation to the activity of thought, the more they also have hermeneutic talent for this side. The more difficult the hermeneutic task is, the more its completion demands collective work; the more the necessary conditions are lacking, the more individual directions must unite to complete the task.

As far as the N.T. is concerned, in the historical texts as we have them, there is almost no opportunity for such interference of the secondary thoughts of the writers.

[*Translator's summary of omitted passage*: The author of the first three Gospels is not obviously apparent from the text, but the author always has some effect on the presentation. The question is whether the judgement of the author is his own or that of an earlier author which has been taken up into the Gospel. In John the author is more apparent. What ideas do the authors of the N.T. have in common with their audience that are different from the material they are dealing with? The main point they share with the Jews is knowledge of the O.T., which is the location for the secondary thoughts of the authors, but they do not share this with the Gentiles, so the life of the Gentiles could not play a role in the secondary thoughts. The role of reference to the O.T. is, however, highly contested. Is the use of the O.T. by the N.T. writers in terms of the literal meaning of the passages in question, or is the use determined by the limited amount the writers and their readers otherwise had in common? If the literal use was the only one possible, then there is only one interpretation, but if not, there are many possibilities. One therefore needs a general overview of all the uses in the N.T. There can be no general rule about the use of the O.T., because there is no one kind of emphasis in that use.]

If we look at the issue more in the context of the investigation so far, it will immediately become very probable that where there is a very small but at the same time very generally available literary heritage it is also natural that use is made of it in the most diverse ways. What is the case for the Greeks

---

[12] *Translator's note*: '*geschehen*', Frank's edition mistakenly prints '*gesehen*'.

with Homer is the case for the Jews with the O.T. Homer, as well, was used in very diverse ways, one interpreted him, like the O.T., allegorically. The analogy is unmistakable. One can think of the issue in general as follows. There is a particular appeal in conversation if two people dealing with whatever it is come to a sphere which they have in common and is immediately familiar, so that they bring in things from it when the occasion arises. A text of this kind takes on the character of a conversation, for the secondary thoughts are only ever taken from an area shared by the writer and the readers, from an area where the writer can presuppose that it can be made just as easily present to his readers as it is to him. Such secondary thoughts can often appear puzzling to unfamiliar readers. If they were also puzzling to the original readers we would admittedly have to reproach the author, for instead of the secondary thoughts giving rise to new appeal, stimulating attention, he would in this case have inhibited the readers by the difficulties he makes for them, and disturbed their attentive reading of what follows. But one should not assume this. If it occurs then it usually is a result of there being too few mediating points in our literature between confidential communication and what is directed at the general public. One should always assume that the secondary thoughts occur in an encouraging, not an inhibiting manner. – If we compare this with what was said above about the nature of digression, we can establish the general formula: Every text is twofold, on the one side a conversation, on the other the communication of a particular, intentionally willed sequence of thoughts. If we think of the latter without the former, and think of the former as absent, then to this also belongs the fact that the writer is not at all determined by the ideas of the readers with which he is confronted. If we think of this, we must say that this kind of thing is not really a text, because the author would only have written for himself. However, as soon as one thinks of a particular text as a communication it is also determined by the ideas of those to whom the text is directed. Everything in this kind of text which bears a dialogical character can only be explained by what is common to the writer and his readers. If the circle of readers is a very particular one, all the more can come from what is common, and then the tendency in the text towards the form of confidential communication is all the greater. If the direction in the didactic writings of the N.T. was towards much later generations, which would really be normal for such texts, then such a direction would have led them out of their domain; but they in fact remained within the domain which they had in common with their readers. But we are thereby led back to a very restricted circle. For among the New Testament writers everything else receded in relation to the domain of the predominant Christian life. As such only the few wavering cases in this domain itself remain. In free communication someone can proceed more from what moves him at the time, or from the ideas that he has of those he is writing to. If one side dominates the other side intervenes in the details. This shift is not easily composed in the way it is in the second Epistle to the Corinthians; this Epistle is so difficult to explicate for precisely this reason. For this reason many people have said that the Epistle has no unity, that Paul wrote it among the distractions of the journey. But such hypotheses are, if they have no determinate foundation, a hermeneutic declaration of bankruptcy; they show that one has lost the thread. The difficulty, however, lies only in the fact that the two directions characterised above merge into each other in the Epistle in a peculiar way. On the one hand the occurrences in Corinth move the Apostle; but to that also belongs what happened to him in Corinth, and this creates a particular difficulty. For if someone speaks in an emotional fashion about themselves, then one assumes one has good reason to believe that they are themselves somehow affected. The elements of the other kind intervene. Only if one considers how Paul describes himself and his whole life as a vital being moved by everything that happened in the Christian Church does one find the key to much that is otherwise not clear. There is, furthermore, much that is polemical in Paul's Epistles. One usually only seeks the objects of his polemic among those to whom he is writing. But that is not necessarily the case. Other things as well can have moved him. If one really pays attention one can recognise in the tone of his polemic whether its object is located where he is writing to, or whether he was moved by something that was happening in other regions of the Apostolic church that was not predominantly located in the community to which he was writing. In this case the explicators have often been very mistaken. But such mistakes arise very easily if one is limited to so few aids. In that case one can easily seek to explain everything via the text to be explicated itself. Whence the fact that however small the proportions of the N.T., and however carefully it has been edited, in this respect it is still very much lacking in firm points of agreement. The already mentioned disreputable habit of making dogmatic use of passages from the N.T. independently of their context has an influence on this. In this way the tendency to take the meaning of the passages in a general sense easily arises. If one then reads them again in the context one then wants to bring in the general sense without even paying attention to the context and the particular circumstances in which they are located. The mistake is then all the greater if the thought is a secondary thought in the context, but taken as *dictum probans* [statement that proves] has already received the character of a main thought. One then gives it a too elevated status and thereby distorts the whole original relationship of the sentences. Admittedly one should refrain from such prejudices and interests in explication, but the evil seems unavoidable because one cannot abolish the practice of considering New Testament passages out of context. But this is a reason why exegesis still progresses so slowly. Added to this is the incomplete state of the exegetical aids with regard precisely to the relationship between the writers and their original readers. The aids are always only products of exegesis and not uncommonly of a wrong exegesis. So one becomes prejudiced if one uses them. One therefore may only use them with great care and control.

The task of recognising the real tendency of all thoughts which are to be seen as secondary thoughts is very difficult. But it is made very much easier by the achieving of the hermeneutic task which still lies before us. For if we have a clear idea of the meditation and composition of the writer then a certain judgement on what lies outside the meditation and compositions easily results. Outside of both lie the elements which are only means of presentation, e.g. figurative expression, metaphor etc. For even if someone goes very far into the particular in their seminal decision and determines the order in which they want to communicate their thoughts, they will still not find those means of presentation already prepared, they find their way in only during the presentation itself, and therefore lie outside the composition. It is more difficult with the meditation; but in a certain sense what has just been said is also the case here. Meditation is the determinate moving away of the decision to communicate, but it is the moving away which is not yet connected to the act of writing in such a way that all secondary thoughts would already lie in this sequence. Indeed everything that is a secondary thought lies outside this sequence. One can admittedly not say that all secondary thoughts would only occur to the writer in the process of writing, let alone that they would do so with such liveliness that he would have to accept them and could not refuse them. He can have had them before and they repeat themselves in him in the moment of writing. But even then they lie outside the meditation. The real value of the secondary thoughts must be recognised from the characteristic by which they are also distinguished from what resulted from the act of will.

The technical task in particular

Here we have to consider how the text emerges in terms of content and form from the living seminal decision, how the text as a whole is the further development of the decision.[13] All elements of the text which can be regarded as dependent on the decision are object of technical explication. This is distinguished from grammatical explication in such a way that, whereas on the grammatical side the individual is the location in which language comes alive, on the technical side it is not immediately a question of language. However, what we regard as a development from the first seed must have become language. Here language is the living deed of the individual, his will has produced what is individual in it, via the power of the psychological fact a combination of elements comes about which have not been together before. Via the power exercised by the individual in language extensions and contractions of the linguistic elements arise in relation to the logical side. If we consider the *emergence* of the composition then here it is admittedly different. Here the general laws of order in thought are to be applied. But I must still also understand the writer in his meditation. This, though, is a task whose object is nearly invisible and seems to rest merely on conjecture. We can indeed easily say that the thoughts present here belong to the issue, one just has to see how they are ordered. But it is difficult to say what and how the author thought about this or that object, for every object can be pursued in differing ways. Here we are in the invisible territory of meditation, where it is also a question of knowing what the writer also rejected even though it emerged from the basic thought. Each text has its particular genetic sequence and what is original in it is the order in which the individual thoughts are thought. But the order can perhaps be a different one when they are communicated.

Here we come to the difference between meditation and composition. The fact that the difference between the two is variable has its basis in the first act of will. Looked at as a moment this can include more or less in itself. It can have such a liveliness that the whole, in its main outlines, is already given in consciousness by it. The more this is so, the less is the difference between meditation and composition; the less this act of will has this character, the greater is the difference. However, it would seem as if the difference really only referred to certain forms. For what, for example, has

---

13 Cf. the passage above on psychological explication after §7 and before 'The Psychological Task in Particular'.

meditation to do in the area of history? Etymologically the expression points to inner development of thoughts. Where, then, as in history, the content is external perception, the meditation seems to have no object at all. But this is in fact only apparently so. Although the difference between meditation and composition is different in the different areas, the meditation is in fact nowhere completely absent, not even in history. If we go back to the impulse then we see that there can be no act of will except in the form of a thought. An impulse which is itself not given in the subject itself as a thought is not an act of will, it is merely an instinctual moment. But now we can distinguish the following in the concept of the thought: To the extent that the particular dominates in it, it has the tendency to be an image, but to the extent that the universal dominates, it has the tendency to be a formula. Each is one-sided. The highest is the interpenetration of the two. But the opposition must originally be in every act of will. But one must ask: has he been determined by the object, or independently of it? The latter. The more the original act of will is given as an image, the more it also carries the particular, so to speak, in a rejuvenated manner in itself, but therefore the less it carries of the composition; its whole development is, so to speak, the outside of what is seen inwardly in that seed. But the more the original act of will is a formula, the less it carries the particular in itself, the more, then, it also already carries the composition. In this way the two acts are themselves both already posited in the first moment.

If we now consider the different tendencies that the development of thoughts can have, we find a duality in the fact that if in the impulse the tendency is towards the image, then the more the development of thoughts is objective, the more what is posited in the first seed is the particular which emerges as a thought, but the more the development of thoughts is subjective the more what lies in the seed is the tone and the various modifications of the tone in which the whole thing moves. However, in the case in which the impulse is more a formula, it is more the case that it carries the relationships in itself, and precisely because these come to be represented via the arrangement, the impulse also contains the seeds of the composition to a greater extent than those of the particular content. But both must mutually seek each other, so that we recognise the particular content via the composition and, as the particular becomes more developed, if it is completely given, the composition will also be given along with it. – But how does this accord with the difference between meditation and composition? In that case the basic principle was that we first grasp the particular via the impulse and then the correct attitude according to which everything which does not correspond to that attitude is omitted. But if it is possible that the first impulse carries the composition more in itself, then in that case the opposite route would have to be taken. How is this? If we have a general but real concept then we already always easily find the indication of further division in it. But if we wanted to say that we would arrive at everything particular via further division alone, then that would be untrue, we would only find a type. As such we can indeed think of an inner development of the composition beginning with the general formula of the whole, but the particular can in no way be found thereby. If we initially ignore the subjective direction in the first impulse, which presupposes a specific talent, and if we stay with what is more general, more widespread, then we can perceive a quantitative difference between the activity via which the original seed develops more precisely in terms of its content, and the activity via which the content gains its form. If we now take up the subjective again as subordinate, then we can say that there is a progression in the first development of the particular that we call meditation, which is more led by the general, and a progression which produces the particular more immediately. In that case the first will always immediately determine the form, and there will be an interchange between the becoming of the particular and that of the form. The particular is only found with its particular passage in context. On the other hand the particular content, which only has the character of the particular, is found in its own right, and multiple combinations are then possible. The whole will be a different one depending on whether it is understood in the one way or the other, thus more in relation to the form or in relation to the particular content. But it follows that we can only understand it completely if we understand the genesis. Whence the indispensable task of understanding every product that can be the object of hermeneutics in that twofold respect. As soon as one relies more on one or the other the realisation of the task will be incomplete. In this task everyone will have of their own accord a predominant tendency towards the one or the other. We all want to understand the presentation of the thoughts of another in relation to our own thoughts. Then the consequence can be appropriation or rejection. For this reason the kind of hermeneutic operation will be determined in terms of one's own development of thoughts. There are many people who, when they read, are not interested in the form and only look at the content. In that case a disordered procedure is possible. If I think of the form as separated from the content I can begin anywhere because I regard the content as an aggregate of particulars. Many kinds of presentation allow that more readily than others. But there are also readers who are predominantly concerned with the form. In that case it is usually at the back of one's mind that one thinks that, to the extent to which one needs the whole, one can constitute the whole from the form and the individual points. But in fact, as soon as, in wanting to understand, the tendency towards our own thoughts dominates, one or the other of the one-sidednesses arises, and true complete understanding becomes impossible. To the extent, therefore, that one wants to understand completely one should free oneself from the relation of what is to be explicated to one's own thoughts, because this relationship precisely does not at all have the intention of understanding, but instead of using as a means that which in the thought of the other relates to one's own thoughts. Everything must be understood and explicated via his thoughts. If it is not worth the effort of doing this, then the achieving of the hermeneutic task also has no value.

The relation of the thoughts of another to one's own, to the extent to which it is of a hermeneutic nature, lies wholly on the side of grammatical interpretation. It is necessary here, for in grammatical interpretation the relationship between the thoughts of another and my thoughts is the locus of language. But if the task is indeed completely to understand the thoughts of another as their product we must free ourselves from ourselves.

But in order to achieve the hermeneutic task in this sense one must above all seek to recognise the relationship between the meditation and composition of the writer. We begin with the general overview. But how can we understand the inner process of the writer from this? By observation. But this is based on self-observation. One must oneself be versed in meditation and composition in order to understand another's meditation and composition. On this side one's own composing is so essential in practice for higher studies in literary gymnastics.[14]

After these assumptions have been made, the question arises as to how I can recognise from the second act, the composition, which lies in the text before me, how this act developed in the author, how he came to the content and form of his text. This seems very difficult. – The more in a text form and content merge into each other, the smaller the difference is between

[14] *Translator's note*: in the *Ethics*, Schleiermacher says that '*Gymnastik*' is 'The development by reason of the immediate senses and talents, beginning with understanding and will, which are also organs in terms of their form' (Friedrich Schleiermacher, *Ethik (1812–13)*, Hamburg 1990, p. 36). 'Gymnastics' therefore has to do with the development of the interchange between receptivity and spontaneity in the individual. See the translator's introduction.

meditation and composition. This becomes even more clear if we think the opposite, thus a decision which does not yet include in itself with the full liveliness of consciousness even the particular content. In this case the particular content only develops via the continued effect of the elements of the decision, it develops further by repeating itself. Now we have, though, said above that there was a form which we regard as the form of the greatest passivity, where one leaves the development of what lies in the decision to circumstance. In that case thoughts arise which belong to the decision, or occasional thoughts arise in connection with the development of the thoughts which are occasioned in us from elsewhere. But then the difference emerges that those thoughts which lay in the initial impulse can be more easily brought into a determinate form, but this is more difficult for those which are more occasional, and these will be ones which can only appear in the form as a digression, because of the alien element which is attached to their genesis. These elements will be easy to distinguish as soon as one has recognised and established the main thought and the most essential divisions of that thought, which must both result from the overview.

But in doing this one must immediately also pay attention to the difference of the form, because a big difference emerges in the grasping of the first act and the bringing together of the elements via the form. The essential difference is between prose and poetry. As far as poetry is concerned, what belongs essentially to the meditation and what belongs essentially to the composition is easily shown, for here they are completely separate. If we think of a fairly extended poem, there is no reason at all to assume that it was completely thought up in advance in the first act of will. The thoughts are only there in outline in the first act of will. They have to be rearranged in the composition. It is for just this reason that composition is One act, not in terms of time, but only in terms of the immediate context. There is no such determinate difference in prose. In the case of prose we assume that content and form are immediately given in the first act. But the form here is that of prose. Hence it is not essentially an obstacle that the individual parts of the whole are not also presented in the way they are first thought. Number and euphony in prose do not have such a close relationship to the form as the metre does in poetry. The strict divergence of the results of meditation and composition is the first difference as soon as we assume there is any significant amount of poetry, where the particular separates itself off. But even in the epigram, as the smallest poetic form, we must recognise the same thing. The epigram always rests on something given. But if we think in this respect of the emergence of the epigram, then the poetic form is not immediately attached to it. If this is the case, then it is only the elements which are different in themselves that have come closer together. In the modern form of the epigram the main thing is the point. But this is the relation to the given in as sharp a form as possible. It emerges like a flash at a particular moment, it is a piece of inspiration which does not yet involve the metre. The metre is a second act. So here as well both acts are certainly separate.

If we now move from poetry to prose then here as well, the more it approaches poetry, the more there is a separation of the two acts. This is the case in prose if a particular value is attached to the musical in language. In that case the thought cannot emerge simultaneously with its expression. The expression only arises together with its musical value via the location it occupies, and this only results from the composition. Here we recognise a kind of ladder. If we now ask in what area the separation of the two acts is a minimum and is of no hermeneutic interest, then this is the lecture, which is most purely scientific. There the musical is completely subordinate to the logical. The more the composition connects the thoughts without any other interest, the more it is originally one with them, so there is therefore no difference between it and the meditation. This difference cannot consist in one's being supposed to want to establish the temporal sequence of the emergence of the individual thoughts of the writer. This is something so insignificant as a result of the composition itself that there are only a few particular cases in which something can be established concerning it. If this cannot therefore be what is meant, but instead what is meant is only the difference which emerges via the composition with regard to the elements which were previously present, then one can expect virtually nothing from this in the scientific domain, because here the expressions cannot be altered without altering the thoughts themselves.

However, this is only one side of the hermeneutic interest. The other side leads to wholly distinct differences. Namely, if we have a complex of thoughts before us, whatever the object may be, we will never call the object in it exhausted. Rather, thoughts, which belong in the same domain but which are not present in this case or which contradict the thoughts expressed in the text, will occur to everyone who is involved in a real process of learning when they read. Then the interest is in knowing whether the writer did not have these thoughts at all, or whether he deliberately omitted them. Obviously full understanding requires knowing both what I see as missing and what I find in the author that is in contradiction with my thoughts about the object. If the author pays attention to it, then one must go back to the ground of the difference. If he pays no attention to it, then it is problematic, but the task arises of investigating it, if it is at all possible to do so. Then the interest is to gain as complete an overview of the meditation of the writer in his own terms, including with regard to what is not taken up into the composition. It is possible that the writer had the thoughts in mind that I think are missing, but that he had reasons neither to include them, nor to refer to them. That can lie in the first act of will, e.g. if he did not want to be polemical. But it is still important to know whether the author had those thoughts in mind or not. For his complex of thoughts takes on another meaning depending on the answer to this. In the latter case the value of the complex is diminished, in the former, the interest in investigating the bases of his procedure more precisely is increased. This task is, though, just as difficult as it is interesting. But the interest here is different again, though this time in the opposite direction. The more the whole complex of thoughts is bound in terms of its content, the greater the interest is from this side, the less it is bound, the lesser the interest. If the complex of thoughts is just an aggregate of particulars, then the interest disappears, and the question as to what the author may have also thought lies outside the hermeneutic task. –

In the Synoptic Gospels, for example, the story of the raising of Lazarus from the dead is missing. As the proximate cause of the final catastrophe, as which it is presented by John, this story is of great importance. If we think that the three first Gospels wanted to give a description of the life of Christ, then the question is how they came to leave out the story, or whether they did not know the story. But as these Gospels are obviously more just connections of single stories, that question loses its hermeneutic interest and only retains its critical interest, namely whether and how the story became so little generally known that it did not get into the common source. In this way one sees how the interest in a bound whole is completely different from in an unbound one.

If we now summarise what we have said so far, then we have a twofold interest in getting to know the meditation of a writer in its totality, independently of what went into the composition, namely on the one side, how his manner of presentation is modified by the composition, on the other, how the whole process which develops from the act of will relates to the totality of the object. This dual interest can occur in the various kinds of composition in very different degrees, but there is no form in which getting to know the meditation of the writer in its totality has no value at all. Even the domain of history is no exception, although the expression meditation cannot be used here in the most narrow sense. Even here we ask about the emergence of the writer's memories of his object, about his intention to make notes concerning the object, and his decision.

But the accomplishment of the task in question is determined in a particular manner. In many cases much needs to be done for the task to emerge at all. For if I ask how the meditation of the author relates to the totality of his object, then I must know this totality in advance. If I first take a book in order to learn about an object, then that question cannot yet emerge; it only emerges when I have reached a certain point in the knowledge of the object.

In the case of the N.T. we find ourselves right at the beginning of the exegetical study in the situation of already having a certain knowledge of the object and a general overview of the content. But precisely this easily leads into error and must therefore be regulated.

The question immediately arises as to what the N.T. author thought about the objects which occupy a particular place in Christian doctrine for us, and from what whole the particular thoughts are taken. If we ask the question in relation to the later state of Christian doctrine then we alter the whole hermeneutic process and are on the wrong path.

The didactic texts are more or less fragmentary. The task thereby imposes itself of finding the whole. Without this no true understanding is possible. We admittedly do not yet have any content in relation to the particular didactic text, but we do have the idea of and the relationship to such a content. If we consequently want to say that the writer could not have thought this or that, otherwise he would have said it, then this would, if it is to be supposed with any justification, presuppose that one had completely accomplished the task. But this is not true. Besides, one would thereby have to presuppose that the object was supposed to have been exhausted in the text. The task can only be truly accomplished to the extent that one is in possession of everything that could have been in the meditation of the author, to which belongs, though, that one would have to know the state of the object at the time of the writer with some precision. But how is it concerning the conditions for this in the N.T.? One can see the matter in various ways. If we regard the N.T. as one task, then we know that there are no texts and information of the same period on the state of the object that come from elsewhere. We must therefore rely on the N.T. itself.

But if, on the other hand, we take the N.T. books singly, then the totality of all of them is a means whereby the accomplishment of the task for the single book is rendered more easy. The task is then to be accomplished in the form of understanding the particular via the whole, and only to the extent that that whole is given for understanding the particular can the task be successfully accomplished.

Now it is true that the task of understanding the meditation is dependent on the understanding of the composition. But we have put the former first for a good reason, because we only understand the composition genetically via the knowledge of the whole meditation. The opposite only occurs in relation to the secondary thoughts, for these only emerge in the composition. If we have reason to assume that the whole essential content was not in the moment of meditation before the writer began the composition, then the work is incomplete. But this involves the recognition of every single stage of incompletion.

If we look at the difference of the content and ask to what extent we can at least establish certain rules and provisos, in order to accomplish the task correctly, then we come to the two points of knowing whether and to what extent the meditation became something else in the composition, and whether and to what extent there were things in the meditation that are not in the composition. Here we will begin to ask to what extent a certain boundness[1] occurred in the psychological state of the author. This varies but always present to the extent that content and form are, so to speak, given in the original impulse. The content is determined by the form in its unity and fullness. If the form is also determined it also has its laws, and two people who deal with the same philosophical object, so that one of them does so in a purely didactic, the other in a dialogical form, are both already bound by the difference from each other. The more firmly and vividly the form is imprinted in the original impulse, the less those elements will develop which admittedly belong to the content but which do not enter the form. The dialogical presentation will take up elements which the other purely didactic presentation cannot take up. If the form is imprinted with a certain vividness in the impulse, then inappropriate thoughts cannot occur at all to the writer either. If they occur to him, so that he has to eliminate them, then he has not reached the highest degree of completion. This, though, is the highest degree of boundness by the

---

[1] *Gebundenheit.*

impulse. But if what is essential to the content does not occur to the writer, then that is an incompleteness which derives from the fact that the object has not been imprinted with complete vividness in the original impulse, and that the writer is not in complete control of the object. How is one now to judge in this case? The explicator must have his own experiences concerning the internal process of the development of thoughts. The interpreter must bring these experiences with him, so to speak as a stock of experiences, and seek to recognise the differences in this area by comparison.

If we consider the state of the meditation for itself from this vantage point, then it can either completely correspond to the original impulse, where object and form are then completely unified, to the extent that the latter was posited in the original impulse, or it can relate to the impulse in an incomplete manner. As soon as this makes itself apparent by deficiencies, it is also easy to see. One easily notices, e.g., the insufficiency of a text in various ways in various forms. If one thinks of the didactic form and the author has proceeded by splitting up his original schema throughout, then the resultant dryness is a sign of insufficiency. The part of his original impulse which represents the content did not have sufficient life. If the author began on the other hand with the treatment of the mere form, then a χρεία[15] results, a composition where the form is so dominant that nothing can get into it, except what arises by continuing subdivision. This is the most mechanical form, which is connected to the lack of living inner productivity. If on the other hand we find a lot of elements in the composition which are really alien to it, then that is a richness in the meditation which is, though, not something that makes it complete, because it destroys the form. This is a sign that the form was not vivid enough in the original impulse, otherwise all those things would not have occurred to the writer, or he would have rejected them if they had occurred to him.

If we look at those kinds of communication which begin more with perception, then historical presentation has such a wealth of diversity in the manner of the composition itself that we must consider the original impulse as very different. For one person historical presentation can form itself as a sequence of images, for another as a sequence of causal relationships. Each results in a completely different content. One presentation highlights what the other neglects, one has more the character of a calculation, the other a more picturesque character. Depending on whether the

---

[15] *Translator's note*: χρεία is the Greek word for the rhetorical organisation of a sentence in terms of a fixed formal scheme.

one or the other was thought in the original impulse the discovery[m] and meditation are completely different. There is, namely, discovery in this area as well, in the manner in which the elements are connected, in which this or that is asserted. There are here completely different procedures, which cannot be subordinated to one another. – If someone writes the history in a sequence of images, but these do not have the right character of images and the reader is unable to imagine[n] them, then it follows that the author was not master of his form. This is insufficiency in this area.

Let us consider the form of the conversation. Only to the extent that one understands how to evaluate the conversation can one follow the author in his meditation and get an idea of whether he collected the elements with a great effort or whether he was impelled by a plenitude of inner production, so that he had to reject things, or whether, furthermore, the particular element is in accord with the original impulse or whether there are foreign elements in the development of the thoughts. If we find that a development of thoughts is productive but that it never goes beyond the limits of the form, and that there are no alien elements combined with it, then meditation and composition resolve into each other, and this is perfection in this area. Insufficiency here is the continued operation of logical splitting. In that case the whole is just the presentation of the mechanism of the meditation. Most of what can be the object of the hermeneutic operation lies between these two cases. If one is to be able to pursue and evaluate the meditation, then one would have to know all the differing forms, for only then can one really see the invention of the artist and imaginatively reinvent[o] it. If we consider everyday life we often find acts of virtuosity with regard to conversation which rarely reveal themselves in texts. In such cases one often surmises what the other person wants to say, i.e. one constructs their development of thoughts, – even before one has the result. That rests on exact knowledge of the individuality of the other person in the process of thought. Achieving this is the essence of the hermeneutic task. But one can only achieve it in an indirect manner. There is naturally a difference in this case whether one knows a writer in the totality of his life as a historical person or whether one has the products of living authors in their familiar circle. Here it is easier because we have the relevant basis outside the text. But where this is lacking it is more difficult. In works of antiquity knowledge of the individuality of the writer is only given to a certain extent. But there is

---

[m] *Erfindung*, which also has the sense of 'invention'. [n] *nachbilden*. [o] *nacherfinden*.

a great difference here between those who have immersed themselves in antiquity and those who have not. For the former the type of development of thoughts is clear, even if the personality is not, and in this case one is capable of achieving something analogous. If one thinks of a writer with a large number of works, and if one has thoroughly studied a part of these works and assimilated them, then one gets to know his individuality as if one were living with him. As soon as the inner unity of a text is clear it is also not difficult to reconstruct the meditation.

A large part of the critical task consists in distinguishing between what belongs to a writer and what is falsely attributed to him. In that case it is a question of reconstructing the meditation of the writer. The tactfulness that many critical operations depend upon is formed in this way. – If we compare, for example, the dialogues falsely attributed to Plato with the authentic ones, then, despite the dialogical form, the former are dry, lack their own productivity and are merely directed at logical splitting, of which there is no trace in Plato's works. Here, then, the grasping of the character of the production is the first impulse to critical investigations.

If we now look at what lies between meditation and composition and can now be drawn to the one, and now to the other, then this is the realm of secondary thoughts. If the writer has also recognised them in the way they emerged as thoughts to which he could assign a specific location then they belong to the meditation. If this is not the case then they belong to the composition. We can distinguish two extremes here. The one is that the writer, conscious of possessing the totality of all the elements, was involved in the composition, that the secondary thoughts then occurred to him when the writing down was already finished. In this case the secondary thoughts appear as having been inserted. The other extreme is that in beginning the process of meditation the writer already granted himself the licence not just to remain within the strict development of the original impulse, but also to let the free play of thoughts come in. In this case we say most definitely that the secondary thoughts belong to the process of meditation. From here we can bring the whole process of meditation under two different formulae, of which one is that we think of the writer as strictly directed in relation to his impulse, but as actively rejecting everything else; the other formula, though, is that we think of the writer as directed towards the active combinatory interference of extraneous things in the sequence of his thoughts. Depending which of these is the case the character of the writer will be different.

Looked at from the point of view of the hermeneutic task it is not possible to consider the object in isolation. The object must first be considered in the total domain of the literary life of the people and of the age, then in the domain of the manner of the composition, and finally in the total domain of the peculiarities of the individual writer. This is the comparative procedure. One can also apply the opposite heuristic procedure. According to this we arrive at knowledge of the literary domain precisely via the fact that we have carried out the hermeneutic operation on many authors. The first procedure rests on personal relationships between readers and writers. If there is a personal relationship of inner affinity between reader and writer, e.g. with regard to a favourite author, then one will naturally adopt the comparative procedure. In this way everyone has their own procedure in relation to every writer. It would be wrong, if one easily finds one's way into a writer to stop and want first to obtain that knowledge that one first gains via the heuristic route.

If we now move to the last point, to the consideration of the *composition* itself, then we thereby presuppose that the writer has brought the inner impulse which dominates the whole work to its complete development within himself, that he has all the elements for the text within himself and now begins the composition.

But everyone is aware that this is not always exactly the way it is in relation to what lies in the domain of everyday life. If one has to write a letter, then one does not separate impulse, development and composition, one brings together a quantity of transitions into one. But the more the work appears as an artistic work the more one must proceed from that presupposition. The question of how much first emerged in the composition also belongs in the investigation to the extent that the aim is to reconstruct the whole. If one now seeks to reconstruct the text with that presupposition, then this has a different sense. There is, namely, no thought without words, but there are thoughts in different degrees of dress, we can have a thought without already having its fitting expression. With regard to the expression, the becoming-ready of the elements only begins with the composition itself. One can only understand these if one can see the whole nature of the content which the form shapes, or which one wishes to give to the form. The richness and fullness follows from this. So both points are therefore to be considered: the place given to each particular element and the filling-out of the form by the content, and then the expression which is definitively determined along with the being-together of the elements. The task is particularly important for the exegesis of the N.T.

If the understanding of the meditation is complete, so that the totality of all the elements belonging to the text is given, then what is left is the understanding of the composition as a deed[p] in the author, i.e. the ordering with its motives. If we now think here of different possibilities of how one and the same mass of details can be ordered, of how completely different results then emerge from that, of how, therefore, the ordering depends on the value that the author attributes to the particular elements, so that one is highlighted, the other recedes, then one sees how much in one's own use of the N.T. it is a question of understanding the ordering in this sense.

[*Translator's summary of omitted passage*: Passages from the N.T. are often used out of context, so one must take care to go back to the original context to avoid the mistakes that arise from taking sentences in isolation. The task of historical criticism of the Gospels depends on hermeneutic understanding of the composition. The synoptic approach to the first three Gospels is only appropriate for the life of Jesus, where the relations between the accounts can help establish the facts. The problem is that the relationship of the author to the events is not clear in the case of the Gospels: were they themselves eye-witnesses and do they rely on eye-witness accounts? This could only be established if it is clear that eye-witnesses combine in a different way from non eye-witnesses. In the case of John the report would appear to be that of an eye-witness. Luke does not claim to be an eye-witness, and the principle of composition is therefore different, depending upon his idea of the life of Christ. Mark would also appear not to be an eye-witness, though the text seems to be intended to be taken as being by an eye-witness. This is contradicted by the consistently mannered manner in which the events are unified in the text. Matthew was an eye-witness, but is he actually the author? The question is what the principle of composition is, which cannot be established via the choice of facts, because we do not have access to the sources from which they were chosen. If there is a mixture of direct and indirect testimony the main thing is to determine whether the manner of their combination points to an eye-witness or not. The Acts of the Apostles offer various views of the purpose and the principle of the composition, and the sources seem to have been very diverse. The main purpose would seem to be the propagation of Christianity among the Hellenic Jews and the heathens, but this is mistaken. The Acts are a combination of the available material, which meant the author was determined by what was available and the space he

---

[p] *Tatsache.*

had to fill. The purpose is Christian historiography, to the extent that this was possible in those circumstances. This judgement takes one beyond hermeneutic rules
into their application: the rules for the N.T. can only be very specific rules. John is
a proper historical work, in which the author is decisive. In the other historical
books the circumstances of the time explain the nature of the composition. Even
now it would be impossible to construct a biography from the material available.
The circumstances of writing history now and in the period of the N.T. are completely different. Then the interest was just in keeping details of the life of Christ
alive in the Church and in preserving the memory of the origins of the Church.
There was no sense of writing for the future in a literary manner. The writings of
Luke are addressed to one individual who was interested in the Christian cause,
Matthew is supposed to have written in order to remember what he had said orally.

As far as the didactic texts are concerned, the same applies as was said above
concerning the epistolary form. In the N.T. the addressee is sometimes a congregation, sometimes an individual, sometimes a series of congregations in an area or
congregations of a certain kind. The unity of composition therefore differs. The
perspective of the letter-writer differs in terms of the differing addressees, the
familiarity with the addressees, and the aims of the letter. There are letters which
are more bound that possess an objective unity, and freer letters which possess a
subjective unity evident in the mood of the text. There is no necessary reason to
believe that the basis of the composition lies in what the writer knows of those to
whom he is writing, the basis can be the conditions and relationships of the writer
himself, as is evident in the case of Paul's letter to the Romans.]

As far as the form [i.e. the letter] is concerned, which has a less determinate unity, we must remember that someone can write from out of the
circumstances which surround him, or from out of the circumstances of
those to whom he is writing. The latter case will show itself via a certain
determinacy in the relationships, in the former case a certain indeterminacy lies in the nature of the matter. For if I give advice to another person
from out of the circumstances which surround me that can only happen in
an indeterminate manner. On the other hand, what is said from out of the
circumstances of the other person has a greater relationship to that person
and thus has greater determinacy. That can only be recognised by comparison of particulars, and not via the structure, via which one finds the
unity in the more didactic letters.

Here there is now a point which is often very easy, often very difficult to
find, but which is always important, namely the tone, the mood of the
writer. Recognising this is essential to understanding a sequence of
thoughts as a fact in their mind. Two writers can have the same didactic

tendency, the object in question can be the same, the manner of conceiving it, the attitude, the manner of writing can be the same, but one writes in a calm, the other a more agitated tone. In consequence the details appear different, have a different meaning. That difference reveals itself the most in the treatment of language. But determinate rules cannot be established concerning this, precisely because it is so much a question of feeling. If we take the case of an objective unity in a presentation in a letter, but at the same time of a calm tone, then significant differences can occur in different authors; one treats language musically, the other does not or does so to a lesser extent, without the point we are now dealing with playing a role. There are people who are witty and eloquent in a way they normally are not when in an agitated state, and that influences the musical aspect. Others lose their sense of harmony in such a state. So what is characteristic does not lie in this. Where, then, does it lie, how does it really announce itself? It is difficult to establish what the same writer has written in one state of mind as opposed to the other state of mind. The right answer can only be determined by comparison. But the case can occur that one is unable immediately to make such comparisons. Then one must look round for parallels as one must in relation to the grammatical side. There is some-thing completely individual and personal in the manner of expressing one-self, but on the other side there is a great area of analogies. If one has found these then one thereby has the parallels. I can draw conclusions from related and comparable passages. If one has the feeling when looking over a passage that there is a unity of tone in it, then the conclusion is more easy and more certain. If one cannot establish such a unity then differences arise in the judgement of individual passages about which decisions generally cannot be made. There are certain moods which are connected with the tendency to hyperbole. Everyone knows that one must understand such hyperbolic expressions with the quantitative differences which belong to such moods. Taken out of context and without the tone in which they are said, one will find them inappropriate and intolerable. They are only com-prehensible in the context and in their particular tone. It is more difficult if there is a change of moods in a text. If we now ask how such a change arises we have, particularly with regard to the didactic texts of the N.T., two clear different basic cases before us. If the author wrote more from out of his state of mind and the text was not written in one go, then he could easily have written in various moods if changes had taken place in the mean-while in his state of mind which he did not need to mention because they did not belong to the object he was dealing with. In this way a divergence could easily arise. If the author writes more in the manner that he has in view the state of mind of the people he is writing to, then a difference of tone can easily be discovered if he is writing to several people and a divergence occurs among them. In that case his utterance, depending on whether it relates to one group of them or to the others, can easily take on another tone. We have letters from Apostle Paul which he wrote during his imprisonment. It is possible that during this time he had so much to do with others that he could not write continuously without interruption. In the course of legal proceedings in which Paul was involved at that time changes could easily occur which interrupted him, changed his mood; there was no reason to speak about this, but the consequences emerged in the letter. And so one can, if one finds this kind of thing, also draw the conclusion that that interrupted context points to a change which has taken place. This is an example of the first kind. The Letters to the Corinthians are an example of the other kind. It is immediately apparent that there were significant differences in the congregation which concerned the Apostle himself. If the Apostle comes to something that is connected with this, then the tone is, of course, different; if he is concerned with circumstances where lessons have to be given, then the tone naturally changes; if he is concerned with purely didactic relationships, then a change of mood will also occur. The certainty in the achievement of the hermeneutic task depends on the degree of knowledge which we have of the circumstances themselves.

If we bring to mind the whole task in its various parts and ponder how much we do not have in the N.T. which we must always presuppose, and how far we are from being able to equate ourselves with the original readers, then one can understand how it is that there are so many irresolvable differences in the explication of the particulars. If we go back to the duality established at the beginning, namely that on the one hand the whole can only be understood via the particulars, and on the other hand that the particulars can only be understood via the whole – to the extent to which it emerges from the unity of the impulse via which everything particular, albeit to differing extents, is founded, – then it is difficult to believe in relation to such a beginning point that the exegesis of the N.T. will ever be so complete and its results will appear so founded that there will be no need to undertake further investigations. Given the state of things, in which nothing can be changed in relation to certain main points, – for we will be

very unlikely to obtain more precise information concerning the situation
at that time and about the states of the individual authors – we see how necessary it is in relation to the N.T. to regard the whole as One and every
detail as something particular. The whole forms a distinct individual world.
The documents on the state of Christianity from the same period that we
possess besides the N.T. count for nothing. In relation to the hints in non-
Christian texts we must first ask through which medium the author saw
things. As far as the Apocryphal texts are concerned the period is generally
unknown, of none of them can it be said with certainty that they represent
the N.T. era. Admittedly we have information about the N.T. era in the
writers of the Church, but is it also solid and reliable? Here we find, e.g.,
the indication of a second Roman imprisonment of the Apostle Paul. Some
see in this a certain historical fact,[q] others a mere tradition which was originally an exegetical conjecture that was gradually taken as fact. One can
say that the Christian writers in whom we find that indication assumed that
every detail in the N.T. passages was inspired by the Holy Ghost, and that
everything must also have been true that they say. As such one also thought
that Paul must have come to Spain because of Romans 15, 24. If we now
find that the indication of the second imprisonment is always connected
with the indication of the Apostle's journey to Spain, then that points back
to Romans 15, 24, and so the whole story probably is based on that.
Depending on whether one sees the question in this way or that, a different
exegesis naturally results for the epistles of Paul which can be related to it.
In this way someone[16] has recently even proposed the critical canon that
everything by Paul that one cannot truly locate in the time of the Acts of
the Apostles, or which is obviously from another period, falls in the period
after the first imprisonment. As such, a completely different order of the
Epistles of Paul results: the latest become the earliest, etc. It is also evident
here how exegesis depends on criticism, but also how the art of hermeneutics
must in turn be the basis of criticism.

If we are to understand the whole via the particular and the particular
via the whole we find ourselves in the situation of mutual determination.
If we now posit the same hermeneutic principles for the achievement of
this task as well, but posit a difference of the underlying presuppositions,
then different results will emerge. The sameness of the results points back

[16] Köhler, *Essay on the Time of Composition of the Epistolary Texts in the N.T. and the Apocalypse*, 1830,
p. 8.

[q] *Nachricht.*

to the sameness of the presuppositions. Admittedly, if we can now say that the rightness of the results depends purely on the application of the right hermeneutic principles, then on the other hand the right results must often first decide which presupposition is the right one, for the result has been arrived at via this presupposition.

If we divide up the task we get very complicated rules for the N.T. One must keep in mind all the differences, namely all presuppositions which play a role in relation to each detail. One must use them as a foundation one after the other and be very careful in doing so. The result which, if one begins with the various presuppositions, most corresponds with the immediate context of a text will be the correct one. But without trying this out one cannot say that one has a safe foundation.

In relation to the didactic texts there is the further issue that one is not only to understand what the writer has said, but also that the facts to which what is said refers are to be established. In this way it is also apparent here that the hermeneutic task cannot be accomplished with certainty until we have at the same time accomplished the task of historical criticism.

If so far nothing has been said about the Revelation of John, that is because I am convinced that a hermeneutic solution is least possible here, because in this book all the difficulties which are scattered through the rest of the N.T. books come together in an intensified manner. The interaction mentioned above between hermeneutics and historical criticism is admittedly universal, but in the Apocalypse a quite particular circumstance comes into play. Let us leave, if we are considering the content of the text, the question about the author and the period of the book out of consideration. But this content is in the main a description of visions. If one now asks what the hermeneutic task is here, then it is to know with certainty, from the utterances of the author, what he saw. It is a completely different question: what does what was seen mean? This question would no longer really relate to the text, but rather to the fact of seeing. Even if we keep within these limits with the hermeneutic task in relation to the Apocalypse, then it is still not really to be accomplished.

[*Translator's summary of omitted passage*: With regard to the vision of Peter the hermeneutic task is to establish the extent to which the vision can be known from the description. Was it external or internal seeing? The only certain fact here, though, is the emergence of conviction in Peter. The same question of inner and outer vision occurs with regard to Revelations and there is no obvious solution to it. The question of the prophesies supposedly present in this text is also not solvable in a convincing manner. Given these difficulties the question as to the very place of Revelations in the N.T. necessarily arises. If one does not see the N.T. historically, but rather as a work of the Holy Ghost, then the book is a complete puzzle. Seen historically it can be understood in relation to some of the views of the congregations who wished to have, by analogy with the O.T., a prophetic book in the N.T.]

If we look at the whole area of N.T. hermeneutics, and at how much is still to be done there and at how little prospect in relation to this book there is of getting further beyond the limited space described above, then one can only regret that so much time, effort and acuity has even recently been wasted upon it. Yet there is a useful counterbalance in the more recent works against the false applications of the book. But even there the difference of views in relation to the arbitrariness of the hypotheses is not very large. Some say the apparatus of the Apocalypse could not refer to events that were soon to happen or even to events that were already past. Others say that what was said with a degree of certainty in relation to details could not be believed to refer to something that would only occur after long centuries: it must therefore relate to something proximate or already past. But despite all the difference in these hypotheses there is still the same amount of arbitrariness on both sides.

If we look at the hermeneutic task in its further relationship to historical criticism we still find so much to do there that one really does not need to go beyond the properly canonical texts. But I cannot take the Apocalypse to be canonical because it contains too little really religious material.

Every single book of the N.T. looked at in its own terms lacks the necessary aids for beginning the hermeneutic operations in a completely assured manner, because for none of them do we have certain and sufficient data concerning the time and the specific circumstances in which the book emerged. Instead, what we have to presuppose in this respect we can generally only derive from these texts themselves. Indeed, not even the whole collection really helps in relation to the individual text. For the epistles we have the Acts of the Apostles. But they are not so central that they could achieve what is demanded. We can only infer the circumstances which occasioned a particular epistle from the epistle itself. As such hermeneutics in the particular case must go beyond the epistle itself and accomplish the indeterminate task of establishing how the circumstances must have been for this or that utterance to occur. This is admittedly a matter for historical criticism. But the hermeneutic results must be able to be related to that. The hermeneutic work is not finished for a book if it does not deal with that particular task with the appropriate skill.

Here something else comes into consideration, namely the idea of the total state of Christianity in the Apostolic era. This can be of help to historical criticism. One can admittedly infer this from other evidence. But this has, if it happens in the wrong way, as many disadvantages for the hermeneutic operations as it, if it happens in the right way, must yet be the basis of those operations.

Now this issue is still far from settled, but if one looks at the history of our science one sees that it goes in a zigzag. We have, e.g., information from later times about the formation of Christianity, which one generally terms Gnostic. Now there are in the epistolary texts of the N.T. a lot of difficult passages which point to the fact that particular circumstances, deviations from the right type of belief, were their basis. One concluded that if Gnosticism had already been there those passages could refer to it; as this is so, then it must also have already been there. In this way a hermeneutic principle is made of it. But now one tested this in a more exact hermeneutic manner and found that Gnosticism was not the corresponding foundation, that the polemic against it must have been another polemic. So one therefore said that Gnosticism was not to be found in the N.T. But others, in turn, said that something related to Gnosticism must be the foundation, namely the beginnings of Gnosticism. In this way one went back again, as in a zigzag. The point where this zigzag will cease cannot yet be determined at all.

We now ask from the present viewpoint: how is N.T. hermeneutics to be carried out, in order to correspond to the expectations on both sides that it is to satisfy and which it cannot fully satisfy because it lacks the necessary presuppositions? One must always connect the opposed directions with each other.

The *first* thing that is inherent in this is that one seeks to explain every N.T. book in its own terms, following the general canon of understanding the whole via the particular and the particular via the whole. One has not arrived at a satisfactory result until both directions have been satisfied in this respect. That presupposes a continual recapitulation. The first thing is always the general overview, via which the totality becomes graspable, and the structure of the whole and the specific formula for it are found. If the overview leads to obscure passages which one sees to contain the main points of the construction, then it is to be feared that one may not arrive at a satisfactory result. In the N.T. books this case is made even more difficult by the fact that too much space has been given to the later conception of obscure passages outside their context. In this case the main rule is to remove everything that we have in mind from the pre-theological period of life. This is made easier by the fact that the ecclesiastical translation is generally the basis of the manner of dealing with the individual passages in their dogmatic significance outside the context, while the hermeneutic treatment can only have the basic text as its object. In this way those conceptions are already distanced and the observance of the proviso is thereby to a certain extent made easier. If now in some text an obscurity which contains the key to the whole is present that is not occasioned by interferences of the kind mentioned, then this is precisely the most difficult case because a method cannot easily be found to shed light on that obscurity. But that is of course also a presupposition which cannot be satisfied. For the fact that such passages occur presupposes such an incompetence with regard to language on the part of the writer that he ought really not to have written at all.

Here one should draw attention to something which often occurs. The N.T. writers have the reputation of not being men who had a literary education, except Paul. Now this is often intensified to the point where it is said that they had no idea how to use language in such a way as to make themselves clear. If an exegete now refutes the explications which have been made from the position of biased interest by saying that it is unthinkable that someone should have written in this way if that was his opinion, etc. – then it is often objected that this is much too sophisticated for the N.T. writers. But if one thereby wishes to leave open these writers to every arbitrary interpretation then that is a completely false application of the fact, undeniable in itself, that they did not have a literary education. If these writers belong to the class of the first preachers of the Gospel they were penetrated by its principles in an important way; it is precisely they who made it possible for Christianity to take its particular place in the world, so one should assume better of them. A further factor comes into consideration here. One can say that those obscurities did not result from their inadequacy in thinking and in the communication of thoughts through language; they did, though, have to speak Greek and this was not their real language: the necessity of transferring into another, foreign language is supposed to be the real basis of their inadequacy. However, no N.T. writer could get into the situation of having to write Greek if he had not previously been in the situation of having to speak it. Indeed it can be assumed that when they were teaching even in Jerusalem the Apostles must have had to express themselves more in Greek. In this way, then, the basis for arbitrariness in explication also disappears. They admittedly make no claims to rhetorical sophistication, but rather to the natural ability, to be assumed in every person, of communicating their thoughts intelligibly in a language they often used, even if it was not their first language.

It can admittedly happen that a N.T. text has an insurmountable obscurity in central passages. But this, then, can only arise for us by the fact that didactic texts refer to relationships of the writer or their addressee that are unknown to us. Then the task is therefore to free the passage in question from its obscurity by a detailed hermeneutic operation and to shed a light on the prevailing circumstances. Until an explanation has been found which makes the whole clear the path of the hermeneutic operation is not certain.

The *second* thing which is inherent in the general canon of connecting the opposed directions is that one progresses from the general view of the whole to the details, and goes back from the general view to the general circumstances of the text. But that includes in it a going beyond the single text to the realm of historical criticism and its hypothetical foundation.

The *third* thing that is inherent in that canon is that the N.T. is a collection of different texts. Here there are two directions. The whole collection is first of all the production of a new ethical potential which became part of history, then every detail is also a whole for itself, which arose out of special relations and situations. As such, all the rest obviously relates to each individual text as the natural location from which the parallels are to be taken for the hermeneutic task in the particular case. But on the other hand the task is not to be forgotten, that if we explain the circumstances which are its basis in relation to one text the results of the operation must accord with all N.T. texts, so that they give an image of the Christian state at that time as a unity, for it was from this that the whole emerged. Without this test we have no certainty. But it is precisely this which has still been very neglected. The hypothesis, for example, of the so-called original Gospel is a result of such regressive operations. One took the many passages of the Gospels which agreed with each other and asked how this agreement may have come into being. But the principle which one found is too much of a merely arithmetical, abstract nature and too sketchy. It is said that what the Gospels have in common is the earlier, what is particular to each is the later.

The former constitutes an aggregate of details of the most sketchy kind, the original Gospel, which was supposedly established as a schema by the first preachers of the Gospel and was extended by each teacher in his own way. If one now tries this idea out then one finds first of all that the Gospel according to St John cannot be understood in this way. The Apostle John would have had to have given his agreement to that schema. But the view which is the basis of his Gospel is completely different. So the authority of this Apostle is already lost for this original Gospel. If we now ask further at what time such an act of the Apostle was supposed to have occurred then we find, at least in the Acts of the Apostles, no circumstance of the kind via which such an act would become probable, no trace even where Luke would have had the opportunity to speak of it. – In this way all hypotheses about the common basis which derive from the particular will fail as soon as one looks at the whole all together.

Here a further point comes into consideration with regard to the didactic texts, which is a source of great difficulties and which one must therefore keep in mind the whole time during the explication. Written communication at that time was, namely, always and in every respect only secondary. As a rule the texts are only intended for people with whom there had already been oral communication. Not only the epistles of Paul but also the catholic letters presuppose the oral preaching of the Gospel as it was carried out by certain not unknown persons. As this was originally something common to all everyone could refer to it without fearing they would not be understood or would be misunderstood. For us, on the other hand, a further obscurity must result from this. Wherever one encounters obscure passages one must presuppose that primitive preaching and infer back from there.

In this way, then, the connection of the opposed directions is always to be applied and, even if perhaps less in profane texts, then preferably very much so and everywhere in the New Testament.

Closing observation[17]

If the hermeneutic task can only be completely accomplished at all by a combination of grammar with dialectic, of theory[r] and special anthropology, then it is clear that there is a powerful motivation in hermeneutics

---

[17] From the lectures in the Winter semester 1826–7.

[r] *Kunstlehre.*

for combining the speculative with the empirical and the historical. Consequently, the greater the hermeneutic task which is set before a generation the more hermeneutics will become such a moving force. An attentive observation of history teaches also that, since the revival of the sciences, the more concern with explication has investigated the principles of explication, the more it has contributed to spiritual development in all directions.

But if the art of hermeneutics is to have such an effect then it belongs to it that one is truly interested in that which is represented by discourse and writing. This interest can be of varying kinds, but we distinguish three stages in it.

The *first* stage is interest in history. One goes no further than the establishing of the individual facts. Much that is scientific can be included in this. Someone, e.g., reads the ancients in terms of natural history. Neither the linguistic nor the psychological context is touched by this. At this lowest stage this would be common human interpretation.

The *second* stage is artistic interest or the interest of taste. This is more limited than the first, for the people are not interested in it, only the intellectuals. This concern already leads further. Representation through language constitutes the appeal and it encourages knowledge of language and artistic products. The theory was particularly inspired by pleasure in the works of antiquity.

The *third* stage is the speculative, i.e. purely scientific, and the religious interest. I see the two as equal, because they both emerge from the highest aspect of the human spirit. The scientific interest grasps the matter in its deepest roots. We cannot think without language. But thought is the basis of all other functions of the mind, only by the fact that we think in speaking do we arrive at a definite degree of consciousness and intention. It is of the highest scientific interest to know how humankind proceeds in the development and use of language. It is equally of the highest scientific interest to understand humankind as appearance via humankind as idea. Both are most strictly connected, precisely because language leads and accompanies humankind in its development. – Even if the interest in taste grasps the task in a deeper manner, the task can still only be appropriately accomplished by scientific interest. But an even smaller part of the population raises itself to this speculative interest than to the interest in taste. But that is evened out by the religious interest, as this is also a universal interest. It is at the lowest stage that the religious consciousness is not yet awakened. The more it awakens and becomes ubiquitous, the more is humankind itself awoken. Now, though, it is possessed and felt by all as something universal. But one can only agree about it via language. We see that humankind only becomes clear and certain about its highest interest to the extent to which it knows communication through language. Everything, therefore, that is a normal expression of the religious, that is in some way a sacred text, must contribute to making this task a universal one. We admittedly find religions which have sacred texts without the interest in them being universal among the mass of the people. Even in the Christian Church the Roman Catholic party is an exception. Even if the hermeneutic task in relation to the N.T. text seems very subordinate, compared with the totality of the object of the whole task of the Christian church, and much cannot be fully accomplished because of the peculiarity of the language and the mass of the material, it is yet on the other hand the most universal interest that is attached to the hermeneutic task, and we will be able to say with certainty that if the universal religious interest were to die, the hermeneutic interest would also be lost. Our view of the relationship of Christianity to the whole of humankind and the spiritual clarity with which this has developed in the Protestant church is the guarantee of that. Admittedly the task in this area cannot be so completely accomplished as in the area of classical literature. But our interest should not be any the less for this reason. Even if we can never achieve a complete understanding of the personal individuality of the N.T. writers, the highest aspect of the task is still possible, namely to grasp ever more completely the life they have in common, the being and the spirit of Christ.

Criticism

In[1] the science of criticism it is initially a difficult task to orient oneself appropriately in relation to the object of criticism.

If there were more time it would not be without interest if we tried to show how the task and the name of the science have been modified in the course of time. As it is we can only look at the present state of things.

If we consider the expression *criticism* etymologically, then two things come into consideration, one the one hand, that criticism is in some sense a court of judgement, on the other, that it is a comparison. Both sometimes coincide, but also sometimes diverge.

As it has become a technical expression the word is very difficult to consider as a real unity. We use it in relation to scientific works and to works of art. If we combine this double relationship, then for this kind of criticism an expression of Fr. August Wolf might not be inappropriate, namely that of doctrinal criticism.[2] The real tendency is always to compare single products with their idea: that is the court of judgement, but also to consider details in relation to other details, and that is comparison. But both then go back together into One, form *one* doctrine. In this way the opposition between historical and philological criticism still persists. Summarising its

---

[1] *Editor's note (Lücke)*: The hand-written unpublished manuscripts of Schleiermacher consist for this part of the Lectures of only a few sheets, the oldest of which contain only short notes and heading-like sentences for the purpose of presenting lectures; two others from differing times begin a somewhat more complete development, but break off again after a few connected sentences. Given this thoroughly fragmentary character of the manuscripts I have preferred to print the last lecture from the Winter semester 1832, using the beginning of a more complete development that was made last, which is the basis of the lecture, in context.

[2] *Editor's note (Lücke)*: Cf. for this investigation of the concept of criticism, its extent and content, Schleiermacher's essay 'On the Concept and Division of Philological Criticism' in the Academic Speeches and Essays, *Sämmtliche Werke, Zur Philosophie*, Vol. 3, pp. 387–402.

unity as well as possible, the task of historical criticism is to construct the facts out of accounts,[3] thus to determine how the account relates to the fact. Philological criticism is divided into higher and lower. If one asks which is higher and which is lower, the answer is not always the same. From time to time, even among theoreticians who make claims to a scientific approach, it sounds very mechanical.

It is true that one says that philological criticism concerns itself with texts, particularly of classical antiquity, with regard to their authenticity. But precisely this last concept is again very difficult. One understands by it the question whether a text is really by an author to whom it is attributed; in this there is, however, a big difference whether the text attributes itself to the author, like, e.g., the second epistle of Peter, or whether it is attributed by others to him, like, e.g., the Gospel of Matthew, where the heading is not an original part of the text. The cases are different. In the latter case the question is just whether the person is right who gave the text its title and heading, and whether the name designates what we think thereby. But that is not at all the investigation concerning the authenticity or inauthenticity of the text itself.

Now it is said that lower criticism relates to the authenticity or inauthenticity of the single letters and words, higher to whole texts and whole parts of texts. But this is a mechanical and untenable difference. Are the words not also parts of the text? Can the authenticity or inauthenticity of a word not be of much greater significance than that of a whole part? – The conjecture of the Socinian[4] Sam. Crell to read John 1,1 as θεοῦ ἦν ὁ λόγος [the word was of God], instead of θεὸς [God], would according to this belong to lower criticism, but the question about the pericope[5] of the adulteress to higher. And yet the former is more important to know because of the whole context of the Gospel than the latter.

There are obviously cases where both become so mixed that one can no longer distinguish them. The question of the authenticity or inauthenticity of a sentence, thus of a part of the text, often depends upon a single word. One will not be able to say that a word is not really part of a text, but also

---

[3] *Translator's note*: As elsewhere, in the following Schleiermacher sometimes uses '*Tatsache*' with the sense of its being both 'fact' and a 'deed' – '*Tat*' – on the part of the producer of the piece of language in question: the context usually makes this clear. '*Relation*' has the sense of 'relating' a story, thus giving an 'account' which is not the original thing and can therefore diverge from the original.

[4] *Translator's note*: A supporter of the beliefs of Faustus (1539–1604) and Laelius (1525–62) Socinus, who rejected the doctrines of the divinity of Christ, the Trinity, and original sin, and held that those who followed Christ's virtues would be granted salvation.

[5] A passage from the Bible, from the Greek for a piece cut out of something.

not, if the issue is sentences, that that is the realm of higher, if the issue is the elements of the sentences, the realm of lower criticism. There is no boundary here. The whole manner of looking at the question is unsatisfactory, and it is better to discard the whole difference.

If we look at the two above cases from another side we will find that a much greater multitude of operations, including activities of a higher kind, belong to the decision on that θεὸς and θεοῦ than to judging the authenticity of the passage on the adulteress. Here it is really just a question of the value of the manuscripts which have the passage or do not have the passage. But we have no trace of the version[a] θεοῦ in the manuscripts and one must have read and investigated much to be able to talk about it. As such, then, the expression higher and lower criticism in the sense in question cannot be justified from this side either.

In order to get to the correct purpose of the concept of philological criticism and its division we must look at it in relation to the other critical disciplines, thus to historical and doctrinal criticism or criticism in reviews.

One could go even further back and ask: what is criticism at all in all its different relationships to the scientific task? But success will teach us whether we can and must go so far back. If we get so far via the comparison of the different kinds of criticism that we can give a satisfactory explanation of philological criticism, one which at the same time contains the principle of its division, then we will not ask any further. But if we were to find definite indications of the relationship to the scientific domain then we would be able to go back without wasting much time. As things stand, however, we will put the question like this: To what is philological criticism more related: to doctrinal or historical criticism?

We want for the time being to consider all the individual tasks as a pure aggregate, without looking at them in relation to each other. It belongs to philological critique that if we encounter differences in one and the same work which cannot exist together we select what is right and reject what is wrong, and establish the original form, if possible, from the differing ways in which the text appears, present it therefore in its original context of life, decide therefore whether it is a deed of this person or that person, or a deed of this person or not of this person. In the cases where it is not a question of the author the question will be of the time in which a text belongs. Let us now for the time being regard this as the aggregate of philological criticism,

---

[a] *Leseart.*

and ask: how does this relate to doctrinal or reviewing criticism? The business of these consists in correctly assessing works of men solely with reference to their value. The word work is here taken as a whole, according to which all human products, from the mechanical through to the realms of art and science, are included within it. According to what does the assessment take place here? For every human work there is a primal image.[b] In accordance with this the particular must be judged as appearance. But then the question occurs from time to time: have the author[c] and the one who judges the same primal image? This is a different relationship if the second assessment derives from the first, namely the assessment of whether the author had a primal image or not. But the whole task relates to the relationship of the appearance to the primal image. And this goes right through the whole domain. Even in judging mechanical works I must be able to say what belongs to perfection and I cannot do this until I have formed the aggregate of perfections into a whole, which is precisely the primal image. It is the same in both the domain of science and of art. I must include the work in a specific genre, attribute a specific purpose to it, and then the question is: to what extent does it achieve its purpose, and is it appropriate to its genre? If we apply this to ethical actions which are transitory moments of life then they are assessed in terms of the ethical primal image and their relationships to what is to be effected. The two together determine the perfection or imperfection of the action.

Among these there are many objects which are at the same time objects of philological criticism. All texts which can become the object of philological criticism are at the same time objects of doctrinal criticism. But the task of each of them is very different. In the realm of art the same task can occur which philological criticism entails for literary works. In relation to a work of plastic art there is, e.g., the question whether it belongs to the person to whom it is attributed. The attribution can lie in the work itself, if the name of the artist is engraved on it. But the name can be attributed to the work from elsewhere. Then the question is again whether the parts are real, whether something is restored, etc. These are the same operations which philological criticism has to carry out. But here we see the difference of both kinds of criticism, of doctrinal and philological, in the same objects. For the former is not at all concerned with the author, but with the idea of the work, whether the latter corresponds to the former. But now one can

[b] *Urbild.*   [c] *Urheber.*

161

say that doctrinal judgement, e.g. about an ode, would be false if isolated elements of later origin were found in it; in this way doctrinal and philological criticism are more precisely connected. But for doctrinal criticism as such it does not matter whether an imperfection of the work originally derives from the author or from someone else. On the other hand philological criticism says that if it has once established and proved that an ode derives from Horace or not, it does not concern itself in either case with whether it is better or worse. In this way, then, the tasks and functions of doctrinal and philological criticism are indeed different, whereas the operations of archaeological and philological criticism are essentially the same, despite all the differences of the material.

However, doctrinal and philological criticism do nevertheless have something in common. The latter, namely, has largely to do with judging how correctly a text has been transmitted. But this can to a certain extent be brought under doctrinal criticism. To this belongs ethical criticism, the judging of human actions according to what they should be in relation to certain laws, ways of life, etc. Now a manuscript is the action of a person, and so it is a question of the faithfulness and precision with which he wrote it out. If one says the manuscript is inexact, badly done, etc., then that is indeed something which belongs in the philological domain. But such an evaluation is always only a temporary measure. The real task of philological criticism is to present what is correct in the text itself.

The next thing we have to do is to investigate how philological criticism relates to historical criticism. Of the latter one generally says that it is the art of establishing the real truth of a fact from the available accounts. The task in this area is to be set quite generally. For we find everywhere a difference between the account and the fact. The difference can be larger or smaller, but it is always present to some extent. If someone tells what he himself has experienced, then the analogous situation is when someone describes with words what he saw for himself. Describing something with words and what is seen with the eyes are irrational quantities in relation to each other. Perception is, namely, a continuum, the description cannot be. The task of representing the object correctly by description can only be accomplished in different ways, never in the same way. There is always a transformation of the continuum, of the concrete object, into a discrete object, – into a description which consists of single sentences, in which a judgement of the describer is always contained, and certain things are necessarily not described, are passed over, other things are abbreviated, because otherwise the description would have to become endless. This transformation of the continuum resembles the transformation of a surface into a single point. One can set about this in various ways, and in this way what is passed over can also be added to in various ways. – If two people produce independently of each other a picture of an unknown animal from a description, the pictures will be very different. In the same way with the narration of a fact. Of course it is particularly important to know how the narrator proceeded. The more he is known to me – his manner of perceiving, his tendencies to overlook something in perception, to take up and leave out things from what he has perceived – the more the fact can be established from the narration.

So the establishing of the fact from the accounts is the task of historical criticism. But here we stand on a boundary point. For if we only had One account of a fact, then the accomplishing of the task would be a purely hermeneutic operation. But if we apply the rules of hermeneutics to historical works in particular, then the establishing of the fact goes beyond the hermeneutic domain. Only the establishing of the perception from which the account resulted is a hermeneutic task. Knowing how what the narrator perceived was is admittedly establishing the fact in the mind of the narrator, but that does not depend any more on his utterance, but on knowledge of him from elsewhere, in short it goes over into adjacent historical criticism. If there are several, and different accounts of the same fact, then the task is more complicated, more difficult, because we must elicit a result via which the way the various accounts emerged can be explained, – but the certainty becomes greater because the accounts complement each other and the differences can be more easily smoothed out. As such, this is a higher position.

Now how does philological criticism relate to this? If its objects can somehow be brought back to this concept of historical criticism, then they are related and to be subsumed into each other; in the opposed case they diverge and philological criticism would be determined in terms of its relative opposition to the other two.

There are very many tasks for philological criticism. One has, as already mentioned, distinguished the realm of higher and of lower. The latter one also terms documentary, certifying criticism, the former, divinatory criticism. But, if one expresses the difference in this way, then the oppositions cancel each other out. For if we grasp the task of higher criticism in the way it is presented above, then it can in one case just as well be accomplished by documentary as it can in another only by divinatory criticism. And the same goes for the lower. For if I can make a certain evaluation of the quality of the extant manuscripts, and the best agree in a version, then this is without more ado the best version. In that case the task is accomplished in a documentary manner. If, however, I must take refuge in emendations, then that is divinatory criticism.

But the question of the relationship between historical and philological criticism is not adequately solved in this manner. We must look at the different tasks more precisely and compare them with one another. As philological criticism is not a concept a priori, but has only formed and developed itself with the business of criticism itself, then one can also only reach its correct explanation in this way.

Texts which are no longer the original texts can be seen as accounts. The text should only communicate what the author wrote. This fact is now to be investigated. So it seems as if the task of philological criticism is the same as that of historical in terms of form, but not of content. Here we do not find at all the same irrationality between narration and fact as in historical criticism. The author writes successively, as does the copyist. If we now take the case in which the author wrote his work and another copied it correctly, then original text and copied text etc. are the same and the difference between the fact and the account becomes irrelevant, so that the task disappears as a task. But the matter immediately becomes different if we think of the case somewhat differently, namely, if the writer or copyist has not correctly written out or copied out the text. Here a difference emerges between the fact of dictation or the original writing, and the account in the dictated text or copy. Even if this difference is not necessary it is still there and must be dissolved, and so we are again in the domain of historical criticism and the task is, it appears, to be subsumed under the concept of historical criticism. This is admittedly only one case, and one where philological criticism could also be subsumed under doctrinal, because it is a question of comparing an action with its rules and laws.

It is another task when we encounter something in the work of a writer that gives the impression of a stranger; the suspicion of forgery arises, in which one can think not just of a single word, but also of something larger. Is this case to be subsumed under historical criticism? Of course. If the suspicion is well-founded then the account does not agree with the fact of the original text, in the other case they both agree. It is a question of finding this out. So the task is to find the fact from the account.

Let us take a higher task. A manuscript contains all texts of one and the same author, but among them is one which lacks the appropriate identity with the others, so that the suspicion arises that it is not by the author: how is this case to be regarded? If there is enough evidence and there are enough reasons that the manuscript is only supposed to contain texts of the same author, if it is, e.g., clear from the heading that the person who produced the manuscript regarded everything as text of the same author, then this testimony states as a fact that the author also wrote that text. If the text is now still suspicious then there is a difference between the account and the fact, and this is to be investigated. This case belongs to so-called higher criticism. But it leads just as much to historical criticism as the one above which belongs more to so-called lower criticism.

We will, then, therefore say that philological criticism is to be subsumed under historical criticism, that it is a particular part of it. This is the case for the task in its fullest scope.

The scope of historical criticism is, though, wider than the classical, indeed than the literary domain as a whole. Taken in its most universal sense we have continually to undertake it in everyday life. Every time someone makes a slip of the tongue we have a case for philological criticism, even though there is no written letter present. What is supposed to be One, thought and speech, has become two. Whoever makes a slip of the tongue says something different from what they think. So we have a difference. The difference can often not be immediately noticed, but only afterwards. One might notice it straight away, but not want to interrupt to ask for an explanation, and so one seeks oneself to establish what he wanted to say. – But in such cases it should always be established what the speaker really wanted to say, as what he said is something different. In the same way the task emerges in the slips of the pen in original texts and copies. But even tasks of higher criticism occur in everyday life, e.g. in relation to anonymous texts. In this way the compound critical problems of classical antiquity have at least an analogy everywhere in life, and the universality of the task is unmistakable.

If we now compare the three main critical tasks with each other we find that doctrinal criticism, including ethical criticism, has a completely universal task which occurs everywhere in every state of humankind. It is concerned with the relationship of that which is determined as particular to the concept. Here the last grounds lie in the dialectical and speculative domain. Historical criticism is a task which also occurs everywhere that past and present confront each other. In that case there is always a comparison to be made between the fact (in the past) and the account (in the present). The task is universal where there is historical existence.

Philological criticism has to do with the gradual transformation which results from the play between taking up and giving back, between receptivity and spontaneity.

If we wanted to unify all three this would take us too far astray. It is just a question of deciding whether we should subsume philological under doctrinal or under historical.

If we do the first then we would say that the task of philological criticism is to make a judgement about the faithfulness of the tradition.[d] But this judgement is not yet the accomplishment of the task itself. For if I know that I in this case have a correct and in that case an incorrect process, then the first is only the case to the extent that the particular has not been obscured in some way, and only in the case where this does not occur in any way at all would a further accomplishing of the task be unnecessary. But if I have an incorrect process then the task arises of producing the original utterance from the text. But this task is not yet accomplished in the task of doctrinal criticism.

If, on the other hand, we subsume philological criticism under historical criticism, then this subsumption at least affects the accomplishment of the philological task itself. For it is a question of producing the original fact from the extant evidence. Now this admittedly seems better, but what do we gain by it? We would have more than half the whole if historical criticism were already a developed technical discipline, if it had firm universal rules. But that is not the case at all. Historical criticism is everywhere only at the beginning, for it has no certain theory to which we could reduce the philological task.

However, we have gained a formula from the comparison with historical criticism to which we can reduce all tasks of philological criticism if we put the case that there are everywhere different quantities, fact and account, and an assumed relationship between the two which is to be established whether it is right or not. The copy wants to be a precise writing out of the original. The original is the object, the copy a description, account, the assumed relationship is identity or complete agreement. Now it is to be investigated whether this assumed relationship really occurs. Details can

---

[d] *Überlieferung.*

be dubious, or even the whole text, but one must always establish what relationship the account has to the fact. In this way one can think of the task of philological criticism as a unity.

But the philological tasks are different in the details, and so the procedure of achieving them is also different. So it is necessary to find a correct division in order to group the different tasks in an appropriate manner.

The division into higher and lower criticism mentioned above is interpreted in various ways. The term higher and lower criticism can mean either that the tasks are more and less important according to their objects, or that their accomplishment presupposes a different amount of knowledge and talents. But this latter at least can only be seen after the operations themselves. If one takes the division in the sense that the higher is called divinatory, the lower documentary criticism, then a difference of procedure or method is admittedly hinted at, but it is questionable whether the term is valid for different tasks, such that some tasks can only be accomplished by diplomatic[e] criticism, others only by divinatory criticism. But this is not the case, instead the tasks often fall into both domains, or both methods of the procedure coincide in many tasks. In this way, then, the tasks themselves are not divided by that division.

Is there another more correct way of grouping the philological tasks? Something more, something higher, than grouping cannot be demanded where one has to do with details. Here it is just a practical question. The tasks arose and arise via the relationship of a later period to the productions of an earlier period, and are of a very different kind. Now the question is: can these different tasks be summarised under certain main differences? How do we find them? By going back to the relationship assumed between the account or the testimony and the fact. Now the question is in how many ways the assumed relationship of identity gets lost, or in how many ways in different cases the difference between the later, which is supposed to be the same as the earlier, but is not, can arise.

We take the task in the above mentioned complete universality, according to which it can, e.g., also occur in everyday conversation. The universal presupposition of conversation is the identity between thought and word. All understanding rests on this. Now how does a slip of the tongue arise in a conversation? It can have very different causes, and in many cases it can be very hard to find the true cause. In conversation we have two

---

[e] *diplomatische* in the sense of 'documentary'.

operations, that of thinking, the purely psychological, and that of speaking, which rests on a purely organic function. We can call this the mechanical, at least in comparison with the operation of thinking. The impulse to it, that which is freedom in it, is really just the transition of what is thought into the activity of the organs of speech that rests on muscular movement, which has its particular mechanism. If we also think of the impulse of the will continuing to have its effect, then we always distinguish this moment of freedom and what is purely mechanical. Now we can think of divergences of what is spoken and what is thought whose basis lies purely in the mechanical operation, and, on the other hand, of those where the basis lies on the psychological side, where the slip of the tongue arises from simultaneous thoughts which admittedly do not come in the sequence but force their way in momentarily. In this case one knows more easily oneself how the slip arises. Mixing up of names is of this kind. If we can take this completely generally and develop it, then we can say that the difference between the fact and the account or the testimony either arises mechanically, or via the influence of a moment which lies in the realm of freedom. A greater, more extensive division of the task could not then be thought. But the question is: can this be put so generally?

If we move on from this first operation, where someone has made a slip of the tongue and the task is to establish what was thought from what was heard, then we come to the analogous case of the slip of the pen. Here we have the mechanical operation of the hand. Via this something has arisen that did not want to be written. The reason for this is the same as with the slip of the tongue.

But let us consider this case more precisely in the form in which it is usual in criticism, namely the act of copying out. If a copyist writes what he has seen, and it is a mistake, then he did not really make a slip of the pen, the mistake lies back in what he saw. But the mistake that he makes himself can rest on an oversight. A greater degree of attention would have prevented all such errors. But lack of attention is something that does not really belong in the realm of freedom. The oversight can happen in various ways. If we begin in this case with the fact that should have been written here, then we can distinguish two cases: either what should not have been written is written, or what should have been written is not written. The latter is the very common error of omission. This can take place in two ways. On the one hand, if two words have the same beginning and the copyist mistakenly omits what lies between, or if two words have the same ending and the copyist writes on from the first to the second and overlooks and omits what lies between. In both cases the omission is not intentional and has its basis in the mechanical operation.

But let us think that a copyist finds something in his original text written between the lines or in the margin, and becomes uncertain whether he should add it or ignore it. What has been written over can relate to the real text as a change or as an addition. The relationship should have certainly been indicated, but this is not the case. If the copyist omits the addition because he considered it to be a change, or adopted the change because he considered it to be an addition, then in the first case something will be missing, in the second case the same thing will be there twice, thus there will be too much there. In the same way with marginalia, which can be either additions or explanations. In all these cases the difference rests on a free action, because it rests on a judgement about facts. This genesis of the critical task is completely independent of the size of what is included or omitted. What is left out via merely mechanical error can be significantly large, whole lines, what is included or left out through freedom, through judgement, on the other hand, can be significantly small. It is not a question of the quantitative difference, but of the genesis of the difference if rules are to be established.

The case of how a doubt about the author of a text arises is still to be looked at in particular. Think of a codex which contains several Platonic dialogues, but only under their heading, and without the name of the author, because one assumed that this was known. Behind it is another dialogue, also with its heading, but like the first dialogues, with the same assumption, also without the name of the author. If someone just copies the last dialogue and puts, because he thinks it is also a Platonic dialogue, the name of Plato as the author above it, then that is a mistake that has arise from a free action; the same mistake can reproduce itself *optima fide* [in the best faith] in otherwise completely correct copies. The question now is whether the judgement corresponds to the fact or not, whether the dialogue stems from Plato or not? – The question can be more easy and more difficult to decide. It is easy if an ignorant person has made the judgement and written the name Plato on a work which no one can take to be Platonic.

Such a mistake can, though, also be thought of as arising in another manner, if, namely, someone wrote the name Plato questioningly or doubtfully in the margin and the copyist of such a manuscript took up the name. There it is also a free action, but of quite another kind: he perhaps did not think about the matter, but just thought that because the name was in the margin it belonged in the text. Had the first person made a sign of uncertainty the second would not have made the mistake. But one can imagine that a similar sounding name has been taken up, or that an epithet that specifies the difference between two writers has been overlooked and left out. In that case a mechanical mistake can be assumed. In this way the two ways in which the mistake can arise converge.

The main cases of philological criticism are summarised in the examples above. We find that the two ways in which mistakes arise are distinguishable in very few cases indeed. In order to determine the critical procedure in every given case one must go back to one or other of the ways mistakes arise. This is always hypothetical. But the tasks can only be separated and assigned in this way.

We can go even further back and say that all operations of criticism are determined by the emergence of the suspicion that something is there which should not be. Where there is no such suspicion no critical procedure can be begun either.

The suspicion can arise at the very beginning in relation to an apparent mistake, as, e.g., when someone makes a slip of the tongue, mixing up a name or a number; but it can also only arise later in the course of further following of the utterance.

If we take the case where a text is falsely attributed to an author, many people can read it and notice nothing, and have no suspicion of it. It can be an object which the author in question could have dealt with, and the manner of dealing with it and the kind of writing correspond, but circumstances occur which the author could not have known. The text can therefore not have been written by him, except if there is a suspicion that the passage in question does not derive from the author, and is therefore interpolated. But those circumstances are overlooked by many readers. A certain qualification is therefore required for the reader to become suspicious. Now if the critical procedure cannot arise if there is no suspicion at all there, then one could divide the cases or tasks according to whether suspicion must arise or not. This could be the occasion of that division into higher and lower criticism. –

Let us go through the cases more exactly. If, e.g., an omission has arisen through a mistake of the eye, so that the sentence becomes lacking in context and incomprehensible, then everyone easily becomes suspicious. If an unfavourable use of language has arisen via a mechanical error, the mistake can often be obvious, but often one needs a thorough knowledge of the language to discover the mistake, especially if the different periods of the language come into consideration. If one wants to distinguish higher and lower criticism in these terms one must really be certain not to consider the amount of text. A triviality can demand just as much knowledge of the language as the inauthenticity of a whole text.

One might say that a person for whom no suspicion arises where it ought to is an uncritical person, and, on the other hand, that a person is critical who is good at suspecting things. But if one wanted to make giving instructions as to how one becomes a critical person part of criticism this would be going too far, because different natural predispositions and degrees of practice compete with each other here. Criticism can only locate itself at the point where it can teach what is to be done if the suspicion has arisen and is acknowledged, and how one succeeds in resolving the difference.

Now we have an overview of how the task is to be divided and what one must begin with in order to proceed certainly and safely.

We must abstract from the extent of the suspicion, because it is contingent. Now should we begin with the way in which the mistake, the error arises from which the suspicion begins, or with how the suspicion arises? The latter depends, however, as we said, on what lies outside criticism. So we must begin with the way in which the error, the mistake arises. The rules of the procedure depend on this. But here we must begin with the original presupposition with which all operations of criticism begin, namely the suspicion or supposition that what is extant does not correspond to the original fact. If we now divide the business according to the above then we will certainly separate *the suppositions which suggest a mechanical mistake, and those which suggest the interruption of a free action through which the difference between the fact and the account was occasioned or caused.* In this way an analogy arises to the division into higher and lower criticism.

The task itself now consists (there as here) of two moments, of the recognition of the mistake and the restoration of the original. But as the grounds of explanation are different in the two main parts, the former must remain the main division.

Part One
Criticism of mechanical errors

Here we first ask what the most general case is in which the suspicion of a difference between account and original fact arises.

If we now take, as stated above, the copy as account and the original text as the original fact, – then the most general case or indication of critical suspicion is that if a sentence in a text does not make any coherent sense, i.e. is not a real sentence, the specific assumption arises that the original fact has been altered, for nobody wishes to write something that does not make coherent sense. This is the formula for the cases where one must always infer back to a mechanical mistake, because one cannot at all presuppose that someone wants to make a sentence incomprehensible, but only that he tries to put another meaning into it. – The indication is as valid for the case that someone makes a slip of the pen in the original text as for when someone makes a slip of the tongue and the sentence becomes meaningless.

It is a different case if we have several accounts of the same fact, several copies of an original text. In that case a suspicion can arise quite independently of whether a passage is meaningful or not, if, namely, it has a meaning in each of several manuscripts, but a different meaning in each. If we have two readings we have two possibilities, one can be false, or both can. If the suspicion only arises by comparison of several accounts, then not everything intentional is excluded, both free intention and mechanical error can have intervened. As in this case the degree of suspicion lies in the difference of the accounts, the task is to decide between the differences.

We therefore have to distinguish *those tasks which arise from looking at a text for itself, and those which only arise from the comparison of several texts.* The former rest on the general fact that mechanical errors occur, the latter presuppose that more copies have been made of the original text and that they are different. These are then to be compared like different testimonies.

Here again two tasks and two procedures emerge. One task is: if we are certainly confronted with the fact of a mistake, how are we to proceed? The other is to discover mistakes which otherwise would not be discovered. It can be that nothing at all occurs in a manuscript that would give rise to suspicion, but the possibility of mistakes is in general always possible; the multiplicity of copies and their difference shows, if we compare them, that mistakes are really present. We therefore have the double task, *first of discovering differences, mistakes, second, of deciding about the differences, thus of determining what is original.*

Now let us look at the most simple case, when the suspicion of a mistake arises in reading through a text. Here we must divide the task according to its content, then divide the resolution, according to whether there is a difference in the manner of proceeding.

The most general indication of suspicion is that a passage occurs which does not offer any coherent sense. In this case two things are possible: the sentence either does not offer logically, or does not offer grammatically coherent sense. The latter can take place without the former. In a sentence noun and adjective can fail to agree, but the belonging together of the two, the logical sense can in this case be indubitable; the case where the logical sense is not coherent is possibly the more difficult, because if the logical connection is missing an infinite number of possibilities arise. Only the context contains indications of what can be meant. In this way, then, the task is indeterminate. On the other hand, if the sentence is logically determinate, but not grammatical, then the task is more simple, it lies then purely in the transformation of the forms and in the grammatical rules. If the noun is right, then the adjective must be made to accord with it, just as, if the conjunction is certain, the mood is easy to determine. But with regard to preposition and case one can waver, because several prepositions used with different cases can mean the same thing. For the hermeneutic operation it can to a certain extent be immaterial whether I accomplish the critical task completely correctly or not. But looked at purely philologically in relation to the totality of language it is not immaterial. In this case the task therefore arises of finding out and determining from the various possibilities what is appropriate both to the language and to the sense. In order now to be sure that the original is established, several copies must, as here only a mechanical error has occurred, necessarily be compared. Here the difference between documentary and divinatory criticism emerges. If several copies are extant, but one of them does not have this error, then it is presumed to be the original and the task is accomplished. But if we have only *one* manuscript, then the decision is only possible for internal reasons. In this way the same task can and must in certain cases be accomplished for internal reasons, in others for external reasons. The decision for external reasons naturally has preference. But there are cases where the decision for internal reasons is just as completely certain, such as if the sense is logically determinate and the grammatical mistake which is present can be corrected with grammatical necessity, i.e. if there is only one grammatical possibility.

The decision for external reasons can very easily be one where the task for the hermeneutic operation seems to be accomplished. But it is possible that in other manuscripts something else is there in the same place. This forces one to decide between the two. Now as long as the documents are not so completely available that we can say that the copies taken together completely represent the original text, so that they mutually cancel out their mistakes, the decision is incomplete and always only provisional. The decision is apodictic only if there is grammatical necessity. But the cases are surprisingly different and the process not at all always so easy.

In the above we have only related the case of the grammatically and logically incoherent to the general logical form of the sentence and the general grammatical rules. But much more individual cases can now arise. A sentence can be logically coherent in itself, yet one can still assert with the greatest certainty that it must involve a mistake, because, as it stands, it either does not fit in the context or cannot be taken as a sentence of the particular known author. In the same way a sentence can appear grammatically coherent and correct and yet there can be a mistake in it; it can be coherent in terms of the general laws of language, but not in terms of the particular linguistic conditions in which the text arose. The suspicion begins in these cases with the hermeneutic operation, it is linked to the perfection with which one strives to carry out the hermeneutic operation. In this way cases of suspicion arise for the attentive and practised reader who is familiar with his author which would not arise for others. The more the task multiplies, and the cases become more specialised, the less the general procedure is adequate and must become more specialised and individual.

In the further investigation of the tasks the relationship of the documentary and divinatory methods next comes into consideration, all the more so because each has been one-sidedly over-valued.

As soon as we encounter an abnormality in reading which makes one suspect a mechanical mistake, a grammatical abnormality, then the question is: do I need to understand anything else in order to accomplish the task? If one looks at the issue only in relation to the hermeneutic task, then in such cases one does not need first of all to restore what is correct. Only the necessary sense need be established. In the easier cases, at least, what must be the case is already given in the grammatical abnormality itself, compared with the rules. Here what happens is hardly to be termed an achievement via the divinatory method. If we now think of more difficult cases where there is a logical abnormality, where the sense is not logically coherent, then the necessary sense can result from the context. As soon as I know that, I now ask how this sense can have originally been expressed. If I look at the case merely in relation to the hermeneutic task, then it can be all the same to me whether the difference between what has been established and what is original is a minimum or is larger than that. From this point of view I can say that the documentary procedure, the comparing of other manuscripts, is only necessary in the cases where the divinatory procedure cannot come into play, i.e. where there are not enough determinate tasks for one to decide what the meaning of the writer was.

But if criticism were related solely to the hermeneutic task, and was limited just to correctly understanding the sense of an extant passage, then our whole philological procedure would soon get into great confusion. For then it is immaterial whether I have correct or incorrect copies, as long as I just have the meaning. But precisely this would also come completely under the concept of true hermeneutics. In this case it is also still a question of the relationship of the author to the language. But in order to recognise this it must also be known with certainty what was originally in the text. In that case it may not be left undecided whether the difference from the original is a minimum or whether it is greater. Otherwise an empty space is left for the relationship of the author to the language and the more such empty spaces I get, the less I can acquire an image of the relationship as a whole, and the more uncertain the whole image of literature and language becomes.

If nothing is unnecessary or unimportant from the philological viewpoint, then the task is as follows: to strive for the greatest exactitude and certainty in the restoration of what is correct. Added to this is the fact that for criticism the handwriting is also something for itself outside of the language and has a positive aspect which does not appear if we abstract from the handwriting in spoken discourse. As in French where single sounds, indeed whole syllables which appear in the text, are swallowed. In the same way in Greek the *iota subscriptum* does not appear in spoken discourse. But for the text this is something positive. Nobody will be able to say that, if we regard the whole critical operation as the completion of a historical fact, what is positively given in the handwriting would be immaterial; instead, precisely the accomplishment of the critical task often most requires the knowledge of that positive aspect in the simple cases. For if I do not know that this or that has been written, then I lack that which leads me to explain what is false from what I suppose to be original, which I can often only explain as false from the strokes of the handwriting to which these positive elements belong. Now it is also significant for the history of language to know how writing related to language at different times. Writing has its own history. Changes take place in it independently of changes in spoken discourse. But those changes are indeed essential moments in the totality of the history of language. Documentary criticism appears in its complete extent from this point of view.

If we now put the philological task as investigating the history of language and writing in a precise manner, then everything that is left of the texts is to be compared. But that is the task of diplomatic criticism[a], of which palaeography is only a part. In that case the content of the text is completely immaterial. That task also exists in its own right. The accomplishment of the critical task by comparison of several copies is only an application of it.

If we now go back to our critical task, then the cases which can arise in reading an old text are of very differing kinds. The most simple are those where the task is to be accomplished via that through which it arises. If the task arises, e.g., via a grammatical mistake, then I also accomplish it by grammar. If, on the other hand, the task relates to a turn of phrase, an expression, which otherwise does not occur in a writer, then it must have emerged via an unfamiliar analogy, and the simplest case is then the one where the task is accomplished precisely by the analogy. But I must know the analogy, both general and special, of the particular author. But if one thinks that someone who has found mistakes in a copy expressed the whole thing in terms of how the meaning seemed to him, or of how the whole thing appeared to him as being as little different as possible, then so much

---

[a] *Diplomatik*, in the sense of 'documentary'.

that is alien can have come into it that no analogy can be certainly established with regard to the diction of the writer. Here once again the result is that the immediate hermeneutic need cannot be the measure of the critical operation.

If one now asks how the documentary procedure relates to the divinatory, then the former is the real basis of criticism; the divinatory is only for the purposes of the immediate hermeneutic operation, where the documentary is not sufficient. If one comes upon a corrupted passage and one only has the one edition, then conjecture, the divinatory process arises. But if there is an accessible critical apparatus and one deals with the matter in a philological sense, not just in relation to the corrupted incomprehensible passage, then the documentary procedure is necessary. If one assumes a mechanical error, then one must also investigate how the mistake could have arisen. But this procedure also admittedly goes over into the divinatory. One can look at the various versions as the known quantities to the true unknown quantity of the original version.

The canon that the divinatory procedure is only admissible where there are no documentary means, or even, that where there is no lack of these one is not permitted to apply the divinatory procedure and that one must then remain with what the manuscripts offer, this canon is not absolutely valid, indeed it may not be proposed in this manner, because in that way the hermeneutic interest would be too neglected. The true assessment of both methods always depends on the particular relationships. From the general philological point of view the documentary procedure is a task in its own right. But there will, on the other hand, also be a divinatory process in it, depending on how the task is set. If we go back to the point from which we began, and consider ourselves as simple readers, so that we have no other interest than to be able to continue with an awareness of being satisfied, then we can leave the critical task completely to one side. But this is not the viewpoint from which criticism can be dealt with as a science. If we have a writer for whom only content is important, whose forming of language is of no particular interest, then one can most easily pass over the critical tasks as soon as one has corrected what is deficient hermeneutically. On the other hand, in relation to a writer whose forming of language is of value for the whole language, the interest in knowing what he really wrote is also greater. There the critical task is to be accomplished. As a simple reader one can content oneself all the more with the divinatory procedure the more one thinks one is familiar with the diction of the writer, so that one can decide in terms of assured analogy. We can therefore generally say that if one takes the hermeneutic task in its immediacy the critical task does not arise at all in very many cases; the critical task only gains its true, deeper sense and its inner necessity from the general philological viewpoint.

There are cases in which no critical task seems to arise in reading, because a determinate sense is really there which also corresponds to the context. Nevertheless it can be that what one reads does not actually come from the writer. One therefore has false elements for the consideration[b] of the language of the writer, from which errors then arise. Here the elimination can only arise via documentary criticism.

But how do the documentary and divinatory procedures relate to each other? Are we to say that if we assume there are mechanical errors the comparative, documentary procedure is to be carried on where a divinatory decision can no longer occur? That would assume that the task could only be completely accomplished via the documentary procedure. But this assumption is not correct. The most immediate tasks are not accomplished via documentary criticism, divinatory criticism is always an indispensable aid. But if we begin from this point divinatory criticism does just appear as a stopgap.

Let us now try to establish the end-points of the documentary procedure more closely and let us begin with those where it does not take place. If, e.g., we have a book that has just appeared, then we presuppose that all copies are the same. Copies do occur in which misprints are noticed later during printing. But in general, and if it is not expressly noted, we presuppose the identity of the copies. Now if we do after all find a mistake we cannot engage in the comparative documentary procedure, because the manuscript of the author from which all the printed copies flowed is not accessible. In this case we are therefore reliant solely on the divinatory process in relation to every misprint.

On the other hand, if we have several editions, not impressions, and they are printed differently, then the possibility arises that some have a mistake which the others do not, etc. Here, then, comparisons can be made. Even in relation to this minimum of difference the comparative documentary procedure comes into consideration, and only to the extent that the divinatory procedure gives an absolutely convincing certainty can one dispense with the documentary procedure.

[b] *Anschauung.*

If we go back beyond the use of book printing, then, because the cause of mechanical errors is always present in manuscripts, we always have the task of the documentary procedure, as long as the task does not extend into a wider perspective.

But here the question arises: are all things which derive from antiquity the same in this respect?

If we take up the general philological viewpoint it is initially a question of how language has been treated in all its different periods. In that case it is necessary to investigate the manner of writing of the writer exactly. To this end, though, one must know what period the author is from, because otherwise the procedure would be void. As such, the task is already more limited. Furthermore, if the author has no literary character, thus no constancy in his use of language, then no result can emerge which would be significant for the general task. Such a writer can just as well represent the manner of his time as he can write haphazardly now in this way, now in another. So there can be several products where we can admit that applying the philological procedure is not of such particular usefulness that it would accord with the expenditure of effort and time. So the task is also limited here.

Now, though, a secondary task arises. Copying is a mechanical task that can be done now in this way, now in that. Alphabetic writing has had different forms at different times, which can also give rise to differing mechanical errors. If the difference of period between the original text and the copy is known, and if there are differing forms of writing in this intervening period, then it is possible that every error has its own history. Errors can derive from completely different periods. In order to know this *palaeographic knowledge and studies* are required.

There are written characters which are connected with the grammatical position of the words, but which are different in different periods. As soon as a copy follows more the character of its period than that of the original text, completely new and more complex errors arise. Here, then, we find the immediate philological task of investigating the history of the language and the writing in its various circumstances of existence. Comparison of the documents has again at the same time the purpose of establishing these historical moments, precisely because we only have them in these traces, of which the writers who have written about them are only the complements. Here a writer who in his own terms is of little importance and does not repay any effort in literary terms can yet be of great value in palaeographic terms. In this way points of view and values arise which one does not find at all from the simple hermeneutic standpoint. Palaeographic study is purely historical in its own terms, one cannot really count it any more as part of criticism. But it cannot exist without criticism, because one has to judge whether a form which occurs at a certain time was really a customary form at a certain period or whether it is a mistake of the copyist.

We now ask: in the accomplishment of the critical task can one always set oneself the same goal in all circumstances?

From the general philological point of view we are, as stated, always interested in asking how the writer originally wrote. Can we establish this in all cases?

We distinguish the divinatory and the documentary method. If one knows exactly how people wrote at the time of the writer and if one can establish his use of language with certainty, then one can set oneself the goal of establishing by divinatory criticism how the author originally wrote. But how much is required in order to make those assumptions with certainty! As far as the documentary method is concerned there are admittedly often cases where it cannot set itself that goal. Namely the cases where, as in Homer, it is doubtful whether there ever was an original text, or where the temporal difference between the original text and the oldest copies that we have is significantly large, so that many intermediate points are missing, where unknown sources of mistakes can lie, and no transition to the original text can be discovered with regard to mechanical errors, – in such cases that task really cannot be accomplished any more, and one must, as e.g. in relation to the Homeric works, be satisfied with going back to the manner of writing of the Alexandrine grammarians. Here, then, the hermeneutic and general philological interests are to be separated. The latter can set itself a limit with which the hermeneutic task cannot be satisfied. The procedure is then accordingly necessarily different.

If we have a printed text of an ancient writer before us, then the question is naturally how this text came into existence. Various ways of proceeding are conceivable. If I do not know how and according to which rules and viewpoints the editor proceeded with the text, then I also cannot deal with his text correctly. We must, in order to find this out, construct the different cases, but the construction of the cases leads one to different ways of proceeding and their rules. These are then to be compared in terms of their appropriateness. But this question cannot be answered without the comparison between the case where I have a printed text and the case where

I have a single manuscript. Is there always a difference between these two cases? Or are there cases where the difference disappears? The latter can take place if a writer is printed from a single manuscript and with the greatest possible precision. But the difference only disappears completely if the characters of what is printed adhere completely to the characters of the manuscript. In that case it is as if we really did just have a single manuscript.

Let us take the differing cases of a printed text itself, and take first of all the most simple case, where I know that the printed copy represents a particular manuscript of the work. In this case the whole critical task is left to me because I have every reason to assume that there are mechanical errors in this copy.

A second case is where the printed copy has arisen via a judgement whose principles I do not know. There I am in a more difficult situation. For I do not even know what has a documentary basis and what only rests on an intervention that I do not know about. It can be, e.g., that the editor had a pair of manuscripts before him and took from each what seemed more satisfactory than in the other. He has also, of course, applied the divinatory method if something seemed more appropriate or necessary to the meaning and circumstances of the book. If documentary and non-documentary material, etc. are mixed together and in such a way that the circumstances cannot be made out, then this is the most difficult task for criticism. Editions made in this way are completely useless in a critical sense and are only useful for assuring oneself of the content of the book in a rough overall manner; precise, certain knowledge of the details is unthinkable in this case. Now if even the content of a book edited in this way is at the same time the object of controversy then the suspicion is unavoidable that the editor, especially if he takes part in the controversy, took much as wrong that is correct, and brought in much that was extraneous. In such circumstances such editions are to be completely rejected.

A third case is that we have a printed copy, and yet know that the editor did not make any arbitrary changes. The editor drew from older manuscripts and always took what he was convinced was the best from these sources. But he did not indicate the sources from which he drew, and did not put us in a position to trace each detail back to its specific source. In this case we admittedly know that there is nothing in the text that was not already extant once before, nothing that is not documentary, but even such an edition is always insufficient, both for the interests of philology and for the simple hermeneutic operation. It does not guarantee any certainty for the precise knowledge of the original manner of writing, and, if the text is put together from different copies, different ways of putting it together can be thought of, which give a different meaning, at least as far as the strength or weakness of the expression is concerned. We then have the case where we cannot adequately distinguish the author and the mere reader who made the combinations.

If, then, different forms of the same book already exist, which deviate from each other even just in trivialities, a complete philological use is only possible on the condition of a critical apparatus. This must contain two things; first the genesis of the assumed reading, then the totality of all critical differences. The former is not sufficient. For, in order to be able to test the critical judgement of the editor and to reconstruct his operations I must also have before me everything he had before him. Now this can, if it is a question of the comparison of three or four manuscripts, obviously only be achieved via a certain limitation of the available aids. We can admittedly extend the presentation in the case of a particularly significant passage, but the apparatus must still be limited if it is to be usable. The abbreviation of the material is, e.g., completely acceptable in the case where all the manuscripts but two agree. In that case just this difference needs to be registered; it then follows that the others have the same text. But if we think of the case of a large quantity of manuscripts which involve a great multiplicity of critical difference, if one wanted to put all these differences together the apparatus would become an enormous mass. If one then had to work through the whole mass for each single case, then the task would become in every respect endless. In this case the completeness of the apparatus is unachievable and also not beneficial. But what should then happen to produce the greatest possible certainty and to enable the readers to make a judgement from all that is extant? It is then necessary that the editor first comes to an agreement about certain main issues with the reader, namely about the reasons why he pays no attention to this or that manuscript whilst particularly valuing others. There are obviously different principles and viewpoints in the preparation of a critical apparatus. Let us take the case where a text is involved in a controversy. Now if the editor says that he excludes those manuscripts and pays no attention at all to them in disputed cases precisely because they are involved in the controversy, and there is therefore a danger that the meaning of the writer has been altered, then some readers will be satisfied, others not. The latter can say that this exclusion is quite justified where the differences have to do with the controversy, but where this does not take place even such manuscripts are useful. It is the same if the editor excludes all later manuscripts just because they are later. Some people will be satisfied with this because the later manuscripts in themselves admittedly make one suspect a mistaken text, especially if the manuscripts used already contain significant material and significant differences. But to other people this procedure can, as it were, appear too cut and dried: the more recent manuscripts can derive directly from a very old source, and in this way an essential aid would be cut off. Now the more reason there is for such a suspicion, the less such a general rule for the procedure is to be welcomed. But if the apparatus has to be limited in order not to become immense, the happy case can be thought in which different apparatuses have different maxims as their foundation. In that case one then complements the other and in this way the reader can be put in a position where it is as though he had the whole apparatus before him. But then it once more all depends on knowing whether and to what extent I concur with the maxims of the editor. For this, though, I myself need, as a critical reader, to have a judgement about the correct procedure of an editor. In this way I will correctly judge and employ the different editors according to their differing points of view.

It is almost unavoidable that one is impressed[c] by what one has before one's eyes. If we have an old writer before us, who has already been punctuated, then we know that the punctuation does not derive from the writer himself, but we know that punctuation has an influence on the way in which we understand the sense. Only a few people will be able from the start to get rid of the punctuation that has been added and put themselves in the original perspective. In this way one is usually inhibited by the punctuation that is there, takes it as correct, and only if one encounters difficulties and the possibility of a different sense if the punctuation is different does one become doubtful. But one is already under the influence of what was formerly clear to one, everything else has the disadvantage inherent in an opposing position. If we wanted to require that the old writers should for this reason be printed without any punctuation then this would be too much contrary to what most readers are used to and would entail new difficulties for them. It would admittedly be more strictly correct, but it is not feasible. However, every possible care is necessary in relation to punctuated text.

[c] *bestochen.*

The reader can equally be impressed by the available text. This takes possession of one before one compares the deviant readings. For this reason it is good if the editor established from the very beginning the maxims which he has followed in the constitution of the text. The more precisely they are expressed, the more easily one can orient oneself. There is a significant difference whether the text consists just of documentary material, or whether there are also results of divinatory criticism in it, whether the text consists of documentary material of the same or of different kinds. But in this it is just a question of the determination of the work. If one thinks of the edition of a classic made without any philological slant for use elsewhere, for example just for the aesthetic enjoyment of book-lovers, then the editor himself can incorporate his own emendations. In this respect the real critical task has little to do even with editions for use in school: the critical apparatus would only get in the way. But for strictly philological use it is necessary for the editor to present the complete critical apparatus, so that what is based on judgement and what is based on documents can be distinguished. This distinction is necessary, even though it cannot always be perfectly carried out.

But how far does the obligation of the critical reader extend, thus of a reader who goes beyond the immediate hermeneutic task? He has above all to ask about the relationship of the editor to the original deed[d] and about the specific purpose of the edition, and he has to judge whether this purpose is one with which one can be satisfied.

The cases are different. If the original circumstance was that the text was intended for publication and reproduction from the beginning, then the question is whether this happened from the beginning or only later. If later, then the question arises, as to what state the original text was in when the reproduction began, and in what way this was carried out.

Let us think of a collection, e.g., of letters of a historical figure. One cannot assume with certainty that the letters were intentionally public from the beginning. We must therefore assume that their being public only began with the collection. If the collector did not demonstrably have solely original texts, but rather had copies, then the critical character is not always the same in the latter case. He can have got more faithful, better copies of some pieces than of others. Then the question is whether the original manuscript of the writer can be established: to what extent and on what conditions?

[d] *Tatsache.*

If we have a productive writer and other works by him which have come down to us fairly exactly, so that we are in a position to get to know his use of language in an assured manner precisely from these more exact sources, then in this way it would perhaps be possible, but only via divinatory criticism, to establish the original text with some certainty, but still only where specific indications of the incorrectness of what is there are present, be it via the diversity of the copies or via the meaning. However, many readers will overlook many things without suspecting anything. What sort of goal should be set in such cases? We will have to rely, instead of upon the author, upon the time of the collection and publication. If one manages to establish what was read at that time, that is all one can achieve. Not that the divinatory procedure might not here and there eliminate many errors, but overall evenness can no longer be achieved.

There can be cases where one must be satisfied with a modest goal. The reproduction of a text can, namely, be carried out in various ways. If this happens in the case of one person because of the desire to possess such a work, of others for other purposes, then a great diversity of copies can arise at the same time. If the reproduction at a particular time is carried out in a particular way as a particular business, then there is greater certainty. In that case, if the copies are made in the same way, particular rules can be established. As a rule what comes earlier is that individuals have a certain interest in the products of a writer, and only when this interest becomes general is the reproduction more even, more systematic, or is carried out commercially. But if a writer has written immediately for the public his work is also immediately reproduced commercially. In this case one can also much more readily try to establish the original manuscripts, in the opposed case one will not be able to do this.

One can, then, set the task in two ways. First, an editor can aim to provide evenness in all parts, second, he can aim to give what is best and most certain in every single case by sacrificing evenness. Both kinds are equally good for the reader, they complement each other. But every editor must be expected to let the reader know the slant and the basis of his procedure.

If we now apply what has been said up to now to the N.T. then we first of all have to consider the relationship of the reader to the editor.

[*Translator's summary of omitted passage*: The secular reader can be content with a simple hermeneutic approach: the theologian must have the most precise knowledge of the use of language in the N.T. The text of the N.T. relied initially on differing manuscripts, not on one text alone. These were later made into one text, the *recepta*, but not according to any consistent principles. Comparison of all the manuscripts is unrealistic, but the *recepta* is not suitable for the task of establishing the text. It would be better to use the text of one manuscript and establish a critical apparatus on the basis of comparing deviant texts from other sources. The fact is that there are no original texts of the N.T. as a whole: it is made up of an aggregate of different kinds of copies. There is no obvious way of getting back to the original texts: there are deviant readings even in the oldest available texts. In this case one can either seek to establish something which evens things out, or one can, though this is not reliable, give the oldest available texts. What are the real theological thoughts of the N.T.? Protestant ideas that are important for the modern Church do not appear in this form in the N.T. As long as the N.T. text is older than the controversy involved in such ideas there is no problem in this respect, because the controversy arose on the basis of a text accepted in the Church. The correctness of deviant readings only matters where they have an effect on dogma. From a philological point of view we must only go back to what can be established with certainty.]

We will try in vain to take up the viewpoint of the original readers of the particular texts, and it is just as vain to try to reach the viewpoint of the readers of the collection. The differences are older than the collection. We can only approximately go back to a time for which we already have sufficient critical editions and documents. But if we ask what was the most widespread form of the N.T. we will never find anything completely of the same kind, but instead always different things next to each other.

[*Translator's summary of omitted passage*: What is the role of the reader in relation to the differing kinds of edition? On the one hand he can use the editor's apparatus, on the other he can use divinatory criticism. If one proceeds in a divinatory way one must distinguish between simple hermeneutic and strictly philological tasks.]

If we remain with the simple hermeneutic task, then one can think of cases where all the documents do not make any sense. Should I then leave the hermeneutic task unaccomplished? I cannot do that and even if I only wanted to leave in doubt what the meaning of the given passage was, this has no influence on the understanding of the whole text. It can be that I find another passage in the same text in which there is an indication of how to understand the dubious passage. In this case I can manage with the hermeneutic solution without solving the critical problem. The relationship can, though, be different: namely, that later passages can only be understood via an earlier passage where the meaning is dubious or there is no meaning. In this case the critical task must really be accomplished, including by divinatory criticism, if documentary criticism leads to nothing. If one does not treat criticism as independent and as its own philological discipline then it can easily happen that we judge the differences of the extant documents in such a way that we consider a manuscript which contains less passages where the meaning is dubious as good, another, which contains more dubious passages, as bad. But this is a false judgement. The latter can be much closer to the original text than the former, in which what is objectionable can have been arbitrarily changed. In this way one sees how critical judgements based on purely hermeneutic interest deceive and are false. Where the documentary material of such a text is not sufficient it sometimes happens that, if there is help to be found even in completely worthless manuscripts, these are already presented by the exegete as documentary evidence, and it is then said that one perhaps must read in this way. But this then only has the value just of a divinatory operation.

[*Translator's summary of omitted passage*: In the synoptic Gospels and the Acts of the Apostles there are statements by Christ whose context of utterance is unknown. Here one needs historical, not divinatory, criticism, which judges what is less complete by what is more complete. Divinatory criticism is less required for the N.T. than for other kinds of text. How is one to choose between different documentary materials for the N.T.? Is it possible to classify the documents in such a way that a general preference for one kind can be established? There are few positive rules for this, only rules for eliminating what cannot be seen as reliable. The situation is no better with translations: they are no use in grammatical questions because each language has different rules, and are of very limited use otherwise.]

Part Two
Criticism of errors which have arisen via free action

Here all the cases are to be investigated in which the deviation is not based on the mechanism of the senses and of ideas, but on a free action.

The question arises as to whether and how it is possible that one brings something that was not already present in it into the utterance of another. Someone who is just reporting, and doing nothing else, will not do this. But, if someone has a particular interest, it can happen that he foists something onto the other person. If someone is interested in making other people believe that the author of a text thought in such and such a manner, then he will seek to produce something which corresponds to his intention by changing the text. That is a real deception, scientific falsification. But one can only assume this in very particular circumstances, not in general. If we think that someone has as their profession the intentional falsification of a whole text, then such a person will avoid changes in order to keep their reputation as being reliable. But if someone cites a writer with the specific interest of showing that he belongs to their party or shares their opinion, then this interest can lead to falsification. Then one must ask whether someone really had such an interest. If I find this, then the passage loses its value as evidence, even if one cannot exactly prove that there is dishonesty. But even the mere copyist, whose trade is copying, can, e.g., have an interest in giving the text an appearance of being by an author who is not the real author. So he can give the text the name of another author to whom it does not belong. But even this can only happen at a later time in quite specific circumstances.

In fact real intentional falsification can only take place in quite specific circumstances. If someone has a manuscript, finds extra text written in the margin, and puts this into the text, this can in certain circumstances be an intentional falsification. But this is not necessarily the case: it can be a correct or supposed correction, to the extent that something in the text was missed out and written in the margin.

We can more or less reduce everything of this kind to the following two cases: 1. If someone brings something into the text that they have done themselves, of whatever kind, then it is always an intentional falsification. 2. If someone adopts something as a correction where what he has in the text before him does not seem to him able to be legitimated, this is admittedly a free change, but one of the kind every editor makes, just that, whereas the editor normally indicates it, or can indicate it, this person says nothing about it and can say nothing about it, and uses the right to correct in the same way as the type-setter does these days. The change can be meant as an improvement, and really be one, but it can just as much rest on an error. In all such cases there is something intentional, but in differing ways.

Something alien can come into the text via the procedure of a copyist or reader, and these are cases which are closely related to the preceding ones. A copyist can bring something into the basic text via a merely mechanical error that is in his mind from the translation. But the same thing can happen intentionally, as a correction. Furthermore, someone can put a more clear expression which is in his mind from what he has read instead of an obscure expression; he can find it as a comment, and only take it as such, and yet take it up into the text. These are changes via free action. The question is to what extent we have grounds for assuming this.

The issue is how one has sufficient reasons for thinking about the reproduction. If one thinks of it in terms of several people at the same time making several copies of an original, then this happens by dictation. In that case everyone is bound to keep up and nobody has time for reflections and changes. Such changes could only derive from the person who dictates and would thus get into all the copies; the writers or copyists will all the more avoid making changes the more they carry out the business as a trade and are concerned with a reputation for reliability. Free changes in the text are only conceivable in the case of a copyist who does not carry out his business mechanically, but is himself adequately versed in the matter itself. Initially the change can also only have been written in the margin by such a copyist or an attentive reader, and later have got into the text.

So the emergence of mistakes of this kind involves a certain amount of leeway. But such mistakes in changes are actually always only infrequent and not very widespread.

There is no question that anything alien that has got into the text in this way must be removed. The question of the original is independent of this and exists in its own right.

In the genesis of such changes one has to distinguish between what is intentional and what is unintentional. The former always presupposes something else; something alien must already be present. We assume it is possible that there are no mistakes in the original text, apart from those that arose via mechanical error; what is mistaken can be by the hand of the author himself. In this case the change will be the restoration of what the author himself wanted. He would acknowledge this as his own, as original. But the one who changes can also deal with the passage differently from how the author would have dealt with it. Furthermore, there can be cases where two things are given, on the one hand something completely correct, then something which cannot be kept, possibly occasioned by a mechanical error, via which, however, the former cannot be explained. In that case there are again two possibilities. Either what is completely correct is also the original, and what arose via mechanical error is the later, or, conversely, the former is the correction, the latter the original. For the latter to be assumed certain indications must be present. There will be no lack of these in relation to the mechanical aspect of language. In many periods one wrote differently from how one spoke, spoke differently from what is entailed by the rules of writing. Now as soon as such a deviant form predominates, it is also possible that it is the original reading. If what is correct can only be found in a few manuscripts, then it is possible that it is a correction.

In the same way as it is possible that changes come into a text via good intentions, they can also come in, not without intention, but via a false free choice, in which case only a critical fact is assumed already to be present.

If a comment in the margin is taken up into the text, then this is intentional if the copyist knows that it is something alien, but adopts it as an improvement. If, on the other hand, the copyist thinks the comment in the margin belongs in the text, then it is unintentional. That changes of the latter kind often occur is generally established, as long as a text has been reproduced individually only by copyists. It has always been the case that diligent readers made comments on what they were reading. If such manuscripts got into the hands of others, such changes easily occurred.

Now in what case can intentional changes arise?

We here distinguish good and ill intention. Good intention is rectifying a mistake that has been made, restoring what is authentic. Such a change is a critical operation. How is this case to be dealt with? Differently, depending on whether one takes up the simple hermeneutic, or the general philological standpoint.

If a writer has not expressed himself with grammatical precision, or has used an inappropriate expression, but someone else has corrected this, then we can adopt this for the hermeneutic task as an improvement. We can say that the author admittedly only chose what was worse because he had nothing better at hand, so the improvement hit upon the real meaning of the author.

It is different from the general philological point of view. From here we must seek to preserve the hand of the author in complete purity and originality; otherwise we deprive ourselves of the materials for a determinate judgement about the writer and the treatment of language of his time and area. It can turn out that what has been changed, has been apparently improved, is not a grammatical error but the usage of the time and the area.

Now as far as change via ill intention is concerned, there are significant differences. There can be very specific tendencies which are not meant to harm the author, but also those which are.

Someone can change the utterances and expressions of a writer if he thinks he knows better than the author. This is easy to imagine in relation to historical objects. As soon as I know that the mistake was not a momentary action but the specific way of understanding of the author, then the change does not happen with good intentions towards the author. The work is altered and what is original is not represented. Whoever changes things in this way *can* have good intentions towards the reader, by changing in order to protect the reader from error.

Furthermore, someone can want to make a writer into an authority for their own view. The writer does not thereby exactly contradict the view, but he has hardly expressed it. By a minor change one makes it such that the author seems to express it. This is admittedly not a good intention, for something is foisted onto the author which he did not know and which he did not will. It is an injustice to the author, but the intention is also not ill against him, but good for the cause in question.

Finally it is possible that someone makes a change in order to attribute something to the writer which he did not do, to accuse him of an error which he did not make. In what circumstances can this be said? The indications must be very clear: only on the presupposition of a personal bias and on the condition that the author can no longer complain, but is still not so far off that the change in his text could not have an influence.[1] But such cases occur rarely. Let us imagine one. Tertullian has, e.g., written against Marcion. His text is a text for a cause.[a] Now if he often cites passages from Marcion and we know that he has really often wrongly interpreted him, then it was easily possible, as Marcion had the name of a heretic, could no longer complain, and the situation was volatile, that Tertullian distorted the man's words and foisted things on him that he had never thought about. Only in such circumstances can something of this kind take place. –

On the other hand the *pia fraus* [honest deception] of falsification from good intentions can easily occur in certain classes of text. Here one has the interest of establishing a text, a writer as authority or witness.

Are, then, the people who reproduced the texts in antiquity such that one can suspect such intentional falsifications of them?

It is hard to think this in a straightforward manner. For if we go back to the time where a work was reproduced by written hand, then we must distinguish an individual reproduction from reproduction in quantity. The latter was really a business that was completely separate from the interest in the object [of the text]. In that case such intentional falsification, deception – is unthinkable. Individual reproduction was only for private use, and as a rule could have no repercussions for public reproduction. In that case there is no space at all for intentional deception in the falsification of a text, and quite particular circumstances were necessary if it was to become probable that something of the kind happened.

Such changes can occur in individual reproduction for private use. But these could only become real changes of the text at second hand, if the text of manuscripts made for private use with added comments was reproduced for general use.

Now how is it in this respect with regard to the N.T.?

[*Translator's summary of omitted passage*: Much depends upon whether the changes are intentional, rather than mechanical. Copyists' main interest lay in being reliable. It was hard for individuals to make changes that really became widespread. Mechanical errors are therefore the more likely cause and should be looked for first: this is in opposition to the conception of Griesbach. In relation to the N.T.,

[1] *Translator's note*: Syntax as in the German.

[a] *Parteischrift.*

neither hermeneutically nor philologically is it a question of whether it makes good sense, but rather one of producing the original text. There are no consistently applicable a priori rules for decisions on this.]

We can, then, establish the following as the result for N.T. criticism: Wherever there is a difference, where there are differing texts, the task is initially to explain the manner in which the difference emerged. The decision always lies at the same time in this. Explanation via mechanical errors is always the first thing that must be tried. If a decision results in this way then this is for the time being to be regarded as the correct decision. For the time being, for indications can result in context which point to an emergence or difference that comes from elsewhere. But if such a decision does not arise, then the probability emerges of an originally intentional change. But this must always remain the last thing. If we must reject all readings except for one and this one makes neither logical nor grammatical coherent sense, or no sense in the context, then we must say that this is the reading from which we have taken away all distortions or possible later changes, but certainly not what the author himself wrote. In that case one must seek to produce the original text in another way, whereby it is all the same whether one takes the help from some corner or other of the critical apparatus or gets it from conjecture. Both are equally uncertain from a critical perspective.

The issue seems to be different in the realm of classical literature, although we can never admit another principle. The difference is just that we have only a few manuscripts of most of the classical authors, but a great many of the N.T. We are therefore more in the situation of taking refuge in conjecture than in relation to the N.T. In relation to the classical authors one can say that the conjecture should only be temporary, for manuscripts could still be found which give what is correct. It has already often been the case that conjectures have been confirmed in this way by manuscripts that were found later. While one can hope in this case to find better manuscripts and better material in them, we do not have the hope in relation to the N.T. If now, as already remarked, conjecture is in fact admissible even for the N.T., despite the large manuscript apparatus, then this is not a difference of critical principles, but only a difference of the state of things in the two domains.

The question now arises as to where the boundary is in the N.T. between the two classes of manuscripts that have been kept apart, about one of which we said that its confirmation had no more weight than a conjecture.

This leads us into the realm of diplomacy or of the art of estimating the value of the manuscripts. We already distinguished between uncial and italic manuscripts.[2] Usually the latter are more recent, but not always. There are no strict boundaries. One can only distinguish precisely between uncial manuscripts from a period when nobody yet wrote italic at all, and italic manuscripts from a time when no one any longer wrote in uncial handwriting. The latter are in this case certainly more recent. But how is it with manuscripts from the same time? Italic writing was invented for reasons of speed. Uncial handwriting is therefore presumed to involve the greater carefulness that is already involved in the decision to use it. As the signs are more clearly separable a mistake is also easier to discover. Admittedly mechanical errors cannot be banished from uncial writing, but rules can be established concerning the mixing up of signs from which precisely the mechanical errors arose, and one should note these rules. But if copies had been made as often from italic writing as from uncial writing the number of mechanical errors would be greater by far.

How, then, did manuscripts of both kinds arise at the same time? Whoever could expend more time and money, and also thought the matter more important, made or acquired uncial manuscripts. Furthermore, italic manuscripts were more for private use, uncial manuscripts more for public use. For this reason as well the latter have more in their favour.

But one should not just consider the age of the manuscripts but also their country of origin. Here, then, as already noted, the difference between the purely Greek and the Graeco-Latin comes into consideration. What is to be found in the manuscripts of the older period and in Greek as well as Graeco-Latin manuscripts is a reading which is backed by the most complete evidence possible.

In the *textus receptus* we do not find many of the best-attested readings. Among these there are admittedly many of no great importance, they often only contain a peculiarity of grammatical form. But often one cannot even leave the best-attested reading as it is. Worse manuscripts make better sense. But the older manuscripts are still the most certain, what is later is probably correction, which was often made very thoughtlessly in the later manuscripts. One must therefore keep to well attested old manuscripts which are widely available, and, if they make no sense, should build the conjecture on them. But one builds conjectural criticism on these much more safely than on the later text.

---

[2] *Translator's note:* In an omitted passage.

Can rules be given for conjectural criticism? No, no positive rules, but only provisos. One can give positive rules as little as one can give a theory of invention/discovery. Conjecture is a question of talent developed through practice.

Can the original that one is seeking be brought out by conjecture alone from a difficult passage, or must one look for assistance from elsewhere? The question alone already leads to the analogous area of hermeneutic operations. Here one is to try to understand the difficult point via the surroundings. These surroundings are often sufficient, often not. It is just the same in criticism. Sometimes one does not need to seek help and guesses from the passage itself what the meaning must be. But then it is a question of finding the corresponding text via which the emergence of what is extant can be most easily explained. This is the correct critical test. This task appears, though, in relation to the massive critical apparatus of the N.T. to be endless, if it is understood in such a way that all differences are to be explained by conjecture. The manuscripts lie centuries apart and the difference has often only arisen via a long sequence of mistakes which we cannot possibly pursue as a whole. The task can therefore not be set within such dimensions. It must therefore be divided.

The first thing is to carry out the test in relation to the best-attested readings. If a conjecture does not pass this test then it is only a temporary conjecture for the needs of hermeneutics; it is possible that something better will still be found. But if this test is passed, then one can go further. Initially one would put together the remaining differing readings in terms of age and origin. Even from this explanations of the later by the earlier may result. If this operation were successful, the conjecture would be proved in the most complete manner. But even if the critical apparatus were put together and dealt with in the most careful way, we could still not establish an uninterrupted ladder back to the oldest text for a single book of the N.T. We will always encounter gaps. For this reason one must be satisfied if one can explain the best-attested text via what one would like to assume to be the original. The principle is to be adhered to, that even where one must construct the original for the purposes of the hermeneutic operation, one may only begin with what is extant as the oldest material. What arises in this way has its value via the artistic critical operation, but is never to be regarded as authoritative.

For divinatory criticism there are, as we said, only provisos, and no rules. But what are these provisos?

First of all the analogy between the divinatory and the hermeneutic operation should be indicated. In the same way as in this case the immediate surroundings, or even the more extended surroundings, and analogous parallel passages lead to the right meaning, the passage itself can initially also contain indications for critical conjecture of how the text is to be completed if the mistake in the text is one where the grammatical or logical unity is the only thing which is endangered. There can admittedly be passages where this only appears to be the problem, but is not. In that case so much becomes clear that the grammatical completion or the adjustment of the hermeneutic operation is not sufficient. For then the task arises of preserving the result and considering the passage from another side.

If we now take the provisos according to which the find is to be tested, then the first is that the conjecture should be adequate to the hermeneutic operation. The conjecture must not only relate to what is extant in such a way that the differences which are present can be derived from it, but it must also fit into the meaning and the context of the passage, otherwise it cannot be the right conjecture. Both must, if possible, come together, for one must assume that the author wrote what was necessary in the context, and that the mistake arose via mechanical error.

But cases are imaginable where the two do not correspond, where one can explain all the differences immediately via what has been found, but where it is not completely sufficient for the hermeneutic operation, and in the same way vice versa. To which of the two moments is the preponderance then to be given for directing the further procedure? In that case one must admittedly presuppose that the result did not arise in the most complete manner. But the question is not to be solved simply and universally. It all depends on the state of the material. The more complete the succession of documents, the more completely everything that is extant must be able to be explained via what has been found; but if the succession is very interrupted, then nothing so complete can be demanded. If one has very old and very new manuscripts which give completely different things, then the task cannot be set in this manner; all hypotheses for the explanation of the emergence of the difference do not help, because the intervening elements are lacking. Then the task can only be to find something that corresponds to the context of the utterance.

But here another proviso now comes in. What is found must not just be given in the language in general, but in the usage of the author. If I cannot show this then the conjecture is uncertain, and, in case the opposite is the case, actually false. There are certain turns of phrase and expressions which are only usual at a particular time in poetry or in a certain area of prose. If one takes an emendation from this for another area, then it is incorrect. The more complete the demonstration of the corresponding usage is, the more the conjecture can be asserted. Here the dependence of the philological disciplines upon each other shows itself. There is in this a limitation of certainty in accomplishing the task. For we only achieve knowledge of the usage in the same manner, namely by critical operations. If many corrupted passages are cited as a demonstration of the usage, then something false can arise; those passages must first be established. In this way it becomes clear that the complete certainty of the emendation is only a product of time. It can be thoroughly welcome where and when it arises, but one must wait to see whether it is confirmed with the extension of the knowledge of the language and of the documents.

If we apply this to the N.T. in particular, then the real difficulty here is that N.T. usage is hard to specify.

[*Translator's summary of omitted passage*: The first printed editions have been substantially altered in being edited. The linguistic domain of the N.T. is still very imprecise. One approach begins with the individual authors, but this fails for lack of sufficient reliable material. The other tries to see what they have in common with regard to the Greek language and Ancient Greek culture. It is clear that divinatory criticism is much more unreliable in the N.T. than in classical literature. The gap between the oldest manuscripts and the original text cannot be overcome, because even the collection of material was a copy. The first reproductions of the N.T. were for private use, not, as for the O.T, for use in the synagogue. The unreliable passages of the N.T. are, though, generally not those which affect the essential aspect of the N.T.

To what extent should theologians concern themselves with N.T. criticism? If one accepts received authority it might appear that one has no need to do this. But which authority does one choose? 'If one does not wish in this choice to submit oneself to a further authority, then one must make one's own judgement.' Concern with the text in the Protestant church cannot just be a matter for the few. 'What aids do we possess to liberate ourselves from the domination of the *recepta*?' The first thing is to note how far they deviate from the oldest manuscripts: this already will make one lose one's respect. An organisation of the textual apparatus which omits all the manuscripts which have no authority and permits comparison only on the basis of real authorities is preferable because it removes a great mass of useless material. By comparing readings in terms of their genesis one gets a better general view of the text and can judge where divinatory criticism is required.

Collections in which the usage of ancient writers is compared with N.T. usage give an analogy for the divinatory process in the N.T. Use of divinatory criticism for passages where documentary criticism is of no help can only even be negative, in the form of 'if I read the passage in this way I can use it as evidence for such and such a dogmatic idea, but if in this way, I cannot'. An essential doctrine may never rest on a single isolated passage, which limits the value of divinatory criticism. 'One should note for convenience sake on every page in one's N.T. which manuscripts exist and where gaps exist.' Manuscripts with special grammatical forms are particularly valuable, and the critical apparatus should always include them.]

But difficult and complex operations, palaeographic knowledge etc., belong in all this if the task is to be completely accomplished. For this reason the complete critical task also cannot be regarded as a universal task for all theologians. But if we do regard complete hermeneutic understanding as the task of the theologian, then already included in this is the fact that the reader and explicator at least cannot everywhere rely on the editor. Added to this is the fact that there is something universal in criticism, and that we are continually involved in a critical operation in every area of reading and listening. As such, nobody can wish to release themself completely from it. One must just treat the task correctly, according to its use and the time it takes.

[*Translator's summary of omitted passage*: What must one be able to expect as a minimum here from every theologian? As far as the hermeneutic task is concerned everyone must have their own principles of decision because even the authorities rarely agree, and one must be able to see if they are biased. To decide which textual critic to trust one must have got to know the critical principles in a general form. All existing critics, such as Griesbach, Wetstein and Bengel, cannot be completely trusted.]

In such a process it is, by the way, self-evident that one completely forgets the German translation. As long as one still has it in mind there is no independence in the use of the N.T. The determining consciousness of the translation is always what is to be corrected, it removes the true analogies from view and tempts one into false ones.

Now the general task of making one's own critical judgement is limited to what is necessary for the hermeneutic task. But the work on this is already a preliminary exercise in critical virtuosity, and there are in this enough occasions to go beyond that necessary minimum. It is just that a greater inclination and ability leads one person further than another, – and it is precisely in this that virtuosity already begins to make itself noticed.

All critical work can be preliminary exercises for the development of critical judgement, not just the exercises in relation to the N.T. Such exercises can be done in relation to other authors and even in everyday life.

It is part of the character of philology that the critical orientation is always an accompaniment, and so it also is part of the character of theology.

In what does the difference between the reader who forms the text for the purposes of the hermeneutic operation, and the critical editor of the text consist? –

There is a certain difference between the result of diplomatic and divinatory criticism. In diplomatic criticism both take up the general philological standpoint, they both want to establish the original where possible. In relation to divinatory criticism both are in the service of the hermeneutic operation. This forces one to supplement and to choose between different things. If the accomplishment of the task is to take the right course the result of diplomatic criticism should not be mixed up with the result of divinatory criticism. The reader begins with what has been established in a diplomatic manner, and everyone performs the divinatory aspect for themselves, and everyone brings things to light for themselves[b] according to their nature and convictions in relation to the hermeneutic operation. Thence it will become ever more the principle of editors not to take up the results of divinatory criticism into the real text. They can be conveyed outside the text. There is something between strict presentation of the text and conveying of the hermeneutic operation, namely commentaries with text and texts connected to a commentary. If in the first case the commentary is the main thing and the conveying of the text only an aid for the reader, then even in this case the text may only be given in a purely diplomatic manner; if this result of divinatory criticism is taken up into the text then there a corruption arises, even if an account is given of it afterwards in the commentary. If the text is the main thing and the commentary only a secondary matter, then it is all the more necessary to convey the text in a purely diplomatic manner.

It was shown above that mechanical errors are rather to be assumed than intentional changes. Now there are cases where the two are combined. Think of two readings, a longer and a shorter. According to Griesbach's

---

[b] *fördert sich jeder*: the sense is not entirely clear.

canon the shorter is to be preferred, the former always being an addition. According to our canon we first try to see whether the phenomenon can be explained by a mechanical error. If I find two beginnings or two endings that are the same, then the possibility of an omission by mechanical error arises, and the longer reading deserves to be preferred. But an addition, an epexegesis can coincidentally have the same form; indeed an epexegesis will generally agree in the grammatical form with the text, so that same endings arise as a matter of course. How is this? Because both cases are possible in general, one must have both in mind all the time. In this way a probability calculus emerges. Is it probable that the longer reading is an addition? An occasion must be sought for this. Or is the shorter reading faulty? For that the possibility of a wandering of the eye must be made probable. The wandering becomes all the more probable if the two endings stand quite close to each other, if the difference between the longer and the shorter reading is small, or if one ending stands immediately beneath another in the following line. But for this an exact knowledge of the manuscripts is required.

In the Synoptic Gospels the matter is peculiarly different. In that case there are translations from one into another which could not easily have immediately arisen when they were copied. For it is not probable that a copyist should have made such interpolations from memory if he was doing copying as a business. But they could have arisen indirectly, as marginalia by the reader. Here, then, where a longer reading in a Gospel contains something from another Gospel, the probability lies on the side of the shorter reading. On the other hand, the probability of a longer reading could arise if, coincidentally, a wandering of the eye were also thinkable. But this probability would also be reduced if the difference between the longer and the shorter were significant.

In relation to the peculiar nature of the N.T. we must also admit the possibility in relation to the didactic books that additions were made as explanations and supplementations in terms of a certain conception. For even in the didactic texts there are such parallels, because it is always a certain sphere of ideas that is being dealt with, in which the same elements are often repeated, but are just differently expressed. So other similar passages could have been written in in relation to a passage. In relation to the didactic books, after trying to explain them via mechanical errors, one must therefore also look, with regard to the difference of the longer and shorter reading, to see whether something does not have the character of a gloss.

In this there is, though, no intentional wanting to change the text, but something has later been brought into the text that originally did not belong there.

Another task of criticism is linked to this.

Certainty or uncertainty about the author of a text also arises via single words, minor changes or differences. What about this task, which seems to be a completely different task?

The question whether the Epistle to the Hebrews is Pauline or not is not a critical question in our sense. For there is no text which would give rise to it, no manuscript that bears the name of the Apostle in the title or which has it occur in the text. From this point of view the Epistle is anonymous, and the task of establishing the author is a task of historical criticism, which we are not concerned with here. It is the same with the question whether the second Epistle of Peter is authentic, and with the question whether Matthew's Gospel is a work of the Apostle or not. As far as the latter is concerned, there is no heading which would attribute to the name the title of an Apostle. Here there is just as little a critical question in our sense as the question in relation to the third Gospel and to the Acts of the Apostles as to whether it stems from the Luke who accompanied the Apostle Paul.

How must things be if such a question is to become a properly critical question?

The proximate case is the one where the manuscripts assert different things about the author. Then a decision must be made in the same way as it is with regard to readings. But here there is a big difference whether the assertion is made in the text itself or outside it. If outside, then it is uncertain whether the heading is a part of the text in the first edition or not. If the former is clear, then the question is to be decided like all critical questions. On the other hand, if it is probable that the heading is later, then the judgement is a task that is to be separated from the text itself. Is the heading a mere judgement or does it have any authorities in favour of it? As soon as the question becomes one where it is asked whether the heading is just to be seen as a judgement it ceases to be a critical question and belongs to historical criticism.

But can that question not become a critical question in another way?

If we have a text which presents itself from within the text as a text of a particular author, and there is also no other dispute about this, but we encounter passages in reading which we find hard to think of as words of the author, then doubts arise because we feel disturbed in the hermeneutic operation which is based on that assumption. In that case it is a matter of deciding from the perspective of the interest of the hermeneutic operation about the diplomatic question of whether it is original or not. But with this we enter our territory. We can only understand the matter from this view-point. The philological domain is everywhere where there are difficulties or disturbances in the hermeneutic operation to be removed, or diplomatic decisions to be made.

Now how do such doubts arise and how do we reach a decision? We must seek out the end-points, decisive cases which immediately decide the issue, on the one hand, and, on the other, cases which leave a sting behind, an uncertainty that cannot be overcome without the existence of what would really bring about a decision. A different procedure results on each side. If a decisive point is given which completely cuts off the possibility that the text is by a particular author, then the matter is settled. Then the question just arises as to how the text could have been attributed to that author.

If we look at the matter in a more general manner, then we first have to investigate whether there is a gap between what we have just dealt with and what we now want to deal with.

The applicability of the rule that mechanical mistakes are always likely first is limited, as observed above, to a certain number of cases, a certain amount of differences. But cases occur where differences by omissions or additions occur to a much greater extent. We seem to have omitted this. For this is not the same as when we are talking of a particular text in terms of whether it belongs to the person it is attributed to or not. Is there really a gap here? We said above that, in all cases where there are differences, along with the possibility of mechanical error the other possibility must also be considered, namely whether they may not perhaps have arisen via a con-scious action. How can it be decided whether an addition originally belonged to the text or whether the omission was what was original? One must first take account of the hermeneutic operation, but here assume both cases. Assume, then, that the addition is authentic. If there is then nothing that is disturbing for the hermeneutic operation, one can continue with the assumption; if a definite reference to the dubious passage is found in what follows, then this is a confirmation. But if one cannot carry on undisturbed with that assumption, then that is a reason for the opposed view. If the diplomatic aspect is in the balance, then one must let in the probability calculus by beginning with both assumptions. If one then puts the moments of the results of both assumptions together, then one of them will become predominantly clear. But it will also often remain in the balance, and then one person will take one of them, another will take the other.

Assuming, e.g., that the inauthenticity of 1 John 5, 7 was diplomatically not decided, then one could be uncertain whether something would be missing if one left the passage out, so much does it appear not to fit the form. But if I look at it materially in terms of its content and context, then it admittedly appears as a superfluous addition. In this way the judgement fluctuates as long as what is diplomatic fluctuates.

But all such larger passages certainly do not require any other rules, but are to be treated completely in accordance with those established earlier.

Let us now go back to the new theme of deciding about the authenticity or inauthenticity of a text and investigate it more precisely.

If a text has for a long time always been taken as the text of a certain author, and doubts only arise later, then the doubt itself is not detracted from by its coming later, but it only follows from this that the hermeneutic operation has not previously been carried out with such precision and completeness.

Let us now distinguish the various essential cases. The first is where a passage occurs in a text which is in contradiction with the idea of the author that I have had so far, where I therefore become inhibited. In the passage there is talk of a fact of which the author certainly could not, in terms of his life circumstances, have been informed, about which he therefore could not possibly speak. A single passage of this kind is therefore a complete proof of the inauthenticity of the text, to the extent to which that impossibility is really there, and it is there if the passage really belongs to the text. The question therefore arises as to whether the passage originally belongs to the text, or is an addition from elsewhere. If nothing at all confirms this doubt diplomatically, then it is still conceivable that the passage came into the text before all the copies which we possess. If this becomes probable, then the passage loses all its value as evidence. Here we come to a point where we can judge the correctness of a certain critical procedure. It is often said that there are cases where every individual reason for suspicion proves nothing, but that several together provide a complete proof. Everyone approves this rule with their feelings, but if one subjects the rule to calculation it seems false. However, if we begin with our position, then it vindicates itself after all. We have said that the value as evidence of a passage which gives rise to doubts is weakened, but not abolished, to the extent that the probability arises that it is a later addition. But if I imagine six such passages, then these are just as many reasons, and each of them would alone be sufficient, if each did not contain something that gives a contrary possibility. The question is, then, what is more probable, the repetition of such confirming passages or the interpolation of the passages? The degree of probability of interpolation obviously diminishes to the extent to which many false passages occur. For this would imply a thoughtlessness which is not very probable. In such circumstances that rule therefore is completely correct.

The case in question is taken from the domain of historical interpretation. The most precise knowledge possible of the circumstances of life of the author is required as an apparatus for this. But something similar is presented by psychological interpretation. If I encounter a thought in a text which does not correspond with the way of thinking of its author, then I thereby equally become inhibited in the assumption with which I have been reading up to that point. In the same way as one had in the previous case to assume that the author could not have been at all informed of the questionable fact, I must also assume here that the author never thought this way in his whole life. In this lies a limitation of the case, for there are few objects about which people do not change their opinions. But the case is exactly the same as in the historical case, only that here the assertion of the contradiction is more difficult, not just because inner circumstances of thought are more difficult to prove than external facts, but also because interpretation of thoughts is inherently more difficult. If it is possible for me to think that such a passage is an addition, then it is the same with it as in the case above: the more such suspicious passages there are, the more probable it is that they originally belong to the text and that it is inauthentic.

These are the essential applications of the general formula to the two main areas of interpretation.

The same thing can now occur in relation to language with an analogous duality.

If a word occurs which was not in use when and where the author was writing, but the word is diplomatically certain, and did not arise via a mechanical error, then that is a decisive factor against the authenticity of the text. But the complete proof that the word could not occur at that time is precisely what is very difficult. The other case would be the one where expressions, turns of phrase occur which admittedly do not lie outside the linguistic area of the author, but do lie outside his individuality. If there is then no analogy for this to be found in the rest of his writings, and there are instead many which contradict it, then a single passage can suffice to justify the suspicion. But for this a complete knowledge of language which very much goes into the detail and into what is individual is required. Here the path of such an investigation can now be more precisely described. There can be cases where a single passage is completely decisive for the expert who is familiar with the author, but where it appears to others as only one reason for doubt. In that case the critic must seek out several things in order to communicate his certainty to others, and in this way a thorough critical procedure arises, the whole text is looked at in critical terms. If there is just the one passage, and if even in an intentional comparison several passages are not found, then the evidential value of the one passage is admittedly weakened. One will then try also to explain it in a different way, indeed one will even be satisfied with a more improbable explanation. But the question arises as to how the fact can have arisen that the text is attributed to an author to whom it does not belong. The text can have arisen as an intentional deception, by the author himself arranging it in such a way that it is supposed to be taken for the text of the supposed author. But this case can rarely be assumed, because the circumstances in which it could be carried out are very complicated. As long as the supposed author is alive somebody else will not easily succeed in circulating a text under that name. Such a text would have to be kept away for a definite amount of time from the circle of the supposed author. This is inherently improbable. And the more a text has the reputation of belonging to the circle of the fictional author, the less the suspicion of deception is applicable. It is then probable that the attribution of the text rests on a false judgement. Where a text appeared anonymously such a false judgement was easily possible. This was carried over into the text and the later copyists could already present it in the heading as certainly a text of that author, not via mechanical error, but intentionally and consciously, though not deceptively. As soon as one is led to such assumptions one must bring them back to this case and prove one of the two possibilities, and set up the critical operation accordingly from the beginning. Where the matter remains in the balance one must begin with both possibilities and allow a probability calculus to enter.

If we look in general at the fact that a work has been falsely attributed to an author, then the reason for doing this, if it is supposed to have happened intentionally and seriously, will have to be very particular. It must be shown in a probable manner, if one's mind is to be put at rest, how someone came to do it. The fact can arise at one remove, thus not really intentionally, if a text is anonymous, and someone makes the judgement that it is by such and such, and this judgement is afterwards carried over into the text itself. Here several cases can be distinguished. The most frequent case is the one where such a text is not separate, but is found in a collection. As soon as such a fact occurs suspicion is aroused against the whole collection. What follows from this, when individual parts of such a collection are falsely attributed to an author? First of all the question is: how did the collection come into existence? These days it is usual for authors to collect their own texts themselves. In that case the collection has the same authenticity as any individual text. But it is completely different if others make the collection. Then such mistakes can occur, but only in relation to anonymous texts. If the author is still alive, then it is up to him to object. If he does not, then that can be seen as a tacit guarantee. If a collection is only made after the death of the writer, then it can all the more easily happen that individual anonymous texts which had been attributed to him in his lifetime without him protesting against this are falsely taken up. If the collection is made long after the death of the author, then the possibility is still greater. In this case there is no precise connection any more between what is collected and the period of the author. The rule is that, as soon as such a suspicion arises, the whole collection must appear as suspicious and every single text must justify itself in another way than via the fact that it is in the collection. In antiquity we almost always find false works in the *operis omnibus* [complete works]. But on the other hand doubts often arise which, when looked at more closely, have no basis. This uncertain path of criticism demands a specific rule. In the light of what has been said so far one can establish that as soon as it is notorious that a collection is not by the author himself it is not authentic; furthermore, that if it was still made at the time of his contemporaries, they can stand in for the author to the extent to which the collection was the object of public interest; finally, that if it was made later it has no original certainty and only has authority to the extent that we can attribute correct judgement and the relative impossibility of his erring to the collector. In this way the presumption that a work of antiquity really belongs to the person to whom it is attributed is very much reduced.

If a work from an earlier period is attributed to an author then the eye and thus one's judgement is admittedly initially impressed by the name which is placed before the text or the collection. One must seek to free oneself from being impressed in reading the text. But in just this way a suspicion which is already present can also sway my judgement. In this way a dual process arises, two maxims which are opposed to each other and equally one-sided. The adherents of the one are called the believers in authority, who keep hold of everything that is transmitted and in this way pass over much that is really suspicious. The opposite of these are the hypercritical ones, of whom the others say that they, because they only set out to find reasons for suspicion, destroy all calm and simple study. It is just as difficult to avoid this duality as it is to establish something in the middle between the two directions. The opposition admittedly has its disadvantages, for as long as there is conflict in this area the hermeneutic operation cannot calmly be pursued. But the question is whether the whole procedure is to be considered only in relation to the hermeneutic operation, or whether it has value in itself. If one starts with the relationship to the hermeneutic operation then it follows that one may not carry on the critical dispute about things which have no value for the hermeneutic operation, and thence that one may not stop the hermeneutic operation until the reasons for suspicion have reached some degree of certainty. The critical procedure is thereby admittedly pushed back and deferred to a later time. On the other hand, though, general philological interest is aroused. For even if a text is as hermeneutically insignificant as it is possible to be, if the particular circle and the time to which it belongs have been established, it is still a document of language for precisely this circle and this time. Admittedly, if this cannot be established, then the philological interest is also nil. But one sees, however, how differently the interest is graded if one starts from the general philological point of view. There are, for example, in the collection of the Platonic Works, several of which it has been made probable that they are not Platonic, but which still belong to the immediate school of Socrates. In itself the question thereby loses interest for the general philosophical point of view, because those works still belong to the area of the Atticism of that time. In this respect their value is determinate, with only a small difference. We can indeed say that Plato was a completely different virtuoso in relation to language than every other pupil of Socrates. But this would, of course, relate more to the style than to the language. On the other hand, for the person who is concerned with the history of philosophy, the question will also be important even in this respect. He recognises in it a particular doctrine which emerged from the Socratic school along with the Platonic doctrine. In this way the interest is graded differently, depending on the point of view adopted.

The result of all this is that the rule is not just to be established from the point of view of the hermeneutic operation, but also from that of the general philological interest.

The case of the collection leads us, more immediately than if we look at a text in isolation, to the question of how texts can positively prove that they really belong to this or that author. In isolation, namely, a text *originally* has nothing in it which it would give rise to suspicion, but in a collection, in the circumstances cited, this is easily possible.

We have said that if a collection is made by the author himself or made in his lifetime it does not need to carry out a proof. Proof by *testimony* is what first emerges here if it can be shown from undoubted texts of contemporaries or other specific information that the contemporaries already certainly attributed the text to the author. But this proof is only complete if such a context can really be demonstrated, thus if the texts are from a time for which we have a coherent literature. Where we have only a few fragments of language and literature this proof is impossible. But there is a further proof which connects to the first, proof by *analogy*. If I have some reliable texts of the same author and the most complete memory of them does not arouse any suspicion in me while reading another text that is attributed to him in the collection, then the text admittedly can be presumed to belong to him. But this proof does not possess the reliability of the first proof, for the correctness of the judgement here very much depends on the nature of the person judging. In accordance with this one will be able, in a larger collection, to distinguish works of the first and second class, those which are reliably documented by testimony, and those for which judgements of people whom one trusts to undertake a correct procedure can be cited. In the latter case there is, though, already submission to an authority.

But if we find in going further that those upon whose authority the second class is founded say in relation to other works that there are admittedly no grounds for suspicion, but that we could also have carried on reading undisturbed if we had taken them as deriving from someone else, nothing reminded us of just that particular author, then these are ambiguous texts which will also have to be established. In the same way as we find less perfection in the language, in the thoughts and the execution, or find this or that which fits less well, but can yet say on the other hand that the text could still derive from the same author if we assume that he was careless of himself in this or that respect, uncertainty also remains.

These are the laws of the critical procedure in relation to collections. If one looks at the result then such a significant tidying up in the domain of ancient literature has arisen via that procedure that both general philological interest and the interest of the actual disciplines rests on much firmer ground than before. It is also very good that those two maxims exist side by side. For if only one, the belief in authority, had been valid, then a large number of errors would still have pertained. If the opposed maxim alone had dominated then it would have brought an arbitrariness into the whole matter, whereby the results would have become far more uncertain than they now are through the opposed action of the other maxim. For the latter demands a strictness of proof and has the effect that one is less quick to surrender to the influence of individual moments and takes account of everything that can be cited from the opposed side.

If we look at the task from another side then the question arises as to whether it is interesting to know and what is interesting about knowing from whom a text originates.

In relation to a collection of texts which belong to One author that question is of great interest. If a text belongs to an author then the total idea of him is thereby more closely determined, the picture of his life, his nature is made more complete. If on the other hand a single text is attributed to an author of whom nothing else is extant, then it can be immaterial whether he is this or that person. It is enough to know the era and the circle in which the text arose. But circumstances, relationships can even occur in relation to a single text where interest in that question arises once more. If, e.g., I have a philosophical text whose author I do not know at all or only dubiously know, and there are also no further determinations present, then it can often be quite indifferent to me whether its author is Simon or Cebes; but if I know that one of the two was closely connected with this Socratic thinker, the other with that, and they are men of great significance who have developed the doctrine of Socrates in differing ways, then their personality is important, for their thoughts will belong in the domain of one or the other school, and thus the more precise knowledge of them will help to complete the concept of that school. In the same way it is interesting to know the author of a historical work, because here it is a question of knowing how the narrator relates to the events. If it is attributed to a man of whom I know that he lived at the time and in the region of the events, then the text has an authority which it would not have if someone else from a later time and from another region were its author. If on the other hand I do not know anything more precise about the relationship of the author to the events, then his name is also immaterial to me. As such, then, the interest of this question is very different. But one more thing is to be noted. To the extent that the knowledge of the whole region in which a text belongs is not complete, one can also not yet determine the interest of that question. In a very thoroughly researched area of literature one must be able to determine the interest of the question. But in that first case an absolute interest remains, because, in order not to neglect anything, the greatest interest is to be assumed.

All these differences can be found in the domain of classical literature. Here there are texts in relation to which it is immaterial in the highest degree who the author is, and which are only important as linguistic monuments of a particular time and region. The text itself then reveals at what stage its author was located, both with regard to the language and the content. The personality is immaterial in this. But the more the personality is woven into the language and the object of the text, the more the interest of the question grows.

Now as far as the N.T. is concerned the critical tasks of this kind are partly transmitted from ancient times, have partly newly emerged, many have already been decided and made doubtful once more. We have here an extensive history of critical endeavours.

For a Roman Catholic theologian all those critical questions are of no interest, for the canon is a work of the Church, and as it is transmitted in the Church it also has the same value and the same authority of infallibility as the tradition of the doctrine. It is immaterial for the Catholic theologian whether he says it follows from the fact that the second Epistle of Peter has been adopted that it is an epistle of Peter, or whether he says, the Church adopted the Epistle without concerning itself whether it is a work of Peter or not. The Epistle has canonical status in any case, and in that case the critical question is without interest.

But this view lies completely outside our viewpoint, because we cannot accept any authority of the Church in criticism. Admittedly the canon is transmitted without our knowing just how it got that way. But even if we knew that we could still not accept it without examination. For since one had to go to work according to certain rules when one organised it, the question is whether the organisation was correct.

If we now ask what interest the question of the author of every text of the N.T. has for us Protestants, then the question cannot at all be easily answered. The interest is very varied.

The N.T. is a collection, but not of the works of One author. The rule above, in which the collection of the works of One man was presupposed, is therefore not straightforwardly applicable to the N.T. We must make distinctions. The N.T. is partly a collection of collections, partly a collection of individual texts of different authors. Each of these is to be looked at separately.

We have in the N.T. a collection which was previously called ὁ ἀπόστολος [the Apostle]. That is the collection of the Pauline Epistles, but now more complete than in earlier times. If critical questions now arise from the Pauline Epistles then we have the case of a collection examined above. But if we ask whether the author of the Epistle of James is one of the men of this name who occur in the N.T., and ask which of these, or whether it was a completely different man, then this question is in itself of no interest because we do not have anything else by any of them, and the actions that are recounted of one or other of them have no essential connection to that letter. But put in another way that question immediately becomes more interesting. If we ask, namely, whether the author is one of the Jameses mentioned in the N.T., thus a man from the Apostolic era, an immediate contemporary of the Apostles, an Apostle himself, or whether he is later, – then precisely this is interesting to know. The difference of time is in this case admittedly fairly limited. At the same time the personality could only be immaterial up to a certain point. The same with Judas. However, the matter seems to change from another side, if the content of these Epistles were of the kind that our conception of the sphere of ideas in the Apostolic era would be essentially differently determined, depending on whether the author is this or that person. If those texts contained something which the other Apostolic texts do not contain, things that diverge but do not contradict, then the question would, of course, be of great importance. If an Apostle wrote purely as an individual, without communication with the others, isolated, then the question again becomes less interesting because one cannot infer from it to that sphere with which we are really concerned. The interest would then just be in the simple personality. If in a text which was written at the time of the Apostles and emerged from their communal life ideas nevertheless occurred which were superstitious and more Judaic, and were contradicted in other epistles, then the interest here is not in the personality himself, but in certain things he recounts; it would be interesting to know whether such ideas were accepted without contradiction in the circle of the Apostles, thus are to a certain extent permitted to be regarded as theirs or not.

[*Translator's summary of omitted passage*: The question of whether the second and third Epistle of John and the second Epistle of Peter were written by John and by Peter is of little interest in terms of the personalities themselves. These Epistles of John are not really large and significant enough for it to matter. If Peter's second Epistle is by him we have a collection, but only of the two Epistles, one of which is doubtful. In the case of Paul the authenticity is of personal interest because the Epistles have to do with the facts of his life. In John's Gospel the interest is historical: was the author a contemporary witness? This is important, given that the Gospel tells the story differently from the other Gospels, and leaves out much that is in the other Gospels. Of Mark and Luke we only know they did not belong to the immediate circle of Jesus, so it does not matter if they are the same as the persons of this name mentioned in the N.T. It is different whether the author of the Acts of the Apostles and of Luke's Gospel are the same person. In the case of Matthew's Gospel the main question is whether he is the Apostle. If so his relation to the events is the same as that of John. This affects the interpretation of the difference of the Gospels.]

If someone takes the Gospel of Matthew as the work of the Apostle, but does not take John's Gospel as this, then Matthew is the norm for John, and everything in which the latter contradicts the former is attributed to the inauthenticity of John's Gospel. If one says the opposite, then the relationship is also inverted. If both are regarded as works of the Apostles then their differences cannot be reconciled. In this case, then, the critical question is of great interest in relation to the establishing of the facts from the different accounts. In this way we find every different degree of critical interest and the different critical questions about the author together in the N.T., and each must be decided in terms of its nature and significance.

Let us now ask whether these critical questions are to be solved in the N.T. in the same way as we established in general above, or are there particular rules for the N.T. texts in this respect?

We already found a similar question earlier in the realm of hermeneutics, but we found it as an old disputed question, not as one which arose for us in the natural course of investigation. For the consistent theory of the Catholic Church the critical question does not exist at all. For us in the Protestant Church it is necessarily present. And as in the realm of hermeneutics we shall also have to say here that there are no other rules for N.T. criticism than the general rules.

The critical questions arise because a fact was not yet correctly established, or because it was obscured. The matter can always be reduced to these two cases. There can be no other rules for establishing a fact in the realm of the N.T. than there are in other realms.

A decision in the establishing of facts can only be brought about via two elements. *In this first place via authorities.* If these are complete and in agreement then the question is also completely decided. If they do not agree, if one of them contains contraindications, then the question is undecided. *Then via analogies,* if one decides, via the use of language and the relations of thoughts, for and against the identity of the author. Does one judge differently in both these cases in the domain of the N.T. than in every other domain?

There are here admittedly authorities of a different kind from elsewhere. This is inherent in the nature of the canonical texts. These have their particular importance because we ascribe a particular authority to their authors, but only in the domain of their particular calling.

If the O.T. is cited in N.T. texts in a certain manner, for example from Isaiah, from a region of which the critic knows that it is later and not a prophesy, will someone wish to say that because Paul cites him every critical operation is futile? Presumably nobody would now still say this. – Paul cited in this way because the passage was given to him under the name of Isaiah. In this area one will therefore reject the authority of Paul. In the same way as when a Psalm is cited as by David which we cannot take to be so. But if the case were that dubious N.T. texts were cited in other N.T. texts which are certainly authentic, then that would admittedly be something else. But then the authority would not count as Apostolic, but just as the authority who certainly could know what was the case. This is now admittedly not the case. This can therefore be of no assistance to us, and no division of the N.T. area would arise thereby either.

Now if someone even wished to attribute a completely particular authority to the Fathers of the Church, then that would be all right for a Catholic theologian, but not for us, as goes without saying. The former, though, if he is consistent, does not need this authority at all. We regard the testimony of the Fathers of the Church as judgements which must first be tested.

The critical rules are therefore the same as in every other literary domain. There are questions in relation to the N.T. books which are very related to those in the domain of real philological criticism, but which do not belong here. We must separate these out. To them belongs the complicated question of the genesis of the Synoptic Gospels. Philological criticism as such has nothing to do with the genesis of a book, it can only go back to the appearance of the book. But if there are passages in those texts which did not belong to it when it originally appeared, then that is located in our domain. There it is a question of authorities and analogies. On the other hand, if one asks whether individual parts of the Synoptic Gospels were already extant at an earlier time, whether they arose from continuous memory or materials collected at an earlier time, whether they are wholly or partly compilations of extant materials that had been further elaborated, – then these are questions which do not belong in our domain: they are tasks of a particular kind which do not have many equivalents, for which there are, though, analogies in the classical domain, such as, e.g., the well-known Homeric question. Where do this and similar questions belong if not in the domain of historical criticism? They belong to historical criticism. This has as its proper aim the establishing of facts.

The matter now looks like this. Philological criticism leads back to the acknowledged public existence of these texts, as far as it can. It cannot really lead us back to the separate existence of individual texts. For we only have fragments of the history of the individual books. The result is completely lacking. We have the collection of the N.T., but do not know how it arose. The N.T. was not always thus, that much we know. We have individual data about it. But the historical context in the testimony is lacking that would show how the present unity was gained from those differences. There are still copies of the N.T. which testify to the incomplete state, like, e.g., the Peshito.[3] But we cannot fill the gap with them. If one asks, going further back, about the emergence of the individual texts, then this question is, on the other hand, not so isolated that it would only relate to the Synoptic Gospels. The question is also how the individual Epistles came into being. This is also a purely historical question. In this way an area of tasks has formed in this respect which is not restricted to the N.T. and which we must separate from the area of properly philological criticism; it is the area of historical criticism.

---

[3] *Translator's note*: the principle Syriac (a version of Aramaic) version of the Bible.

This is the art of restoring a fact in such a way that it is as though it happens before our eyes. And it is a question of restoring the fact either from deficient evidence or from testimony that is contradictory, thus by supplementation in the one and reconciliation in the other case. Both tasks occur. Let us take, e.g., the Homeric question. Even if we leave it completely undecided whether at the time when the poet is supposed to have lived he could have been able to write and could have produced his works in written form himself, we will still justifiably maintain that they could not have been reproduced and disseminated by the text alone. So the dissemination of the texts will therefore have been more by oral transmission. But they could not be orally transmitted as One whole. That goes without saying. But as soon as one thinks of a dividing up of the text it is necessary to assume a complete and an incomplete transmission. That leads to the positive fact of an individual transmission of individual parts, as a fact, then, which must be supplemented from deficient information. This, then, is the task. The task of reconciliation from differing testimony [is] the same. This occurs continually and everywhere in history, and is the real task of historical criticism. We have separated this task from the real hermeneutic operation. This is also necessary. But one must always remain aware that the hermeneutic task cannot be accomplished without the operation of historical criticism. The directly hermeneutic task is accomplished if I know how the writer of history presented the facts. But if I want to use him as historical witness the task of historical criticism arises.

In the N.T. the task of reconciliation, like that of supplementation, arises in relation to everything in it that is historical. In this way this double task is, e.g., present in relation to the history of Jesus Christ from the Gospels. If, on the other hand, we want to make clear to ourselves the fact of the spread of Christianity outside the period contained in the Acts of the Apostles, then the task is to establish the fact in a complete manner by supplementation. The supplementation consists in filling the space in the middle between two separate historical elements in a probable manner. This task is directly connected to the hermeneutic task.

In the Synoptic Gospels the task is of a quite particular kind because it here affects the hermeneutic operation itself. Among the various hypotheses about the synoptic relationship there are some which to a certain extent destroy the unity of every single Gospel. If one finds it probable that the Gospels emerged from already extant written and oral transmission in such a way that different people made a whole out of them in different ways, then the question is whether the author took up the extant written elements as they were, or whether he presented them having worked them over in his own manner of writing. If the former is made probable then the unity of the text for general philological interest ceases to exist and the hermeneutic task must be accomplished in another manner. The text then no longer forms One area of analogies of the linguistic usage; its usage at least becomes very uncertain. This is therefore a very elaborate task which has no exact equivalent in any area of literature. It is, though, certainly not immaterial whether and how this task is accomplished, not least because the hermeneutic task is immediately affected by it. Indeed the issue itself is also different. If the hermeneutic task is to be accomplished as completely as possible it is desirable for every Evangelist to have worked on the whole in his manner in order to have a unity in relation to the language. But if we consider that many speeches of Christ are in it, which have a completely different authority, then we will find it desirable to have these speeches exactly as Christ originally gave them. In this way two opposed interests arise. But it is not a question of what we find desirable, but of establishing how the matter really is, in order to determine the degree of reliability with which the speeches of Christ are transmitted. This task may not remain unaccomplished, otherwise something essential is lacking for the use of the N.T. in relation to its complete certainty.

But are these two tasks really present? This sounds peculiar. But there was a time when the tasks were not yet present. We must therefore first ask whether they have justifiably been established or not; only then can we give the method for getting as close as possible to accomplishing them.

The questions which really belong to historical criticism of the N.T. are usually dealt with in the introduction to the N.T. This is now a science which has no limits at all, into which one can throw what one will. In that case it is not at all a question of going back to principles, instead one treats the issues according to the particular state of things at the time. But the question is: are there no such principles?

If we conceive of the tasks as they tend to occur in that discipline, then the aim is the establishing of the fact from deficient and contradictory clues or evidence. In this case there is no other method than what presents itself to each person individually as the most probable. If one goes no further than this one only gets something fairly vague. One will sometimes approach the truth, sometimes get further away from it. And in this way it becomes desirable to be able to go back to something firm and objective.

If the border between philological and historical criticism were fixed, such that the former always goes back to documents as what is earliest, or, counting backwards, goes back to the last thing, and excludes what lies beyond this from its domain, then in this direction this last thing is the beginning for the task of historical criticism. If we now ask whether there can be a specific method for restoring a fact when things stand as they do here, then the question is, put like this, so to speak, without foundation, isolated and hanging in the air. But if we assume that the fact is a single thing in a whole, then the question is whether this whole is only a mere aggregate of such single things or something else.

If one wished to assert the former one would destroy all history. For that would mean that every historical moment would be something purely contingent in the sequence of time. If we do not wish to dissolve all history into empty semblance then even the single thing must be able to be conceived of as something that can be judged. Every totality[c] must now be a unity and every fact must be able to be understood in context. It will therefore be a question of how far one will be able to conceive of the totality.

As far as the question of the emergence of the Synoptic Gospels is concerned, the first thing to do is properly to imagine the totality within which that fact belongs. But then an indeterminacy in the task immediately arises again, because we cannot precisely cite the time at which the Gospels arose. We know only that they are present at a certain time and that each of them is in its current state. We do not know how long they were there before. If we stop with the earliest documents of the fact we never find the Gospels mentioned individually, nor do we find isolated occurrences of them, but always all four together. It is invalid to assume they are parts of a whole and were prepared together. They were therefore certainly there individually. But then we have a historical gap. For we know nothing of their individual existence. The first task is therefore, from the very beginning, precisely to find a point in time which is closest to the emergence of the texts, and to find how that point where they occur together is documented. In this way we have kept the indeterminacy within certain limits. We begin with the life of Christ. In this case the worst thing is that the information about this is precisely in these books. However, the existence of Christ is sufficiently attested even without that, namely by the other books of the N.T. which, after all, originally arose independently of

[c] *Gesamtzustand.*

217

the Gospels; otherwise one would have to assume that these as well were made as parts of a whole, and that the whole N.T. was therefore something made up and therefore a great deception. But we now have as attested a collection which is separate from our collection, the canon of Marcion. And although this is a somewhat different canon, there is in it a certain fact for the foundation of the historical appearance. If we now, beginning with this, descend further in order to have attested facts which are older than our Gospels, we find a strange fact. Several Epistles of the N.T. were obviously written at the time of the Emperor Nero. Now it is a fact that many people have asserted that Matthew was written in 48 AD. If we connect these facts the strange conclusion results that the Gospel of Matthew would, on this assumption, be significantly older than those Epistles. But in the Epistles of Paul there is no trace that indicates the Apostle knew a text of this extent and content. Now is it really probable that both things were really together in this way? We are to think of the totality as composed of certain elements, of which one is an attested fact, the other a hypothesis. We can completely develop the principles of historical criticism via this example. If we have several points from a totality the question is whether we can think these together as a unity or not. If it can be thought together that Paul and all his activity, and such a text were around for a significant period of time, without there being any information about the text in the Pauline Epistles, then that hypothesis that Matthew's Gospel was written in the year 48 is possible. If I cannot do that then the hypothesis is refuted. In this way one sees how one must go to work. Under what circumstances could those two points be thought together? If one could show that Paul might well have been without any information about that Gospel, or that he did not need to show that information in his Epistles, then both points could be thought together. However, the chronology of the Apostle Paul is subject to very many doubts; the question of when during his period of effectiveness his Epistles occur is generally not yet completely answered. It still seems impossible to us, though, that he was supposed not to have had any information about that Gospel. According to this hypothesis the Gospel was supposed to have been written in Palestine; that was not the sphere of activity of Paul, but he was still very closely connected to those districts, so that, if it was not intentionally kept secret, he had to have information about it. But it is unthinkable that something written for Christians to fix the facts of the Gospel should have been hidden in Jerusalem and have remained unknown to the one really literary Apostle. But how is it with the other case, that Paul had information about it, but could just not have mentioned it in his Epistles? In order to decide this one would again have to cite points from which a totality was put together in which the moments of decision lay. If the Church at that time had been full of Gospels Paul would also not have needed to talk about it. But according to that hypothesis one is supposed to think of Matthew's Gospel as the earliest, and, for a time, only Gospel. But perhaps Paul did not have to take account of the book in his manner of working? One really cannot say that, for if it was the only Gospel and Paul stood at the tip of a great circle of congregations, whose connection to Palestine he had to organise,[d] then his duty was to disseminate it. Furthermore he had the duty and the opportunity in his Epistles, particularly the ones known to be later, where he speaks of the common life of Christians, including specifically of their meetings, to cite the book. The mentioning of the book would have been a part of his fulfilling of his duty. When he talks of the resurrection of Christ, refers to it as a fact, should he not have referred there to a text which it was his duty to make known? To the extent, then, that we cannot think together such a totality with that hypothesis, the hypothesis must be dropped, because there can be no doubt about the circumstances and sphere of activity of the Apostle.

The whole process of criticism in this content must always be based on constructing a totality in relation to a disputed question, in which one has fixed points according to which one can judge what is dubious, to the extent to which it can be thought of as in harmony with the whole or not.

Up to now and even now one usually thought one had done enough if one had established a single possibility. But the single detail hangs in the air without the construction of the complete context. That is how it went in the dispute over the authenticity of the first Epistle to Timothy. Whereas I began by presenting the totality which would have had to have pertained if the Epistle was to have been written by Paul, and judged the individual circumstances according to it, the younger Planck opposed details to other details without bringing them into a totality. In this way the process which begins with the idea of pure contingency is opposed to the only correct maxim of explaining the particular from a totality and bringing it back to a totality which is equally tenable.

If we now look at the issue of the Synoptic Gospels, the question is in which totality something like this could have arisen. If we set up the

---

[d] *vermitteln.*

hypothesis that Mark used the oldest Gospel of Matthew, and that Luke used both of these, then the question is what totality is to be thought in which that could have happened. How must things have been in Christendom if, after Matthew was written, there should have been sufficient reason and need to write the Gospel of Mark? How is the difference between the two to be understood? Was the difference such that it was worth the effort of writing such a book? How do the two authors relate to each other in terms of location? Could the Gospel of Matthew not get to where Mark wrote, and did the latter write his Gospel precisely for this reason? If we now also take into account that only a very small period of time is assumed between the first three Gospels, then we ask how the state of the Church must have been for the three Gospels to have been able to appear so soon after each other. One would have to assume either a massive deficiency in communication or a massive desire to write. But neither of these corresponds to what we otherwise know about that period. The lack of connection between congregations was no longer so great and writing only expanded later. As such we therefore cannot think this hypothesis without destroying the unity of the image of the period and without denying evident facts.[e] We must therefore cross it out and seek a better one.

Everything so far is only a maxim for judging, not for discovering. Would it not be better if such untenable hypotheses did not emerge at all? Certainly. But how can one get to what is correct? Only by descending from above and remaining from the very beginning within the exact development of the conditions of Christianity. Now, what is given to us in relation to the synoptic problem that we know to be attested? We can only assume that individual oral and written accounts from the life of Christ were present before the time of our Gospels and that our Gospels are products of these, that none had an immediate relationship to the other, finally, that their composition is to be moved down into a time when such a compilation appears founded in the conditions of Christianity.

Let us now briefly summarise in what the sole correct method of historical criticism consists. If it is a question of the establishing of a fact of which, whatever is the case, several individual moments must be given, a decision is only possible if one has a fixed point from which one can begin, and, on the other hand, a fixed point which has emerged from the context together with that which is to be explained. The disputed fact lies between these two

[e] *Elemente.*

known end-points. There must be an adequately attested totality, as location of the fact, so to speak, an earlier and a later totality this side of and beyond the fact. If various perspectives are conceivable the test is twofold; namely, whether the various known moments can be explained together with the attested earlier totality, so that it becomes clear how the fact emerged from it, but then, as well, whether the other end-point and the totality which belongs to it can be explained as having emerged from the fact which has been established. If both correspond, then that is a decision of the only kind possible. Admittedly, as soon as new elements of the fact become apparent the investigation must be renewed. This method precisely rests on every fact being regarded as part of a connected historical whole. For this reason, if one has very precise points for the same whole, they are to be regarded as belonging to the fact itself. The decision can then be all the more definite.

In the N.T. this method is still too little used. But this is connected to the manner of dealing with the real critical task, with the still current, completely unscientific respect for the *recepta*, where one accepts the worst transmission completely without judgement. How has the question concerning the authenticity of the N.T. texts been dealt with? What is the position of the critic here? It is a well-attested fact that certain parts of the N.T. canon were still regarded as inauthentic for a certain time in a great part of the Church. The later fact is that the canon in the Christian Church is as agreed as it could be, after those texts were recognised as authentic. We can distinguish a further duality about which one admittedly did not think at that time, namely the interest in the authors of the texts, to the extent to which they were Apostles, and in the texts themselves, to the extent to which they were canonical. One did not distinguish these at that time, in the same way as one would not have taken up the second Epistle of Peter if it had not been taken as authentic. But the later attested fact is that even the texts that were previously doubted came into the canon, that, therefore, those who took those texts as authentic gained the upper hand among the conflicting parties. The history of how that took place is lacking. Everyone who deals with the question is well aware of this. But if the question is now dealt with anew the issue is posed as if it were a trial, and as if those who assert the authenticity had already won the trial as those who were already in possession, but as if it were up to those who dispute it to carry out the proof. Here judgement is impressed[f] by tradition, in the same way as the eye was

[f] *bestochen.*

impressed above in relation to the text. One introduces the statute of limitation where it is not a question of statutes but of truth. That is an unholy respect for tradition and a Catholic practice. For the core of this respect is the ghost of the manifest Church.[g] Until one has freed oneself from this no scientific treatment is possible.

What does the fact that only those who dispute it have to carry out the proof lead to? The defence is then carried out in such a way that instead of going back to the totalities one cites only isolated moments, without showing that these also make sense. How should it be? It depends what is really to be explained. The fact is to be explained that the party which takes the dubious texts as authentic became the dominant party. The earliest thing is that the texts were recognised by some people as authentic, and not by others. Here one is to calculate what is most probable in looking at what is earlier and what is later. Do we treat the two opinions as two readings, and ask which is probably the authentic one, which has more in its favour? If we had all the reasons before us why some took those texts as authentic and the others took them as inauthentic, we would only need to examine them. But there are not many of them left. So it is precisely just a question of probability. What are we mainly to assume at that time: desire for holy texts or rules of caution? Obviously the first in terms of the totality of the old Church. So those who had that desire will have needed less particular reasons, those who doubted will have needed all the more. As long as particular grounds for deciding do not reveal themselves we must say that those who doubted had better reasons than those who accepted. In this way, then, the general acceptance of such texts was only the consequence of the dominant inclination. To this is added the opposition between the Orthodox and the Catholic on the one hand, and the heretics on the other. In this there are in certain respects contraindications. In the Catholic Church the consolidation of the Church was the dominant objective, and this was connected with the desire to consolidate a corpus of holy texts. Connected to this was the attempt to avoid heresy, if at all possible. There are heretical texts which were used in many congregations and immediately made the questionable claim to be taken up into the canon. But one rejected them. In this way the later totality is the result of the desire of every congregation to have everything that had been regarded as sacred in any other congregation. This desire won the day in all cases where there was nothing heretical in what

[g] *der erscheinenden Kirche.*

was dubious; it did not win the day where there was something heretical. That is how it happened. But one did not at that time examine the texts for the right reasons, but really saw it more as an exchange. In order for some to let go what appeared as heretical from the Catholic side, others accepted what was dubious without being heretical. Now the question comes to the point where it must be decided by internal reasons. Which reasons did those who doubted have, and which reasons did those who accepted have? Doubting presupposes a critical orientation, accepting does not. If we could cite facts in order to establish where the dubious texts first came from and how they were disseminated to such an extent, then we could carry out the proof with really attested facts; as long as that is not the case we can only carry out the proof with inner reasons, following the method described, of only dealing with the details in relation to the totality.

The N.T. offers a further obstacle to critical investigations. If we look more closely at the parts via which the dominant ideas are usually defended we find that much is taken as evidence that was only opinion. In this way the second imprisonment of the Apostle Paul is taken by many as an attested fact. But looked at more closely there is no evidence for this at all. Were there evidence one would also have to be able to say what the Apostle did after the imprisonment recounted in the Acts of the Apostles. There is admittedly later information about it, but it does not have any evidential force. We have already tried to explain above in the hermeneutics how the view of the ancients of the second imprisonment may have arisen from the assumption of the divine inspiration of Holy Scripture.

Something else comes into consideration here, where one can clearly see what happens to criticism if one does not give it freedom. It then only works against itself.

Doubts were raised against many Pauline Epistles, because it was said that points occurred in them which could not be explained via the known totality, the life of the Apostle. But if it is only the Acts of the Apostles that says nothing of this, then this is no reason for doubt, because the Acts has historical gaps. But if contraindications occur in the Apostle's texts against certain information these are precisely not to be understood via that total- ity, they cannot have emerged from it. There the liberation of the Apostle from the first imprisonment was a very convenient piece of information: it was supposed to refute all the contraindications. But as there is no positive evidence for this, and as the explanation of the whole question via the theory of inspiration of the ancients suggests itself, one cannot allow any form of argument from such a fact which has not been attested at all. One must beware of taking mere opinions of the ancients for truths! We often just do have only the tradition of opinions without any real history. One should be careful here!

We will perhaps not get to the point of completely deciding all the questions in relation to individual books and the whole complex of the N.T. For there are tasks where we do not have sufficient points to come to a firm judgement. In that case much must remain uncertain and disputed. But, via the correct method which we have given, we at least free ourselves of false impediments and make and keep the ground of the investigation clear. It is very improbable that aspects of importance which we do not yet know should yet be discovered. They would have to be texts from the period which is the least historically filled, or texts which inherited assured information from this period. It is very improbable that such texts should still be found. But for this reason we must nevertheless apply the correct method to everything that is disputed. These lectures are meant to be a contribution to this, but only in brief, so that the task is left of carrying out the application to the individual N.T. books and further developing the principles established.

General Hermeneutics

General Hermeneutics

by Dr Fr. Schleiermacher
Written in the winter of 1809–10
(begun 24th November 09)

Copy made by August Twesten in 1811 of the original manuscript, which is no longer extant. Transcription by Wolfgang Virmond.[1]

Introduction

1. Hermeneutics rests on the fact of the non-understanding of discourse: taken in its most general sense, including misunderstanding in the mother tongue and in everyday life.
2. Non-understanding is partly indeterminacy, partly ambiguity of the content.
   So it is thought of without any fault on the part of the utterer.
3. The art of explication is therefore the art of putting oneself in possession of all the conditions of understanding.
4. Others wrongly include the presentation of understanding in this.
   Whence in Ernesti the chapter on the writing of commentaries. This presentation is, though, itself a kind of composition, thus in turn an object of hermeneutics. – Cause lies in the Greek etymology of the word.
5. But the explanation seems to contain too much because it presupposes knowledge of the language and of the matter in question in the original reader and listener.

---

[1] The text is laid out as in Virmond's transcription.

227

Hermeneutics first of all sends one to grammar and to the sciences, otherwise it would have to take over all [forms of] instruction itself.
6. But one only arrives at language itself and the knowledge of supersensuous things via the understanding of human discourse.

Hermeneutics is therefore not built upon philology, but instead there is a changing relationship between it and philology, which makes the borders between them hard to determine.
7. As we, in this sense, practice explication from childhood onwards one might think the theory is superfluous.

The more common things are understood of their own accord; the higher things are a question of talent and genius, which also help themselves.
8. Treatments [of hermeneutics] generally originate with people who had an ulterior purpose.

Theologians and jurists. For the latter the main thing is the logical interpretation which goes beyond the real content of the utterance. For the former, it became necessary via the fusing together of the writers in a codex and the dogmatic exegesis and other abuses which arose from this.
9. The real philologists and connoisseurs of the art of discourse did not work on hermeneutics, but were satisfied with praxis.

They seek to reduce the area of hermeneutics via more precise determination of the use of language and by the production of historical apparatuses. What is left is genius, which is not helped by analysis (see Wolf).
10. The relationship [between theory and praxis] is like it is in all theories of art.

They [the theories] do not make the artist. But the more the explicator is an artist the more interesting it is to watch his activity. – An immediate specific need is admittedly better catered for by practical instruction.
11. The business of hermeneutics should not only begin where understanding is uncertain, but with the first beginning of the enterprise of wanting to understand an utterance.

For understanding usually only becomes uncertain because it has earlier already been neglected.
12. The goal of hermeneutics is understanding in the highest sense.

Lower maxim: one has understood everything that one has really grasped without encountering contradiction. Higher maxim: One has only understood what one has reconstructed in all its relationships and in its context. – To this also belongs understanding the writer better than he understands himself.

13. Understanding has a dual direction, towards the language and towards the thought.

1. The language is the embodiment of everything that can be thought in it, because it is a closed whole and relates to a particular manner of thinking. Everything particular in it must be able to be understood from out of the totality.

2. Every utterance corresponds to a sequence of thoughts of the utterer, and must therefore be able to be completely understood via the nature of the utterer, his mood, his aim. The former [i.e. 1.] we call grammatical, the latter technical interpretation.

14. These are not two kinds of interpretation, instead every explication must completely achieve both.

One has often talked of kinds of interpretation; but a kind is what completely includes the concept of the genus within itself. This does not take place here. Whoever wants only to understand grammatically wants only to understand inartistically. Whoever only wants to understand psychologically (one calls this with good reason a priori) will always understand unphilologically.

15. The compatibility of both tasks is evident from the relationship of the utterer to the language; he is its organ and it is his.

1. The language is a leading principle for every utterer, not only negatively, because he cannot get out of the domain of the thinking contained within it, but also positively, because it guides his combination via the relationships which lie within it. Every utterer can therefore only say what it [language] wants and is its organ.

2. Every utterer whose utterance can become an object himself works on or determines the manner of thought in an individual manner. Whence the enrichment of the language with new objects and new potential, which always begin with the linguistic activity of individual persons.

3. Neither language nor the individual as productive speaking individual can exist except via the being-in-each-other of both relationships.

16. Precisely because in all understanding both tasks must be accomplished, understanding is an art.

Every single language could perhaps be learned via rules, and what can be learned in this way is mechanism. Art is that for which there admittedly are rules, but the combinatory application of these rules cannot in turn be rule-bound. This is how it is with this double construction and with the interpenetration of both tasks.

17. On each side of interpretation another one of those two relationships dominates.

The grammatical side puts the utterer in the background and regards him just as an organ of the language, but regards language as what really generates the utterance. The technical side, on the other hand, regards the utterer as the real-ground[a] of the utterance and the language merely as the negative limiting principle.

18. But it is not the case that one side is more oriented towards the lower and another towards higher understanding.

In this way people have talked of a higher and a lower interpretation and then called grammatical interpretation the lower; but the grammatical also discovers very much which is unconscious to the writer himself, and therefore leads to the highest understanding, as technical interpretation often has to do with objects which are only worth a lower understanding.

19. Both sides are not in equilibrium in relation to every object.

In everything which is only meant to reproduce perception the utterer diminishes in importance; in everything which reproduces feeling or which shows itself as the will of the utterer it comes to the fore. In the highest objects, philosophy and literature, both are in equilibrium, for in both there is the highest subjectivity and the highest objectivity.

20. In every case, though, one must intend to develop each to the point where it is as if the other were lacking.

The grammatical side, as if one knew nothing of the utterer or had first to get to know him from this side; the technical, as if one first should get to know the language from the given utterance by dint of the certainty of this side.

21. Understanding is twofold in both, qualitatively and quantitatively.

1. Make word and thing, utterance and thought correspond correctly to each other;

2. establish the currency and the content correctly, not take a minor issue for the main issue, significant for insignificant, higher for lower, and vice versa. – This is therefore the main division for both sides.

23. Whence, *first of all*, no given utterance is to be understood via itself alone.

For the knowledge of the writer which must come to the aid of grammatical interpretation must come from somewhere else. The knowledge of

---

[a] *Realgrund.*

the object which must come to the aid of the technical must come from somewhere else.

24. Every utterance or text is only to be understood in a larger context.

1. Either I am involved in the study of the writer and already bring knowledge of him with me; or I am involved in the study of the object and already know it so well that I can take up the understanding of a particular representation.

2. If I first come to someone who is speaking I find him in certain circumstances. If I come to a writer in the right way I find him where he separates himself from the mass in certain respects. In the same way, when I first come to an object I must begin with what is intended as the information required for initial acquaintance with it, or I must grasp it where it first develops, i.e. separates itself as its own sphere from a larger sphere; in the way that philosophy develops from literature, and the other kinds of literature from epic.

3. Where only one of the two takes place, the other must be added.

25. There is no proper understanding apart from in the progress of a thorough study.

Every thorough study is historical and begins at the beginning. All inadequate understanding has its basis in the lack of thorough study. Where one now goes to work in this way, one must know that one only understands partially and incompletely.

26. Where the historical sequence is interrupted, the gap must be filled in another manner.

This is, as an example, the real purpose of all introductions to the New Testament. Unfavourable preponderance of the critical part, with neglect of the hermeneutic part. The purpose ought to be to present, to the greatest possible extent, the world from which the N.T. immediately arose. Everyone will feel the difference that it makes whether he only gets this knowledge occasionally in relation to isolated passages, or whether he gets it beforehand, and with it a total view.

27. Whence, *secondly*, the understanding of the whole is not only conditioned by that of the particular, but also, vice versa, that of the particular by that of the whole.

For if the particular is to be understood as a member of the sequence, the exponent,[b] the tendency, the manner of the whole must be known; and if

---

[b] *Exponent*, in the mathematical sense of that which determines a sequence of numbers.

[it is to be known as] a product of language, then it must already be known what linguistic usage one is actually concerned with.

28. The whole is provisionally to be understood as an individual of a genus, and the intuition of the genus, i.e. the formal understanding of the whole, must precede the material understanding of the particular.

One can admittedly also only come in the first place to the knowledge of a genus via knowledge of an individual case which belongs under it; but then [one] also [comes] historically [to that knowledge] via knowledge of the earliest genera,[c] and in these one also sees the genus arise as a new genus from a familiar older sphere. Arbitrary products never become genera and are always only to be understood from a subordinate point of view.

29. The whole is even materially to be provisionally understood as a sketch.

This is only in terms of the present presuppositions. In living speech, the less experienced the listeners are, the speaker must all the more bring about this overview himself, and the less he is able to do so, he must speak all the more in such a way that everything remains in the memory, and later understanding is made easier. – Sermons. Speeches before a court.

In written discourse this is the cursory reading. First requirement.

30. Understanding results when both operations complete each other, the image of the whole becomes more complete via the understanding of the particular, and the particular is more and more completely understood the more one gets an overall view of the whole.

This as well proves that understanding is art. If one were only allowed to string the particulars together, then it would be a mechanical operation. But experiment shows that one does not get far with this, but must continually slip back to what came earlier.

The grammatical side of interpretation

1. It is most obvious to us that we should begin with this side.

The language is what mediates sensuously and externally between utterer and listener. On its own the technical side can only take up the analogy [of the sensuous outer world] in the inner process of thought, thus only non-sensuously and internally.

2. The task is to understand the sense of an utterance from out of the language.

---

[c] *aber dann auch historisch der frühsten:* the sense is not clear, and I have had to 'divine' it.

Laws of the language and content of their parts must be given. What is being sought is the same thing in the [inner] thought which the utterer wanted to express.

3. Two elements are to be distinguished in the language, the material and the formal.

The words and the connections. The individual sound elements do not concern us, because they are not to be regarded as significant.

4. If explication is to be a separate art, the elements of the language must in themselves be indeterminate as to their significance.

If one could only think one thing in relation to every word and formulation nothing more would be necessary than to know the elements; there would only be grammar.

5. Explication always consists in determining the grammatically indeterminate via the grammatically determinate.

This explanation is the same for the most opposed members of the changing relationship (See Introduction 5, 6). For in that case the more the utterance is the object of explication, the more the utterer himself forms language (Introduction 15.2), so explication is continuing understanding of language. The principles must therefore be the same for every degree of presupposed knowledge of the language. Much is to be learned from the hermeneutic operation of children. Gradual progress is here also a natural condition.

6. The elements of the language cannot be completely indeterminate, but also not completely determinate.

1. Otherwise the language itself would be neither totality nor unity, [there could be] neither acquisition nor certainty of use for the incessant demands of scientific striving.

2. The latter point is immediately apparent from experience. Even where the elements of the language are explained from within the language, each element shows itself as a multiplicity.

7. For every element one has to distinguish the multiplicity of use and the unity of the meaning.

The real occurrence of the words is different in most cases; the sense is determined and affected by the context. But there is a sphere of the word where all those occurrences, albeit in differing manners, must be included.

8. Every individual occurrence of an element is one of the multiplicities of use; the unity of the meaning appears nowhere in an individual case.

The unity is really the idea of the word, the occurrences are its appearances.[2] The latter are always affected by the context; in them something is always posited via other words, or the whole sphere of the element is limited to a smaller sphere.

9. This is as much valid for the formal elements of the language as it is for the material elements.

The opposition between the two is mediated by the particles, which belong to the formal elements in terms of their content, to the material in terms of their form. Between them and the real words stand other parts of speech which are close to the particles, like pronouns and many adjectives; and these are, in turn, close to the mere form because the form partly follows them of necessity and is also partly synonymous with them.

10. The unity of a material element is a schema of an intuition[d] which can be further determined, that of a formal element a schema of a way of relating.

This view is opposed to the usual view, according to which every real word originally means a determinate sensuous thing, and all other meanings are supposed to be inferred or translated from this meaning. This inference and translation would, though, then be a completely arbitrary and inexplicable operation.

11. The multiplicity of use generally rests on the fact that the same schema can occur in completely different spheres.

Opposition of space and time (form to be imagined via movement), outer and inner (speaking and thinking, desiring and grasping equated), theoretical and practical (believing[e] and deciding), ideal and real (knowledge and operation of the senses) [there is a brief gap in the manuscript here].

12. Every element does not occur straight away in all its different meanings.

Because the language does not always immediately become aware in all cases of the identity of the schema. All the cases also belong here in which one can demonstrate a specific sensuous use as the first use for a word which thereafter occurs in real situations. The schema contained therein stands out more and more emphatically, becomes predominant, and the individual case only retains the value of an example of the schema.

---

[2] *Translator's note*: Schleiermacher clearly means this in the Platonic sense of the difference between the 'form' of the thing and its manifestation in the empirical world.

[d] *Schema einer Anschauung.*   [e] *Meinen.*

13. If the manner of combination takes another direction a word must either become obsolete or the schema must shift somewhat.

E.g. *Fremdling* (alien) and *Feindseligkeit* (enmity) can as effective cause and inner effect have been bound together in one word. If the two become separate the word must become obsolete or it can now only mean one of the two.

14. Many things come into the language of the lesser people by mistaken application.

This is really, if it becomes established before it is properly recognised, the domain of *usus tyrannus* [habit is a tyrant]. Countering this from above then remains an act of daring. To declare something particular to be just common usage is over-hasty, until one can show the basis of its origin.

15. The sense of a single element is therefore not clear in itself in any utterance, and grammatical interpretation is a real task.

For even if the inner essence of a word is known, but never itself appears, then the relationship of the real occurrence to the inner essence must always first be established. But it must be able to be recognised from the context because this determines the sphere in which the word actually plays.

16. What is to be determined every time is a single manner of use, this must be brought back to a unity which is therefore presupposed as known. But we can only gradually arrive at the knowledge of the inner unity via the understanding of individual utterances, therefore the art of explication is also presupposed if the inner unity is to be found.

The difficulty already touched on above (see Intro. 6). It is resolved via the relationship of the utterer to language remarked on above (Intro. 15). Every understanding of an utterance is a continuing understanding of the language. Understanding a language means knowing the unity of the words. So both are one and the same operation.

17. One can only be sure that one has found the inner unity if one can collect the totality of all manners of use. But this is never completed; the task is therefore strictly infinite and can only be accomplished by approximation.

The first parts of this approximation are therefore subject to the same laws as the last parts and the procedure must essentially be the same.

Much is therefore to be learned for hermeneutics from the procedures of childhood.

But precisely because understanding is a sequence one can only ever come to the next member via the preceding one, and true understanding is only possible in a step by step progression.

18. Every individual element in any discourse gives a direction towards a multiplicity.

Because there is a multiplicity of manners of use for every element which immediately accrue to the word.

19. The understanding of the individual element is therefore conditioned by the understanding of the whole.

According to Introduction 27 this is therefore also particularly the case for the grammatical side.

20. The whole for an individual element is first of all the whole utterance, then the single organic part in which it directly occurs. *Canon*: what is grammatically indeterminate in the individual elements must be determined via the context.

For this lies in the descent from the whole through the individual organic parts to the element, and vice versa. The determination must begin with the whole, as that which is most opposed to the element, because help [for interpretation] is precisely supposed to lie in opposition.

21. The general idea of the whole already limits the multiplicity of the individual parts by incorporating them into a specific genus.

For both material and formal elements have a different sphere in poetry and in prose, in scientific and popular presentations.

22. Then also via the fact that it [the general idea] locates it in a certain period of the language.

Already according to 12. One can, particularly in a language which becomes fully developed in a living manner, assume three periods:

1. the pre-scientific, where not all oppositions are yet developed, so that licence and imprecision dominate, significance is not yet exhausted; among the Greeks until Socrates, because of the constitution of philosophy.

2. real flowering. Proof: philosophy and art next to each other. Greeks until the Macedonians.

3. Artifice, deformation,[f] leaning towards what is alien.

The difference of the large periods also recurs in every single period in smaller forms, and at all times individual areas bear the characteristics of individual periods. – For each of these cases the element gets its own sphere of significance.

23. Complete determinacy can only grow from the smaller whole in which the element immediately occurs.

---

[f] *Verbildung.*

236

For here the more precise limitations must first be added, and here is where the different hermeneutic operations first meet.

A. Determination of the material elements

24. The multiplicity (§18) is more determinate, even if perhaps more comprehensive if the idea of the essence of the word is already complete.

Because the multiplicity is then enclosed within the limits of a fairly determinate schema.

25. It is more indeterminate, but perhaps less comprehensive if one only has a small number of manners of use.

Because one then feels the lack of knowledge of the word more strongly, but does not yet know in what directions one has to seek other manners of use.

26. The less particular manners of use one has collected, the less one may easily move away from the already familiar manners of use. The more certain one already is of the schema the more easily one may assume what can be subsumed under it.

In relation to 1. Namely because one is forced into indeterminacy by unfamiliarity with the schema. The context must therefore then be very powerful, or one must employ external help. Both are usually the case when learning one's mother tongue and are therefore also to be imitated in the learning of foreign languages. Danger of a premature use of dictionaries if one does not yet know how to find the principle of relationship or does not know how to separate the spheres.

The 'less' [i.e. in relation to 'particular manners of use'] is not to be understood in terms of a number, but in terms of difference. Less manners of use from opposed spheres are more likely to lead to the true schema than several from the same sphere.

The correct model of external help for beginners are indices, which must be worked out in this manner.

In relation to 2. Occasionally one can establish with the greatest of certainty a still unknown manner of use from a single passage. But the less one knows the schema the more one must be careful with rare manners of use. – Common beginners' mistake in interpretation.

The former progression, in which one only gradually lets oneself be given individual manners of use, is the purely empirical progression. The latter, in which one derives new manners of use from the schema, is the constructive progression, the automatic filling in of the gradual extension of language. One sees how each is determined by the other, but [also] how the first beginning of the empirical in childhood already leads to the constructive.

27. The supplements of one's own experience, in order to come as close as possible to the completeness of the manners of use, are the dictionaries.

They either begin themselves with the empirical view, as a collection of usages, or they wish to be constructive. Usually only as in the note on 10 [on word and thing]. One must in using them put everything that is a judgement to one side if possible, and do the constructing oneself.

One must also at least be able to learn from them which use flowed from which spheres.

28. The idea of the whole limits the multiplicity of the particulars even as a sketched overview, to the extent to which it determines an object.

Of course in this case those elements which immediately designate the main object are assumed to be familiar (following Intro. 24), via these a determinate sphere is then drawn into which everything must fit.

29. A word which appears as subject can be determined in this way if its sentence deals with a part of the object itself.

For it must then belong in a relationship with the familiar main elements.

30. If a sentence does not deal with such a part, only the predicate therein is determinable in that manner.

For only this can then contain the reason why it [the sentence] became part of the presentation.

31. The idea of the whole has an influence on the determination of an element, to the extent to which it depends on the relationship of the musical to the grammatical element.

The language as a totality of tones is a musical system. The musical element also has an effect in every utterance, and as this effectiveness has a different basis from that of the significant, they can come into conflict with each other.

The musical in language has its effect in part immediately upon feelings, in part also by imprinting itself on the memory. Therefore the more the speaker wants to affect feelings, or is compelled to turn to memory, the more he will get into the situation of sacrificing grammatical precision to musical power. The genre must therefore determine where, if music becomes prominent, such a deviation is to be assumed and where not.

For the prosaic side the type where music becomes prominent is the saying, the type where music recedes into the background is the mathematical formula. In more elevated didactic lectures the musical must only be play and must never damage grammatical precision.

32. Every proposition originally consists of two elements, subject and predicate.

That is Plato's theory and certainly that of the earlier [philosophers]. Aristotle was the first to have invented the copula. In intuition the connection of the two elements is not mediated, but immediate. Only the verb is the simple form of the predicate. Adjectives are only derived from verbs and after this derivation a mere form of the verb (copulative being)[3] is left as a *caput mortuum* (death's head). Many original verbs get lost in this way. It is a mistake to dissolve the verb into a participle with 'to be'.

33. The subject must receive its final determinacy via the predicate and the predicate via the subject.

For after their spheres are already more narrowly limited it becomes clear that only that part of the one is valid which can at the same time be part of the other.

34. Every extended sentence must be treated in the same way.

In an extended sentence the two main sections are either broken up into several parts, or are more precisely developed by secondary determinations.

If the sphere of one section breaks up into several small spheres then it is all the easier to compare these with each other because they must, of course, be related to each other.

Secondary determinations can be resolved into clauses in which they are the predicate and therefore offer several other aids, so that what is more complex is again also advantageous.

35. Every compound sentence must be resolved into a simple one.

In all periods which are a true unity this is admittedly difficult, but always possible, and a thorough understanding is not possible without this.

36. Predicate and subject of the sentence are then also to be determined from the predicate and the subject of the opposition.

Both [are] to be understood within the complete sense of the extended sentence.

In the compound sentence the form of opposition everywhere dominates, its compass extends from parallelism, where the second clause is just an echo of the first and the opposition is only spatial, to the strictly logical,

---

[3] *Translator's note*: The 'is' in, for example, 'x is running', which without 'x' and the participle 'running' can be seen as a merely formal connecting word, a '*caput mortuum*'.

and from the partial (subject with opposed predicate and predicate with opposed subject) to the total.

Attention is also to be paid here to differences of genre, as it is to difference of the language. In modern languages [there is] not such a great role for opposition as in ancient languages.

37. The rules just given are not just isolated fragments.

Only when taken together do they take the place of the rule (33) referring to the simple sentence and therefore form a whole in themselves.

When they are applied they presuppose the understanding of the formal element, because only thereby can the sections of the extended sentence be correctly distributed and the compound sentence be correctly resolved, and the task is therefore in fact only to be accomplished by approximation.

Furthermore, the judgement of which of several individual sections or parts is the most strict depends in part on inductions concerning the formal aspect, in part on the hermeneutic feeling for art.[g]

38. The determinacy which emerges from this is only sufficient in the case of faultless composition.

The utterer rarely puts himself completely in the place of the listener, least of all of the listener who is not immediately there; instead he believes a lot of things ought to be clear to the listener as well which are only clear to him. Of the two forms of what is imperfect, ambiguity and indeterminacy, the former is more attached to the formal element, the latter to the material. For ambiguity can only be attached to a word to the extent to which one wavers between two opposed manners of use (11), which is no longer possible after the application of the instructions provided.

39. If indeterminacy remains one must seek means of explanation outside the sentence whose section is the element.

Indeterminacy is attached to the word if there is still a wavering between general and particular, if one does not know whether the utterer had the whole individual sphere or only a part thereof in mind, or if one does not know whether he did not use a general word because he really only wanted to designate some individual cases.

40. Even if the listener does not arrive via step by step progression at understanding, the immediate context can be insufficient for him.

This case is very widespread both in foreign languages and one's own language. We arrive nearly everywhere via a leap.

---

[g] *von dem hermeneutischen Kunstgefühl*, i.e. on what is not given by the rules.

41. The more that which cannot be understood particularly belongs to the specific utterance, the more one must also only seek the means of explanation in its compass.

Because then a usage that is particularly determined by the context is to be presupposed.

42. Canon for this case: the closer the means of explanation are to the passage to be explained, the more sure the help it can offer.

Proximity is not to be understood mechanically. The rule that a word in the same sequence of thoughts may only be taken in one single meaning is subject to a thousand exceptions, and is very restricted.

43. In the same way as the period is to be reduced to the single clause, every complete utterance is to be reduced to the period. Passages that correspond to each other in this way according to the whole structure of the utterance are, of course, parallel passages.

The difference between the freest and the most strict composition in fact only constitutes a relative opposition. An analogy of rhythmic structure is in every whole which does not come completely within the limits of conversation.[4]

44. Parallel passages are of two kinds, word-parallels and thought-parallels.

1. Where the same word occurs in other surroundings via which it can be understood, and in such a way that the parallelism either makes the identity of meaning necessary or makes a specific analogy necessary.

2. Where the difficult word does not occur at all, but where the thought is recognised via the parallelism of thought as the same or as analogous in a specific manner.

45. In order to determine it correctly one must distinguish whether what is to be explained belongs to the subject or to the predicate of the whole utterance.

For the arrangement of the way the object comes apart is different from how the result is gradually produced.[h]

---

[4] *Translator's note*: The sense of this last sentence is rather obscure, though it would seem to have something to do with the way in which the musical element is not directly part of the semantic aspect of language, but can still influence what an utterance means, in the same way as what is *not* said in a conversation may still play a role in its meaning.

[h] *Denn anders ist die Anordnung wie der Gegenstand zerfällt, und anders, wie das Resultat allmählig produ-cirt wird*: the sense is not clear, but probably has something to do with the difference between the way something is constituted that becomes apparent in interpreting it, and the way we actually arrive at our knowledge of that constitution.

46. Greater or lesser certainty arises from the difference of the genres and from the completeness of the writers.

1. Even the freest composition which as a whole is not even in stanzas has something cyclical, via which a sequence of relationships is formed.

2. The less a writer follows the rules of composition the less he can be relied on.

47. The less that which cannot be understood belongs to the particular utterance the more one is driven beyond the utterance in the search for means of explanation.

For the basis of incomprehensibility then lies in a greater area and must be extracted from this area. – General sign of this: the same thing I do not understand could also have occurred for me somewhere else than here.

48. What is introduced into an utterance from an extraneous area can be explained via all utterances whose main object is this area.

That is an intermediate case. The incomprehensibility can here be attributed to the writer, also to the reader.

49. What belongs to the essential aspect of the utterance can also, if it is objectively incomprehensible, be explained via all utterances which belong to the same area.

1. Here the presupposition is already that the incomprehensibility is to be attributed to the reader.

2. The maxim of the explanation remains the same, for all these form, so to speak, One λογοσ.

50. All writers are to be thought of in relation to this parallelism as One writer that is dealing with the same object [the sentence is ungrammatical, in that 'dealing' is used in the plural to refer to writers, rather than the One writer].

[This is the] Canon for scientific incomprehensibility. One must, though, not go beyond its limits and apply it to purely philological incomprehensibility.

General schema [for this is] philosophy. Everything in each nation forms One knowledge,[i] but [it is] enlivened by a large amount of individuality and relative oppositions.

The more a writer has to say and is hard to understand, the more this canon may only be the supplement of the previous canons.

51. Only those writers are really One who have the same type of treatment.

[i] *Bildung.*

1. The concept of the school in the schema of philosophy.

2. The more diversely an object has been treated the more the preceding canon [50] must be limited by this one, and the smaller unit must take precedence.

52. Only those writers are to be seen as One who have treated the object in One period of language.

This relates in part to the main periods of language in general (transition from poetry to prose, from unity[j] into oppositions), in part to the periods of every technical language area in particular.

53. All writers are to be seen as One who belong in One genre of those genres which fall more into the domain of art.

Canon for poetry, history and rhetoric.

The connecting unit is in part the mythical and gnomic cycle, in part the same proportion of the musical aspect of language.

54. Even here subordinate kinds and periods are to be distinguished.

The periods are not strictly chronological, instead the recurrent imitative writers are to be counted with the original writers. – Alexandrine poets and Homer.

55. Both views unite if one initially begins for safety's sake with the smaller unit and moves to the rest only because something is missing, and if one tries to distinguish what belongs in the domain of each unit.

The latter aspect again presupposes precise knowledge of the matter in question, which can only be gained hermeneutically, thus the old cycle with its explication.

56. That which cannot be understood in an utterance taken purely as language can be explained via everything which belongs in the same language area.

General way of identifying this is feeling: the same thing one cannot understand could have occurred elsewhere. Further, guessing of the sense from the context, which is, though, subject to grammatical reservations, and which therefore demands grammatical confirmation.

Here the incomprehensibility is obviously attributable to the reader, except in relation to completely uneducated writers.

57. Even here the same proviso is valid with regard to the larger and smaller unit.

The smallest unit is personal usage; the largest is the overall period of language or the dialect. One-sidedness if one gives too much space to either.

---

[j] *Ungeschiedenheit.*

The rule is also valid here that every writer is his own best explicator, i.e. one must begin by searching for parallels in the writer himself. The domain of the larger units can then be most certainly constructed via this search – the most fertile example is Greek. Even here the parallels should not always be literal, instead one should gradually construct an analogy for oneself.

B. Determination of the formal elements

(Note: almost with regard to all hermeneutic relationships, as opposed to the material element.)

58. In relation to the formal element it is much more difficult to reach the unity of the schema.

Almost the only exception are the persons of the verb, but these contain the disguised subject. – Case, prepositions, tenses, modes, are almost in every case very difficult to find out even from the greatest multiplicity of manners of use.

59. For this reason one may not depart at all from what can be strictly grammatically proved by being led by conjectures from the context. (Cf. 9 and 26.)

This is almost the main characteristic by which philological reading is distinguished from unphilological reading. Main source of lack of thoroughness.

60. The observations of the grammarians are what comes to the aid of one's own experience, but they must themselves first be hermeneutically constituted.[k]

Much over-hastiness: in relation to a clause whose sense is clear one puts something into a formal element which belongs to another element. Whence [there should] never [be] untested use in cases which are at all difficult.

61. The simple clause has only One formal element, namely the manner in which the predicate-word, the verb, is related to the subject-word, the noun.

1. Here only mode and tense are to be thought about. Number and person are only the non-expressed subject or what corresponds to the one which is expressed. (On the clause [formed?] by an impersonal verb.)

[k] *gebildet.*

244

2. The nominative, as the only natural thing in a simple clause, is not to be regarded as a case, and therefore only presents an apparent duplication. The article is actually only formed by analogy with the verbal article because of this apparent duplication, or just belongs to the duplication of gender.

62. Extended and periodic clauses cannot therefore be reduced to the simple clause, even in relation to the formal element.

For the formal element is not extended like the material element from inside to outside, but is rather multiplied from the outside.

It is rather the case that the material reduction already presupposes the understanding of all the formal elements.

63. The additional elements therefore partly designate the relationship of the more precise determinations to subject and predicate, and partly designate the relationship of the corresponding clauses to each other, and of the subordinate clauses to the whole.

To the extent that the whole utterance must be regarded as reducible to the simple clause, the element which links the larger clauses also belongs here, as these are similarly co-ordinated and subordinated.

64. Where difficulties arise for the qualified listener without fault of the utterer, one does not at all provisionally depend for the means of explanation on the context of the utterance.

For nothing that particularly belongs to the specific utterance is to be sought in the formal element, and precisely for this reason the utterer cannot in this respect as well determine the sphere in an individual manner. In the same way as it is in itself the more wavering element, it is, on the other hand, that which allows the least freedom for the individual.

65. The area of parallels is the analogy of the whole language, limited according to its dialects, periods, and genres of verbal presentation.

1. The limitation is admittedly itself in turn limited, for there is much which goes through the whole language without any difference.

2. One can divide all languages into 3 classes, a) Those which present a pure unity of forms, so that one can just as easily see the languages themselves as a greater unit, as their own language, and as smaller units, as dialect, but dialect which has remained unmixed as part of a greater unit.[1] b) Those which, having emerged from a mixture of several smaller roots, manifest themselves for a time as a chaos of multiple equally valid forms, and only then gradually develop determinacy. Schema: Greek (originally

---

[1] *als kleinere, Dialect, aber unvermischt geblieben unter einer grösseren*: the sense of this sentence is not wholly clear, though it becomes somewhat clearer via what follows.

from Hellenic and Pelasgic, perhaps even more composite than this. Three periods are to be distinguished here, the chaotic period, the period of transitions, and the mature period. c) Those which only emerged after they also took up languages of a foreign root into themselves. Schema: German (here the periodic division disappears more into that of certain writers who seek to develop the determinacy [of the language], and others who just follow custom and the common ear).

3. Extremes of the genres are didactic and lyrical. In the former the sense of the formal element must be most precisely determinable, in the latter it becomes relatively vague. In the former the oppositions of meaning (11) in question here are kept strictly apart, in the latter they flow into one another.

66. In the difficult part of the formal element one must regard particles and inflections only as One whole, and deal with analogy via this whole.

The larger units are hard to determine as such, e.g. επι [to] and προσ [from], or subjunctive. Frequent errors via the fact that one found the schemata for these too early. The correct maxim is therefore provisionally to make the wholes as small as the nature of the language allows. But this is more or less the case in every language.

67. Peculiarities of individual writers in the formal use of elements are usually defects.

Because clear consciousness is lacking and spontaneity is only subordinate, one easily becomes habituated to something. Or one follows, in the way children do, an analogy which imposes itself as a strict analogy and yet is not the correct analogy. The extent to which one may form language in this area. (Cf. 14.)

The difference between classical and non-classical writers rests largely upon this habituation, and out of this difference the genius of language speaks purely as instinct, even if it has no clear consciousness of the fact [again the sense is not wholly clear, but seems to have to do with the way in which non-classical writers' unconsciously breaking the rules can produce new meaning].

68. Even the best writers are not able to avoid hermeneutic difficulties.

Ambiguity is the dominant aspect here, as indeterminacy is in the material element.

Causes are 1. grammatical homonyms, more or less in every language; 2. that one cannot decide whether a connecting particle affects a subordinate part or a larger whole.

The more the writer is in the state of inspiration, the more easily he can mistake subjective clarity for objective. Superficially elegant writers without any real content gain an illusory classicism via this ease. Critical readers find this difficulty more often, others often happily read over it.

The freer the structure, the more the difficulties accumulate.

69. For these difficulties the only way out lies in the context.

One must, of course, not think of parallels here. The way out lies partly in the combined grammatical understanding of the whole, partly in the results of technical interpretation.

70. One must put together all the possibilities of relationships and not rest until predominant case of one relationship shows itself as united with the greatest improbability of all the others.

Otherwise the feeling of uncertainty remains. – Knowledge of the train of thoughts must do a great deal. The less technical interpretation can be developed, the more difficult it remains.

71. The difference between more free and more bound structure which is inherent in the languages themselves has only a limited influence in this.

For the freer the structure the less grammatical homonymy and vice versa.

72. But the more bound the genre of utterance and the less imperfect the writer, the more certain the decision.

For the greater probability always rests with the fact that in the rest of the possible cases the expression would be more imprecise.

C. On the quantitative understanding of both elements

Note. Follows on from Introduction 21. The difficulty rests on occurrences in the history of the language which must be elucidated.

73. In all so-called synonyms it is possible to understand too much or too little.

Too much if one accentuates the difference between the one and the other where the writer neglects it, too little in the opposite case.

Elucidation of synonyms. The 'all' depends on the proposition that there are no strict synonyms; 1. that one and the same schema is not expressed by two signs in one and the same language is just as necessary a principle as that two schemata are not the basis of one and the same word. One could not find a principle for the opposite of this.

2. If a language has arisen from a multiplicity of dialects it would seem that several signs would have to come together for the same schema. But then, on the one hand, the common unity of the schema will be divided and a particular determinacy of every sign for a certain sphere develops, on the other, every dialect, like every language, has its own manner of intuition, so even at the beginning the schemata are already not the same.

3. The usual coming into being of synonyms is that they originally begin with completely different relations, but often coincide on the same empirical object, and thereby finally become confused, admittedly always in a more or less indeterminate usage. They resemble circles whose centres are less distant than the sum of their radii. The external part of their sphere therefore coincides, while the inner part remains separate.

74. One understands the relationship of synonyms to one another if one compares the cases where they can be substituted for one another with those where they cannot.

Then the hidden difference must also be discovered in the former cases and what is superficial in the confusion must come to light. The only systematic procedure is to follow these lines of the different usages beginning with the common sphere until the end of every circle, and then from this to construct the centre of every circle.

75. Strictness of usage must be presupposed in the inner part of every didactic presentation.

All the more so the more everything must be constructed, each word related to something internal. Where everything is internal the strictness must therefore be everywhere, as it is in Aristotle. But one may not make this separation in relation to the external, even if it is also materially related to the internal, as it often is in Plato.

76. The less technical the character of the utterance, the more one assumes the difference [of internal and external] is not being taken into account.

Thus in the case of everything which occurs as mere addition, or which basically belongs to the sphere of everyday life, where one is satisfied with a merely empirical designation.

77. To the extent to which the musical element predominates it is also possible that the less adequate word is even consciously chosen.

Because then the rhythmic effect is often of greater significance than a small advantage in the precision of the expression.

78. The application of these rules is modified by the knowledge of the excellence of the writer.

Even in the most free area of poetry the good writer only uses this freedom where the reason for the musical usage is evident and the context gives clear indications. The mediocre writer is always inclined to extend the limits.

79. *Second Case*.[5] In relation to all words which permit a more and a less, which involve a certain intensity, it is also possible to read too much or too little into them.

Elucidation. Almost all words which do not express any substantial forms more or less belong here. In some way they can be all subsumed under the idea of an activity. (Verbs are closest to this, then adverbs, adjectives, and finally the nouns derived from adjectives.)

Every such word belongs to a sequence whose members restrict certain transitions or degrees of intensity. The value of the members in this sequence fluctuates, because from time to time some of them die out as too weak or as common and inferior. Examples: primarily expressions of politeness and poetic expressions. But the cause of the fluctuation is not always corruption.

Normally only what belongs to emphasis is dealt with here. But this is only a stress given to a word for a particular occasion, not what fluctuates in the natural value.

80. One must have an idea of the average intensity-value of a word and therefore have its whole sequence in mind.

But the average value is different in different periods of the language, even in different genres of utterance.

81. Every direct particular usage relates to the average value either as a being-elevated to the higher level or as a letting-down to the lower.

One can divide the writers of every period and genre themselves into those for whom the one [i.e. elevating or lowering] is maxim and praxis and those for whom it is the other. – Overall moderation is the elevating principle for the particular, overall lack of moderation is the lowering principle.

82. Besides there is an indirect usage which brings the highest immediately next to the lowest, and vice versa.

The lowest expressed in a negative manner is often the greatest intensification; this is almost the rule among the Greeks. The highest can be ironically equated with the lowest. We Germans are generally reckoned to be particularly incapable of understanding the latter, and there must be something in this.

[5] *Translator's note*: The First Case is not specified, though it is probably § 73.

83. Everything particular can only be definitely recognised by the accentuation.

Feeling this correctly demands practice in hermeneutics, beginning with inversion as the most easily registered and coarsest means, and going as far as the most subtle rhythmic and musical relationships. – In our language the rhythmic is particularly intended to designate the intensity of the expression. One sees this, for example, in the comic effects which immediately result if one treats the expression in the opposite manner.

84. What emerges from the recurrence of the same schema with different potentials belongs in common to this and to the preceding case.

Elucidation. Potentials of the power of nature, of life, of consciousness.[6] As these potentials are only gradually being discovered, the same expressions are then used for them in a promiscuous manner. Fixed determinations can only very gradually develop, though not everywhere, and they remain valid for those who occupy the viewpoint from which they can all be surveyed. Misunderstanding in the domain of philosophy largely has its basis in this fact. Here it all depends on correctly grasping the dominant ideas via the context of the whole, on not being led astray by the identity of the sound [hence the recurrence of the same schema].

85. *Third Case.* It can be dubious whether secondary ideas that are produced are intended or not, and one can then either take out too little or read in too much.

Elucidation. Every word is admittedly connected to a unity of what is thought, but the fact is that, according to the normal laws of combination, it can awaken ideas via memory which do not belong in that unity. Every time we listen and read we are full of such ideas. Most of them can be recognised as merely a result of our subjectivity; these are not what is at issue here, they must just be got rid of. In the case of others one admittedly has cause to think the writer had them as well, but it remains uncertain whether they were also the kind of ideas which he gets rid of, or whether he intentionally wove them into the utterance.

86. Secondary ideas which emerge of their own accord from the common subjective domain of the writer and the reader should only be regarded as

---

[6] *Translator's note*: the notion of 'potentials', which has Aristotelian and Thomist roots, almost certainly refers to Schelling's *Naturphilosophie*, which explained the development of mind out of material nature in terms of an ascending series of potentials that are generated by the fact that everything particular in nature has an internal contradiction, which forces it beyond itself.

intended if one can demonstrate that there is a particular invitation to do so, and if they bring about a particular effect.

For if the writer wants the secondary ideas then he also wants to be sure, and must do something for the people who could be less inclined to find them themselves. But given that he must actually try to counteract all ideas which insinuate themselves as distractions, he can only want them in order to achieve something specific.

87. To the intended secondary ideas belongs first of all the figurative expression, which, besides the general similarity, is also intended to transfer a particular characteristic from one object to the other.

Elucidation. According to 11, 12 above, we attribute much to the literal expression which is figurative to other people. But precisely because we maintain that in *coma arborum*[7] hair should really be imagined, at the same time foliage is really intended to be thought via an unfamiliar schema, and all characteristics of this schema are intended to be applied to it, therefore not just the growth of extremities, but also lushness, adornment, etc.

88. The power of the figurative expression diminishes via habituation and via this the ideas of the reader and the writer can become different.

1. e.g. when they think of '*Augenweide*' ['treat for the eyes', literally 'pasture for the eyes'] nobody thinks of the original idea, but the secondary ideas have all disappeared, and only the general similarity is left. This gradually happens through use, partly when the utterer uses the expression where the secondary ideas do not belong, partly when the listeners overlook it, so that in this everything applies that was said above about the reduction in the force of strong expressions.

2. If, then, the expression is still new for the listener, but old for the utterer, then the former will read more into it than the latter wishes. But the opposite can also occur, namely that the image has already become old for the later listener and he therefore reads less into it than is actually there. A difference in the effect can also arise via the way a nation thinks, because what appears hard and forced to one person is natural to another. Here, then, correct understanding of the particular can only be produced via familiarity with the whole manner of thought. – Twofold false procedure in orientalism. – Even the habituation to the affectations of later writers, who use images just as *flores orationis*, makes the understanding of those writers for whom they really arise in a natural manner more difficult.

---

[7] *Translator's note*: see § 7 of 'Grammatical Explication' in *Hermeneutics and Criticism*.

89. In order to assess figurative expressions correctly one must bear in mind the whole sequence of changes in the area in question and thus also the character of the writer.

The former in order correctly to judge the average value of the expression at the time of each particular use (cf. 80), the latter in order to know whether it belongs to the elevating or lowering usage (81), and whether it belongs to the affected or natural usage (88).

90. In the particular case one must judge from this and from the contexts how much of what is meant is intended by the writer to be connected to the general similarity.

Example. If we make *Schwarm* (swarm), which for us is not a figurative expression at all, into a figurative expression by inferring it from *Bienenschwarm* (swarm of bees) then we still only understand the disordered mobile crowd; the Greeks also understand by σμηνοζ [swarm], where it is used figuratively, the desire to attack and to sting.

91. The kind of allusion also belongs here which is not just to be explained via the subjective combination of the utterer but has an objective grammatical cause.

The former [i.e. that is explained by the subjective combination] belongs to technical interpretation; grammatical interpretation on its own can only produce the intuition that there is something to be found there, but it cannot explain it.

92. Objective allusion is always hidden quotation, either of a passage or a of fact from the classical domain.

Explanation. In the same way as the secondary ideas from the figurative expression could also be put next to it and then the proper comparison arises, what is to be remembered could also be put next to it, and then it would be a complete quotation.

2. The classical domain is what the utterer can presuppose as known among all immediate listeners, like the Bible, Homer and a certain area of history.

93. Reading too much into something is only possible here by confusion of a universal with a particular or by pure fiction.

1. In the same way as the power of a figurative expression gradually gets lost, so does the power of certain allusions via too frequent repetition. Individual expressions from certain passages and memories of individual occurrences become proverbial, if, e.g. someone calls his wife his rib, it only makes the impression of a stable sphere in which such expressions can be

normal. The occurrences can even become so lost that they appear mythical, e.g. like that of the slap in the face.[m] Whoever then looks for the specific allusion in this reads too much into it.

2. The most complete schema of fiction in this sense is the Kabbala, the multiple sense. The real basis of this is the exaggerated opinion of the content of an utterance, that one looks for particular significance in everything. Nearly everybody 'kabbalises' to some extent with their favourite writer.

94. Reading too little into something is the natural thing to do because quotation is something which conceals itself.

Because everything is made for the eyes we are particularly used to the crude means of cognition, so that when these are lacking, especially among the ancients, we are only too certain to miss them [quotations]. For this reason there are here as well still so many discoveries to be made.

95. Every writer must reckon, even in his immediate circle, with those who are not so good at making connections and he must therefore point to the connections.

The hand that belongs to the finger must be somewhere. Often a single particle is a hidden formula for a quotation. But one must admittedly have first placed oneself in the same sphere as the utterer.

96. Because the classical domain of allusion is always distant in time there must also already be an indication in the language.

That is more the case in relation to the ancients than for us where the situation becomes one of the simultaneity of philosophy and history, and it is more the case in relation to quotation of texts than of direct utterances [I have 'divined' the sense here, as it is not clear in the original]. The Greek of the New Testament is too much formed in accordance with the Septuagint, and here exact familiarity must replace everything else.

97. Both the essential components of the task of grammatical interpretation and the cycle of aids are hereby exhausted.

There is nothing which is grammatically in dispute any more, except what has been examined here, and with the last part we have already approached the domain of the technical.

But because this [the technical] had to play a role everywhere, albeit from a distance, there is no correct way of exemplifying it after all than via the living examination of a totality of discourse.[n]

---

[m] *Ohrfeige*: literally 'ear-fig'.
[n] *giebt es keine rechte Exemplification als nach allem durch lebendige Betrachtung eines Ganzen der Rede*: the sense is not wholly clear.

The technical side of interpretation

1. The point of the task is to understand the particular part of a coherent utterance as belonging in the specific sequence of thoughts of the writer. Of course not only in terms of possibility, but [to understand] just as determinately in terms of this necessity [i.e. its part in the sequence] as it is known grammatically via the language.

2. As progression from one particular to another technical interpretation presupposes grammatical.

For at least two sentences must be known in order to have an element of combination, and they must therefore have been understood beforehand grammatically, with their connection.

3. The technical side is presupposed for the completion of the grammatical side.

For in order to determine what is grammatically indeterminate, knowledge of the whole, which is only present as a sequence of thoughts and can only be understood as such, is presupposed. And in the case of ambiguity the sequence of thoughts is always one of the determining factors, even in relation to details.

4. The technical operation therefore includes the whole business of explication.

I.e. the technical operation must begin together [with the grammatical] and the business of explication is not finished until the technical operation is finished. The possession of the whole spirit of the utterance is only achieved via the technical; for dealt with merely grammatically the utterance always remains just an aggregate.

5. The technical understanding of the sentences rests on the knowledge of the individuality of the utterer as their inner unity.

The general logical rules of combination are only negative, limit points beyond which nothing can be understood. Similarly, the particular technical rules for the individual genres [are] also just more restricted limit points, outside of which the work could no longer be understood in terms of the initial conception. One cannot understand via either of these kinds of rules, because combination does not take place in terms of them, as little as it does in terms of musical rules. The only positive aspect is the individual activity of the person as grasped in this particular direction.

Every completed sequence of thoughts can only be completely understood as an expression of this individual principle in a particular direction, and the recognition of the necessity of the particular part of the utterance only takes place to the extent to which one has reproduced the principle for oneself.

6. Looked at even more closely everything depends upon the individuality of the person in their thought which is immediately directed towards representation.[8]

Everything individual in the person is connected and bears a common character. But understanding and demonstrating its connection, which is everywhere to be presupposed, is the highest test of insight into individuality. One must therefore initially remain with the function[9] whose single expressions one wishes to consider, and this is here the one described. For thought without reference to representation does not belong here, because one can only infer very indirectly from the composition [i.e. the particular product being interpreted] to the meditation [i.e. the thoughts which gave rise to it]. In the same way representations of another kind, which do not begin with thinking, constitute a completely different function, which lies outside the realm of hermeneutics; e.g. when someone is at the same time a writer and a painter.

What one knows beforehand about the rest of the [person's] individuality is always usable, but primarily only materially, as a way of noting merely external circumstances in relation to what is itself to be explained.

7. This individuality we call the individuality of style.

The expression 'style' is also already habitual in other arts, in terms of the whole way in which the inner primary image of the representation gradually realises itself, and is therefore also to be used here in this higher sense. In the same way as spirit is the manner of thought, style is the manner of representation.

8. The maximum in the knowledge of individuality applied to understanding is reproduction.

Technical understanding itself is the reconstruction of what is given; if one is now completely sure about the correct use of the individual principle in doing this, then one must be able also to apply it in an analogous manner to another given. Imitation of external details is, though, just a game of fantasy.

---

[8] *Translator's note: Darstellung* means both 'presentation' and 're-presentation': Schleiermacher, like Friedrich Schlegel, does not use it in a simply mimetic sense, and it is best understood in terms of the 'articulation' of what goes on in the person whose utterance is to be understood.

[9] *Translator's note:* 'function' is explained by what follows, and refers to a kind of articulation, be it linguistic, musical or in the form of the plastic arts.

9. The style of an individual must be one and the same in all genres, modified by the character of the genre.

1. For because the individuality of style begins with inner individuality and representation via language is in fact everywhere the same function, it [the individuality of the style] must be the same.

2. On the other hand, if details in the representation also occur unchanged in different genres we criticise them as mannered, as affectedness or as bad habit,° because they cannot have the same meaning in different genres.

10. Every utterer has an individuality of style which appears everywhere. In common writing it seems to disappear, but it is the same with this as with all individuality. If one first takes what is common in large quantities it yet forms itself again into [recognisable] groups and in this way one still finds further differences. However, where they disappear to too great an extent one must admittedly rely on the next higher individuality.

11. The idiosyncrasy of style is partly idiosyncrasy of composition, partly idiosyncrasy of linguistic usage.

The former is the side which lies more on the inside, [which is the] choice and arrangement of thoughts, the latter lies more on the outside. The two [are] end-points because composition already begins with the primitive sketching out and the language already contains everything presentationalᴾ within it. But the two are not opposed, because they merge into one another, for there are thoughts which themselves belong to the expression, and on the other side there is in every significant work an endeavour to fix language in an individual manner, to form terminology which connects directly with the innermost self and is the thought most proper [to the author].

12. Knowledge of this idiosyncrasy is itself conditioned in turn by the preceding understanding of particular sequences of thoughts.

For to construct this idiosyncrasy from other expressions of individuality is even more difficult and is perhaps the final test. Even less is it the case that there always are such expressions. But there is no third alternative.

For this reason the knowledge of idiosyncrasy increases with the study of particular works, but only the first study can give the first concept of individuality. The relationship is just like the one between the basic

---

° *Verwöhnung.*

ᴾ *alles mimische:* the sense is unclear, but would seem to have to do with the external, objective nature of language as the social means of presenting thoughts.

schema of the words and the specific manner of use. For this reason a technical understanding of the particular part and knowledge of idiosyncrasy must begin with One act and then gradually mutually determine each other.

13. Provisional overview of the organisation of the whole is the first basis of both, so that even here understanding of the whole and of the particular begin at the same time.

Note. The cyclical relationship between the technical and grammatical side is broken up by this overview, for every indication of more exact grammatical determination of the elements begins here.

The idea of the whole becomes clear from the organisation, and individuality must lie in the idea, because it is the particular manner of grasping the object. On the other hand, the particular is only understood technically via the relationship to the idea of the whole, reconstruction.

But one must not regard the image which arises in this way as anything but changeable. It must first receive its confirmation by study of the particular. Success at the first attempt is the work of hermeneutic skill. One must therefore be attentive to every contradiction which is discovered as study progresses.

14. The provisional overview can only achieve its purpose if one comes to it sufficiently prepared.

Only in a coherent study (see Introduction). Without knowledge of the genre one cannot find the individuality of the particular product, and therefore one also cannot do it without knowledge of the period of the language.

15. Looked at technically every utterance consists of two elements: predominantly objective and predominantly subjective.

Even the most subjective utterance of all has an object. If it is just a question of representing a mood, an object must still be formed via which it can be represented. Even if it is originally freely created in fantasy, it still is then present as an object in the mind of the poet and holds his attention.

Now everything which relates immediately to the representation of this object, which so to speak results from it, belongs to the objective elements; everything else, via which in another way the utterer expresses himself more than the object, belongs to the subjective. But this opposition is not a strict opposition. There is nothing purely objective in discourse; there is always the view of the utterer, thus something subjective, in it. There is nothing purely subjective, for it must after all be the influence of the object which highlights precisely this aspect.

16. The overview is the highlighting of the most important objective elements in their organic relationships.

For in comparison with these elements the subjective is only a secondary issue, and the particular objective element is referred to the understanding of the particular parts. The organic relationships are the connection in which the main elements are supposed to represent the whole.

17. The reconstruction of the sequence of thoughts is determined by the general overview.

The utterer is involved in a twofold function: he is in the power of the object in the objective element, and he is outside this power, inhibiting, interrupting it in the subjective, which is the retarding principle in the presentation.[10] Reconstruction rests primarily on understanding the relationship of both functions and the way they interlock. But to that belongs first of all the general separation of their results, and then, that the person understanding should have the particular closest objective element in mind every time, in order to be able to notice the deviation.

18. The individuality of the composition is initially apparent via the general overview.

It is all the more apparent via the unity of the image: the more the objective element itself already has something subjective in it, the more it contains an individual view.

Via the organic constitution of the image: the more only the particular manner of dealing with it can contain what is individual.

Both are never completely separate from one another, but are relative to each other.

19. The more the utterance falls into the domain of theory, the more the individuality of the material treatment of language or of the use of words must already be discovered in the overview.

For the individual intuition must then already reveal itself most in the overview and can express itself all the more in an individual use of words the more clearly it begins to develop. The centre of this area is transcendental philosophy, but from there it spreads through the natural sciences to every philosophical treatment of any empirical object at all.

Individual usage must consist, in accordance with the perfection of the writer, in the words being used according to a particular analogy in a certain part of their sphere, or in objects being named according to certain

---

[10] *Translator's note*: in this passage I tend to use 'presentation' for *Darstellung* (see note 7), though at times I also use 'representation'.

relationships which are not at all taken up in the usual designation. (Examples: opposed usage concerning the electrical poles.)

The further away it is from theory, the more the individuality of the formal treatment of language can only show itself in what is of little importance for and merely coincidental to the given utterance, but which on the other hand must belong in some other theory as something individual.

20. The individuality of the formal, rhythmic usage is more apparent from the general overview if the tension is greater, and less apparent if the tension is lesser, between the objective and the subjective element.

The degree of tension rests on the one hand on the strong, always qualitative separation of the oppositions, where, e.g., the objective itself already has a great element of subjectivity, it is small: on the other hand it rests on the one element [subjective or objective] not being forced back too much. Thus where qualitatively strong objectivity comes together with a quantitative proportion of subjectivity which is also strong.

In the case of the strong tension the opposed members must also be rhythmically highlighted and thereby express the way in which they are One in the utterer.

A small amount of tension is therefore characterised by uniformity of the rhythmic treatment and individuality cannot show itself in this in such a way that it would already emerge in the overview. e.g. a) lyrical with large periods, and distichal; b) philosophical, cut up equally in the Aristotelian manner, because of wholly lacking subjectivity. On the other hand, in strong tension, Platonic individuality which is much more historical and philosophical.q The rhythm must then follow the opposition between both elements and thus already emerge in the overview.

21. As the general overview does not always achieve its final purpose, the possibility of error is present in it, which is to be avoided.

False views of texts often predominate. But once an image of the whole has arisen via the general overview one does not allow it to be spoilt for oneself by details, but instead tries to harmonise the details with the image of the whole. So the incorrectness already results from that image.

22. Objective unity is necessarily found by holding together beginning and end.

Every beginning is in a certain way an advance notice or at least gives a general direction beginning with the first point. The end need not always

---

q *Dagegen in starker Spannung platonische und viel historischer und philosophischer*; the sense is unclear.

be the literal end, for individual explanations can still come after it, so that it perhaps stands in the middle almost as a point of culmination. But the concluding pointing back to the beginning in some way or other is always decisive.

23. The objective unity is, however, not always the theme of the work.

The theme is that which the utterer wishes to bring forth in those for whom he presents, and it is rare that this is just his desire to teach them to know the objective unity. That only takes place in purely objective artistic presentation, where everything must be resumed in the object and there is no external purpose for the presentation, and in purely empirical presentation, where the presenter himself only wants to be the subordinate meaning for other people and wants to supply them with the material of experience.

Now there is admittedly no absolute object and objective unity; every object becomes something for every person and the law according to which it has developed for him therefore necessarily is included in the presentation. But if this is just the same as the object for him then object and theme coincide.

But every object can also be treated as a schema via which something else is presented. This is always in a certain sense the law of its becoming, but only to the extent to which it is particularly apparent objective unity and theme move apart. e.g. Schiller's dramatic representations as examples of his theory of the sublime etc. Many historical examples as examples of great events from small causes, or in order to give political lessons or to highlight moral truths. This even takes place in philosophical presentations; the objective unity can be a sequence of concepts or from a subordinate factual area, and the theme can be a higher intuition or a methodological law.

24. If one has not found the theme behind the object then one has a false overall impression.

The theme often hides itself intentionally, in part to avoid inconveniences and to convince all the more certainly, in part so that the presentation gains the more distinguished appearance of pure objectivity.

Error is all the more dangerous here because the relationship of the subordinate issues to the main issue cannot be recognised if one has overlooked what is most of all the main issue to the utterer.

25. Whoever is themself caught up in a special view of things is easily able to look for a particular theme where there is none, or where it is a wrong theme.

For the latter one already needs a great degree of blindness and it is almost only possible if the subjective is objectified as it is in artificial kinds of explanation. The former easily happens to purely objective representations.

There is an assumption of one's own view which comes from preference, as well as of the opposed view which comes from suspicion. The explanation must be completely false because one always carries on looking in the combination and in the subsidiary elements for what is not there.

26. Every particular theme is to be recognised in part by the way in which it dominates the subjective domain, in part by polemical relationships.

The former because if it wishes to hide itself and remove the suspicion that it has marred what is objective it must yet emerge somewhere, namely in the subjective.

The latter because every particular view is opposed to another in a hostile manner, and the more that view wants to have its effect only in an unnoticed manner, the more must happen expressly to remove the other view.

27. Individuality in the composition of a work is achieved if one recognises the subjective in the objective.

Namely the individual in the spirit, in the organisation. – If one thinks of a pure object, then it is an infinity of representability.[r] For everything, as something visible, can be looked at as One, but it is to be reproduced as something successive, as infinitely divisible. The principle, therefore, according to which some things are taken out in order to represent the whole, is a subjective principle.

However far one goes in the process of separation of both elements and with the grasping of the objective, the same is always valid.

28. The next test as to whether one has recognised it [individuality] is if one recognises it as the same in the single, organic parts of the whole as in the general overview of the whole itself.

For because every organic part, in which one of those main points which has already been found is an objective unity, is the centre, behaves in the same way, the subjective must behave in the same way in both. Where that is not the case the writer shows great imperfection and his work is just an aggregate which has been thrown together, is composed at least of heterogeneous imitations, or the reader has taken something for a main point which was not one. This danger arises particularly from large piece-like subjective aggregates, episodes, digressions, etc.

[r] *Darstellbarkeit*: i.e. of potential for 'seeing as'.

29. To recognise individuality of every kind two methods must be linked, the immediate and the comparative.

Usually one wants the latter to be sufficient; but there is really never anything there which can be immediately compared, rather everything in two works of the same kind is heterogeneous, for the organism is determined in everyone by the subjective principle. What is therefore an organic part in the one work has as its counterpart in the other only an anorganic part. So either the one is made the basis, and is left intact and the other is dismembered, or only anorganic details are compared from both.

The immediate method is the one where one seeks to recognise physiognomically the subjective principle of the work by holding the work and the pure idea of its genre against each other. For the pure idea of the genre is something purely objective in which all individuals are implicitly contained as more precise determinations.

The latter method provides a feeling which can be certain enough, but cannot be elevated to the clarity of being able to be stated. Whence the two must be combined, namely individual works looked at physiognomically are to be compared via the common idea of the genre.

30. Individuality is therefore not to be recognised without a complete study.

1. Only to the extent that one compares several works of the same kind can the knowledge of the particular work be completed.

2. If someone composes in several genres one must also compare his works in the differing genres and seek the identity of the subjective principle of the structure therein. [This is] one of the most difficult tasks, but also one of the best exercises.

31. Individuality does not just show itself in the material side of the writer's way of thinking, but also in the formal side.

Everything so far is only concerned with one side of individuality, and consideration of the objective side alone does not lead any further either. The formal side shows itself only via the relationship of the objective to the subjective.

32. The extrication of the objective elements is the basis of the reconstruction of the sequence of thoughts.

One only sees the writer to the extent that he finds himself in the power of the object (see 17). Every progression from one objective element to another is the product of this function. The function is to be thought of as the act of violence to which all interruptions from the subjective function must subordinate themselves, and which therefore determines the return from the subjective to the objective. One must therefore only think of it during the interruption as inhibited.

33. All subjective elements of discourse have their basis in the flowing individual combination which inhibits the objective process.

See §15. – The objective process is, so to speak, what is rigid, as opposed to what flows. Both are conditioned by each other. Every objective process only develops out of what flows. The first idea of every representation arises in the latter. If the objective process has been initiated, then the flowing process is subordinated. Everything which has been formed is a living unity of the two.

34. Which subjective elements occur in an utterance cannot be regarded as coincidence or as arbitrary. For then there would be no technical interpretation at all. Yet the opinion [that it is coincidence] is fairly universal. It arose via the great army of imitative and affected authors, from whose procedures a shallow theory abstracts its rules.

35. The occurrence of subjective elements is only understood to the extent to which their objectivity is recognised.

For why of all the things which are possible does precisely this occur, except because the object leads to it in accordance with the individuality of the writer.

Understanding these [subjective elements] overall means understanding the individuality of the writer in this respect; in the application to single cases it means reconstructing the sequence of ideas.

36. The first condition is the knowledge of the totality of everything that can occur in a writer as a subjective element.

Natural contrast with the objective. In the former one had first to grasp the unity, here the totality of everything diverse in order also to understand the choice as exclusion.

The *negative* side is that one should not unconsciously or indirectly think possible for him what is only possible for us, that one should not attribute our material to his. Usual mistakes. In ancient and foreign texts the subjective elements often for this reason appear hard to us, because for us much lies between them and the objective that was not there for them at all.

The positive side is therefore knowledge of his era, of his personal circumstances, of everything that he had to know even if it does not actually occur [in his text].

37. The degree to which the material of their consciousness interests every individual becomes clear from the way it occurs as a subjective element.

1. One part of the material, for example, partly does not occur in this way at all, partly only occurs for pressing reasons which can hardly be avoided. This is therefore neglect, lack of interest, if there are no particular reasons to regard it as intentional avoidance.

2. Other parts occur frequently or seldom (for this can purely depend on the objective element), but always in relation to reasons which are easy to explain. This is the common element of consciousness which presents itself of its own accord if one needs it, or which one can very easily use if it presents itself.

3. Other parts similarly occur frequently or seldom, but in such a way that they appear contrived and are the reason for [doubts? – there is a missing word in the manuscript at this point]. These are the objects which almost always only intrigue consciousness at a particular time.

38. The degree to which the objective and the subjective function (art in the more narrow and life in the wider sense) come apart is evident from whether, in terms of the genre, the subjective element comes in frequently or rarely.

1. In terms of the genre. For some genres can take more and others less of the subjective: strict and graceful [genres]. But every genre leaves space on both sides. So it is the character of the writer which inclines every work to one or the other side within this space.

2. Art and life. Whoever is most aware of this difference also tears themself away the most from subjective combination in composition. Plebeian writers are those who are wholly unable to do this.

39. Every work which belongs to art in the wider sense is at the same time an action which belongs to life in the narrower sense. The more it appears in this way to the writer in terms of the genre, the more the subjective element acquires secondary relationships which are supposed to effect something in life.

1. In terms of the genre. There are genres which are much less suited to intervening directly in life: these are universally valid works. Those in which the relationships to life dominate are occasional writings. Works which have a further theme outside the objective unity often belong in the middle between both, but do so while lying on the objective side.

Besides the genre time also has an effect. Public life brings art nearer to itself. Difference between Plato and Aristotle.

But here there is always also a free space for the writer.

Note. This division and the one in §38 should not be confused with each other; every part of one can belong to every part of the other.

2. In the secondary relationships to life one can also include everything which characterises a text as popular, i.e. all taking account and use of specific moods to achieve the aim of the work. The writer admittedly thinks of a certain audience in relation to every word, and finds himself more or less in dialogue with the audience, but keeping in mind what the audience has temporarily in mind means always intervening in life.

This opposition is also not strict. For to the extent to which the writer presents something new, new truths, he will also have to employ popular elements.

40. The individuality of usage which does not immediately emerge from the objective side cannot be certainly inferred from the totality of the subjective element.

In the bringing together of the subjective element one can find many things in the language which appear individual. But, on the one hand, in relation both to the ancients and to foreign authors one can never know whether it is not the common property of a time or of a genre; on the other, if it only reveals itself as such in the subjective element, thus emerges purely from the personality, then one can only notice it as affectation.

41. What can be considered as subjective individuality of usage must be able to be founded in something objective.

That which belongs to the objective element in a work, the more it contains an individual manner of intuition and thus also establishes [new] usage, also occurs again as a subjective element in other works. Everything [subjectively? – there is a missing word in the manuscript at this point] individual in the usage must, though, derive from an individual manner of intuition which in the majority of cases has been formed by an objective element, perhaps in a lost work; but if the manner of intuition is really only established fragmentarily in such a manner, the analogy between its single elements must be able to be found and this is the only true proof.

42. The language itself is an intuition (*Anschauung*); individuality of usage can therefore only be founded on an individual intuition of language.

Most of what we consider to be individual because of a particular feeling, without being able to give a precise justification thereof, depends on this. The individual intuition of the language is generally a particular view of the relationship of organic elements to each other and can concern the relationship of formal and material elements to each other as well as that between the musical and the grammatical elements in the language. Individual writers certainly seem to bring the power of certain expressions into consciousness, 1. to transplant something from one sphere of language into another in a more refined or milder form; 2. predominant tendency to use words in a particular direction or to make words universal which only belonged to a particular sphere, rhythmic games and combinations, word games, anacolutha. In general one must regard something which appears to contradict the laws of language and appears difficult to find and difficult to convey to everyone else as an element of this individuality. If it is to be completely freed of the reproach of being affected one must be able to seek its common principle and develop it to some degree.

43. The living combination of all the moments indicated so far creates complete understanding.

Combination is necessary: for in the strict sense no passage can be understood via the application of one procedure on its own. If one overlooks where there is even only a minimum of the objective and subjective element the error becomes ever greater. Whence a frequent very clear understanding of individual passages without a true understanding of the whole. On the other hand, the obscurity of individual passages in relation to a correct understanding of the whole will always be based on the deficient knowledge of something outside the work itself.

44. Complete understanding grasped in its highest form is an understanding of the utterer better than he understands himself.

Partly because it is in fact an analysis of his procedure which brings to consciousness what was unconscious to himself, partly because it also conceives of his relationship to language via the necessary duplication which he himself does not distinguish in it. In the same way he also does not distinguish what emerges from the essence of his individuality or his level of education from what coincidentally occurs as abnormality, and what he would not have produced if he had distinguished it.

The truth emerges from the fact that when a writer becomes his own reader he steps into a line with the other readers and another reader can be a better reader than he himself; in any case, at least their difficulties and obscurities as well emerge from the unconscious part of his work.

45. The difference between easy and difficult writers only exists via the fact that there is no complete understanding.

An understanding which had to begin at the same time with complete givenness of all necessary conditions would have to negate this difference; for if the language is completely given an isolated element is not more

266

difficult to understand as language than another isolated element, nor is one subjectivity actually more incomprehensible than another. What cannot be overcome in this difference lies outside the complete givenness of the languages, especially of the ancient languages in all their periods and forms, 1. partly in the writers themselves: the difficult ones are namely the confused ones who have partly not grasped the idea of their genre purely, partly do not have the language sufficiently in their power, and have partly not worked out their individuality purely enough, so that one cannot get to the rules for all the exceptions. It is not possible to understand these writers completely and certainly. 2. partly in the readers, namely because not every reader has the same relationship to all domains, rather, like the composition itself, most people's understanding also tends to one side, or, where it is directed to all sides in the same way, it certainly comprehends the grammatical side more than the technical.

The totality of understanding is always a collective work.

Conclusion

46. The prescriptions of the art of understanding are more precisely determinable if they are related to a specific given, from which the special hermeneutics arise.

Because in every single case all the prescriptions given here really must be applied and must therefore mutually determine each other, which is a task that can only be accomplished precisely in an immediately practical manner, but which can only be accomplished via theory and via analysis by dint of approximation, there is already in the nature of every whole partly a negative reason to exclude certain mutual determinations, partly a positive reason to highlight others in a dominating manner. Grouping these together beforehand makes easier the applicability of the general prescriptions and is therefore an almost indispensable mediator between the prescriptions and the carrying out of the task itself.

47. The special hermeneutics of the different languages follow the grammatical side, those of the different genres follow the technical side.

Because for the former the languages are the highest given whole, to which the language's dialects and periods are subordinated, for the latter in the same way the ideas of the genres [are the highest given whole].

In explication itself both must in turn be combined in relation to a given individual.

48. The special hermeneutics are only capable of a less strict scientific form.

Essentially because they have an empirical part. For neither the particular languages in their individuality nor the really existing genres can be deduced.

To the extent that the empirical part dominates they [the special hermeneutics] just present themselves as a mass of observations. But to the extent that one seeks to find the unity in the given and tries to dissolve it into a pure intuition, everything is likewise said with necessity. Both manners of proceeding must be unified in the idea that they gradually coincide, which, however, admittedly never happens.

49. In the same way as the grammatical sides of hermeneutics relate to the theory of language,ˢ so the technical sides relate to the theory of art.ᵗ

Namely the former develop with and through each other, determining each other, and so do the latter. The theory of art as related to verbal art. Neglect of hermeneutics must give rise to mistakes in both. Grammatical observations become too general if one attributes to the elements themselves what is only the case via and for a particular context, and too hesitant if one does not acknowledge the objectivity of single examples. The same is valid for the theory of composition, for it is, after all, reconstruction which presupposes that those who compose have not been correctly understood as such. – Examples from the theory of the French, who nearly everywhere confused the subjective and the objective element in old works of art.

50. Criticism with its two branches is grafted onto both sides of hermeneutics and the disciplines which correspond to them.

ˢ *Sprachlehre.*   ᵗ *Kunstlehre.*

Schematism and Language

Schematism and Language[1]

(from *Friedrich Schleiermachers Dialektik*, ed. R. Odebrecht, Leipzig 1942, pp. 370–81)

Knowledge rests ... on two characteristics: on general identity of construction and on agreement with the being to which the thought refers. As far as the latter is concerned, we have stated: If we do not assume a general belonging together of the inner process with being, to the extent that it affects the organic function, then there is no truth in relation to being affected from outside, and we would only have sensation. For nothing becomes an object for us unless the organic impression becomes an image and is related to something particular. All truth therefore depends on our assuming:

1. The general images which form themselves in us are identical with the system of innate concepts.

2. The relation of the organic impressions to these images expresses what the fixed differences in being themselves are.

Admittedly mistakes are often made in relating the general image to a particular. (If I, e.g., see a horse as a cow.) But then precisely only if one does not possess the organic impression completely enough and does not wait for the meeting [of general image and particular]. But the general image retains its truth (the general concept 'animal' is always there as a true basis), even if the relation is mistaken. If on the other hand I relate the particular image, instead of to a general image, to a higher general image, by saying, for example: 'I do not wish to maintain that that thing there is a

---

[1] Editor's title.

271

horse; but it is certainly a four-footed animal', then the mistake here is always related to the truth, because the higher concept contains the lower in itself.

To knowledge belongs further that it is a thought which is constituted in the same way in all people. Now to what extent will the second characteristic, the general identity of construction in thought, be encountered in this process as far as we have described it so far? The whole process is determined by the organism and this is attached to the individual person, and everyone relates themself to the unity of individual life. We cannot therefore know whether the other person hears or sees as we do. In what, then, does the identity of construction reside? Unconsciously in the fact that we rightly assume the organism follows the same laws in all people. But thought is only knowledge if it has consciousness. This consciousness of the sameness of construction must be contained within the feeling of conviction. Now how do we succeed in verifying this assumption?

Not via the organism. But if we make man himself the object of our investigation, then the process of induction will lead us to the identity of organisms and laws. But we cannot pursue that as far as the complete result, for something always escapes from our investigation. We cannot observe how the outward image appears in the inside of the organism; from here, then, no verification is possible. So we need to rely on the effect of the intellectual function on the senses. We can only bring the sameness of construction to light by exchange of consciousness. This presupposes a mediating term, a universal and shared system of designation, which will be language or something which is substituted for language. The characteristic of knowledge is also already potentially present in this area in the process as far as we have pursued it. For the process of schematisation already produces the general system of designation. If one wishes to pursue this into its innermost basis one will only be able to explain it thus: the general image we project for ourselves is essentially something indeterminate in its generality; for only the particular is totally determined. But it [the general image] is not posited outside the particular, but contained within it; and the whole process of representation is an *oscillation between the determinacy of the particular and the indeterminacy of the general image.*

Language as a general system of designation. The identity of individual and species is posited in this oscillation. The action of being able to synthesise already produces a system of designation. For we can only fix the general image in its difference from the particular by a sign, whether the sign is a word or another image. If I, e.g., paint the outline of an object and fix it by lines, I can in doing so abstract as much as possible from the determinacy of the object; and this visible sign represents the general image. But the word can just as much be a sign with which I fix the general image.

We cannot here examine how the preponderant tendency to fix the system of designation in discourse arises. For language is our constant presupposition when we deal with the art of carrying on a conversation. And without language we could not even have got as far in the realm of schematisation. The word, then, serves to fix the general image, in order to be able to bring it to mind again. And this is the identity of construction of the ideas of one and the same person. If we look at language then we must also admit that the real appelatives [common nouns] are the primary core of language and are nothing but the fixing of the general images. It has admittedly often been maintained that proper names are the core. If this is right we can easily reduce them to the former by what was said earlier. For proper names, like appelatives, seek to fix an identity, but only to the extent that an object is posited and changes at different moments. And in this way the difference would not be significant. Seen historically it is only a particular narrow area where proper names have priority. So, not only potentially but actually, the tendency towards the second characteristic of knowledge shows itself in language.

The emergence of language depends on this process of schematisation and is adequately grounded in it. Everyone seeks to fix the general image for themself and for others. The inner necessity is just as great for consciousness to go out of personal difference in order to compare what happens in us and in other people by putting itself in the middle between the two. The emergence of general images in language for everyone is the first means of avoiding conflicting ideas.

Now that language is an adequate guarantee for us of the identity of the process, i.e. that I am certain that someone who says the same word as I must also construct the same inner image and thereby form the same particular organic effects, admittedly only appears as a presupposition which must continually be proved and, by being proved, will be declared to be true. This must continually be tried out and does occur in many identical moments. The conviction as to the identity of the process grows accordingly and what always remains obscure on the side of the organic function is supplemented via this.

Scepticism has been taken to an infinite extreme here and it has been asked, e.g., whether perhaps one person has a different image from another in relation to a colour of the same name. This can never be established, but is also immaterial, if only the object is the same as the one I have and the other person describes the same actions of the object as I describe. We are continually testing and so are also testing in the perception of the identity of construction. All communication about external objects is a constant continuation of the test as to whether all people construct their ideas in identical fashion. (The norm here should be the rainbow, which is, of course, not something objective, but only appears in the eye of each individual and is designated and described by all people in the same way.) But this identity, both in itself and to the extent that it can be brought to determinate consciousness, has its limits, which constitute the relativity of knowledge. How can error arise from this relativity; and do these limits as well already lie in our domain?

The understanding of language rests on the identity of human consciousness. The identical construction of thought laid down in language is not a complete guarantee for the correctness of thought. Much must be corrected here. Yet error depends on a premature closure of the relations of the particular image to the general. But there are also changes in the use of language as a whole. In this respect we find changes of language in all work on branches of human knowledge which result in a different construction of knowledge (e.g. classification in natural history). Here as well error is very much related to truth and is present in the process of deduction ... So there is error and truth in language as well; even incorrect thought can become common to all, so that thought does not agree with what is thought. How are we to regard this in the context of our whole investigation? The evaluation and use of the scientific content of all formulations which are laid down and developed in language depends on judgements, in which a premature closure, so an error, is possible.

We must look at the matter from another side. Identity of construction of thought as one of the elements of knowledge is only manifested in language. Now there is, though, no universal language, so there is also no universal identity of construction. This characteristic is therefore not realised at all, and will not be realised. All attempts to get to a universal language are failures; for agreement about the universal language itself is subordinated to particular languages. We already drew attention earlier to this limitation by language, so that we say that identity in the construction of thought is not something universal, but is enclosed within limits. The relativity of knowledge already shows itself in language; the limits are different according to the difference or relatedness of the particular languages. Many a language can be more easily resolved into another language because it is more closely related to it; an equivalent construction of knowledge is more likely here. If, then, language is already brought out by the process of schematisation, there must already be a difference and the relativity of knowledge in the process itself, which expresses itself in the difference of languages. The general images are admittedly something which arose via the intellectual function in the mind[a] (the inner side of the organic function), but they are still determined by the organic function. And only by the collision of the two functions, the inner and the outer, only by the connection of the two does consciousness arise. If we speak of the difference of language we distinguish the external difference of the sound and the internal of the content. It is conceivable that only the sound might be different, the content might be the same. But no word that bears a logical unity within itself corresponds to a word of another language. In this way the human capacity with regard to receptivity for the activity of the intellectual function is different in different people. But where this difference of the general images is located is not clear to us. It could derive from a difference in the intellectual function itself or from the state of the external receptivity of the organic function. Is there a Third within which the basis of the difference of language could lie? This cannot possibly be assumed if we do not wish to destroy the assumption that in itself the relation of a particular image to a general image cannot be a mistake. For this relationship is the truth. The first case, that the difference is grounded in a difference of the intellectual function in and for itself is also excluded. For if this were not identical in all people there would be no truth at all. If reason is the same then the system of innate concepts which is the location of reason is the same. So there is no other alternative than that this relativity of knowledge is grounded in an original difference of the organic impressions. The divergence in the process of schematisation of different peoples, from which the difference of languages arises, is explained by this.

We want now to leave this issue here, and assume this relativity, because we necessarily find it in the course of our task itself. We encounter it if we are to mediate between conflicting ideas of two people who speak a different

---

[a] *Sinn.*

language. Now how are we to deal with this relativity in the sense of our task, which is hereby partly obviated because it posits the identity of all people as thinking subjects? If we allow the relativity to persist then it partly negates our task. For there would be no limit here, and in this way the possibility of the mediation of different ideas in one and the same language would finally be removed, because every language is modified in an individual manner within itself (cf. judgements of taste and smell, where the difference is so great that there are no general names here).

There are only two ways to dissolve the relativity. Either we posit via it a difference in what is thought. This difference is then in conflict with the postulated identity of thought. It must be dissolved, otherwise we get no knowledge. This is one of the ways, which begins with a separation of the two domains. The other way is more complex, so it is less direct. If we assume that we could never remove this relativity then we would be left with reducing the relativity of knowledge itself to knowledge. Then we could at the same time take up the task of construction and the mediation of knowledge. All real thinking is subjected to this difference to differing degrees; only in the limits of thought established above is there an identity. These limits are on the one side the contentless idea of mere matter, on the other the absolute subject, i.e. the absolute unity of being within which all oppositions are enclosed. If we say: there is a difference of the mind with regard to its receptivity for external objects, then this means: the difference in thought begins with the beginning of the operation through which subjects are formed. The idea of mere matter precedes the definite impressions via which subjects are determined, and difference is not possible in it, because the chaotic confusion of difference and indifference is itself posited here. If the difference of thought begins as soon as the continual effect of the intellectual function on the inner side of the mind becomes determinate, then it begins with the formation of the general image, which always either belongs to a predicate- or a subject-concept. This formation is only conceivable if an opposition is presupposed. But before the opposition there is the identity of all oppositions, namely the absolute subject, so there is no difference. However, both, the contentless idea of mere matter, and the absolute unity of being in which all oppositions are enclosed, are only basic conditions of thought, not real thinking itself. Everywhere between these points where a thinking refers to them there must necessarily be difference. This is clear from what has been said so far. The difference must be grounded in the organic function as receptivity from outside, and in this lies the fact that the difference must be everywhere where something depends on specific organic impressions. Now all thinking has something of the organic function in itself, thus also something via which difference is grounded, thus also something of the difference itself. Assuming as well that the totality of the general images lay in the mind and was the same in everyone, then it could still only come into consciousness via particular impressions. If this seems to negate the identity of man as thinking subject, then one can say against this: Every person has their place in the totality of being and their thinking represents being, but not separately from their place.

From this the following *canon* results: *The identity of thought expresses the attunement*[b] *of the person to being in the place where they are located; the difference of thought expresses the separation*[c] *of their thought from being in the place.* From this follows as a matter of course that we have no other means of connecting our task with this relativity but to reduce relativity itself to knowledge, so that the construction of the difference of thinking coincides with the attempt to resolve conflicting ideas. We must come to know the individual difference itself and thus remain with our task, namely the task of wishing to know. This, though, is only a new coefficient in the approximation to real knowledge. For the demand is completely to know the individuality of a people or of a single person. And these are objects that we know we can always only ever attain via approximation.

The canon of the critical procedure. All that is left, then, is to make relativity itself the object. Only the limits of thought are excluded from the influence of the individual. History confirms this, for we find the same ideas about it in all peoples. Besides, this difference is visible in all branches of real knowledge. That is already inherent in language. This goes so far that, even though we had to say that the more a particular thinking approaches the limits, the more the identity in construction would have to emerge, even here individual difference is still not lacking. The limit on the side just of the possibility of the subjects is mathematics, where different methods have always occurred; on the other side it is where everything lies that is most related to the idea of the absolute subject, the properly metaphysical. Here as well we find differences in the basic ideas, and individual difference reveals itself everywhere in the form which constitutes the scientific character.

From all this emerges a new *canon* for the formation of concepts:

[b] *Zusammenstimmung.*
[c] *Verschiedenheit*, which also means difference, but here has more of the sense of '*scheiden*', to 'divide'.

There is everywhere as much approximation to knowledge that is really known as the procedure of the process of induction is accompanied by a critical procedure which seeks out what is individual and tries to understand it in its positive aspect and in its limits.
Something is to be divided here that is not separate. The procedure is, therefore, only an abstraction. The division can for this reason never be placed in a particular product, otherwise it would also be affected by the individual aspect of that which divides. The division can only be in the process itself. If the canon is right that there is only as much approximation to knowledge as the individual in thought is sought, then we can see from this how it really is with regard to the demand for universality in science. Absolute identity of knowledge can only arise if the individual factor were completely eliminated. That is, though, only possible with the presupposition of an absolutely universal language. But there is no means of producing such a language, even if it is also a product of the intellectual function. For language is not in all respects subordinated to construction, and it keeps a hold on the realm of nature. Everywhere where science awoke this issue was discussed, most recently by Leibniz (pasigraphy). But this problem corresponds to the squaring of the circle. In the domain of the technical procedure in thought one was never as close to accomplishing this task as when the Latin language was the universal scientific language. But this was at a time when all languages were in a revolutionary state. And this state passed away when the languages had formed themselves according to the character of the people. When the modern languages had developed the Latin language could not sustain its domination, even though everything scientific was recorded in this language; and today it is impossible to present science in it in a living manner.

All the elements of the system of designation which form the canon of language depend on the part of the process of the formation of concepts which we have observed: nouns and verbs = subject- and predicate-concepts. As language immediately develops with the schematic process the root words are to be placed more on the side of the process of induction which relates to perception; everything abstract will depend more on the process of deduction. This is the sense of the expression that in its beginning language was sensuous. All expressions which designate immediate change have the general images as their object; but just as much in language must correspond to the process of deduction as to the process of induction.

The task of the critical procedure of gaining control of the individual factor is to understand the differing characters of language according to their general image-schematism. The perspectives for this are present in what has been said so far. One language will direct itself more to the side of determined thought, the other more to the side of pure thought. One gives the subject- the other the predicate-concepts priority; one will subordinate the action to the thing, the other the fixing of objects to the actions. But it is obvious that even this can only be brought to intuition in the form of a general image, in the same way as anything individual at all cannot be reduced to a general concept, but only to a general location where several particular things are located together. The same task will extend to the process of deduction. In that case one tries to classify the language with regard to its logical content; so one forms oppositions and designates similarities and relations. But the image always remains what dominates; and in such a way that it cannot be completely reproduced in language. We can never express something individual through language, except to the extent to which it is present as an image or a sequence of images. A personality can never be reproduced by a definition, but, as in a novel or a drama, only by the image, which is the better the more all the parts in it cohere.

It is just the same with language and its individual character. Only particular traits can be grasped as formulae, but only to the extent that they are opposed to others. But that is not a proper combination, rather each person has it in themselves as an image. *The last supplement of the incompleteness of knowledge lies here on the side of the image, and the complete cycle of individual images must complete the incompleteness of universal knowledge;* but that is only possible in continual approximation.

Applied to the task of universal knowledge this means: *In no domain is there a complete knowledge, except together with the grasping of the living history of knowledge* at all times and in all places which is taken as a whole in its complete extent by this critical procedure. And there is no history of knowledge without its living construction.

Here we have at the same time on the greatest scale the resolution of the conflict between empirical knowledge and the a priori. For this critical procedure is located in the empirical, historical, the indispensable supplement of pure science, where it is shown how people thought at different times in different nations. But whoever wished to say that all knowledge ought finally to be dissolved into this history would take away its innermost life. Because history presupposes the living images of cognition, in relation to which it has all its value, and it is only fruitful if one develops the science further; otherwise it is dead collecting.

We will pause here and easily become aware that we have grasped the general rules for the formation of concepts from the organic side, thus have grasped for the process of induction how error must be avoided, grasped how much knowledge is in this, and grasped where the supplement of this knowledge lies.

Index

References to the Old and New Testaments have not been detailed, as they are too numerous. Some of Schleiermacher's more complex terms have also not been listed, as they only make sense in the contexts in which he employs them, and occur in too many different contexts and in too many different senses to be usefully included. **Bold** numbers refer to a whole section on the topic in question.

Absolute, xiv, xxiii–xxiv, xxv, xxvi
allegory, 15, 71
analogy, 36, 53, 73, 147, 176–7, 208, 213, 246
analytical philosophy, xx–xxi, xxix, xxxi
Apocrypha, 40–1, 43
art, work of, 112–13, 115, 144, 161, 264
    relation to science, 114–15, 116
Ast, F., 4

biography, 118

Cicero, 14
Collins, D., xix
comparison, 25, 40, 41, 42, 43, 62, 71, 72–3, 88,
    92–3, 95, 98, 141, 144, 147, 158, 172, 178, 262
composition, 105–6, 126–7, 131, 132–46, 241, 255,
    256, 268
context (linguistic area, surroundings), 145, 147,
    160, 173, 195, 208, 209–10, 219, 221
    and meaning, 30, 31, 35, 37, 44–5, 51, 54, 56, 61,
    62, 66–7, 71, 83, 94, 111, 131, 233–4, 235, 241,
    243
conversation, 102, 106, 116, 124, 129, 142, 167–8,
    273
copula, 49–50
correspondence theory of truth, xxiii
criticism, 149, **158–224**
    documentary, 163–4, 167, 174–5, 176, 177–9,
    180
    of errors arising from free action, **188–224**
    historical, 80, 87, 88, 158–9, 166–7, 214–15,
    216–17, 218, 220–1

of mechanical errors, 172–187
    relationship of doctrinal to historical and philo-
    logical, 158–71, 217

Dannhauer, J. C., viii
Davidson, D., xxvii
Derrida, J., xxxi
dialectics, 7, 8
dictionaries (lexical aids), 33–9, 42, 55, 73, 237, 238
divination (divinatory criticism), xi, 23, 92–3,
    163–4, 167, 174–5, 177–8, 180, 181, 184–5,
    187, 194–8, 199

empathy, vii, xx, xxix
Ernesti, J. A., 5
ethics, 8, 73

falsification of texts, 188–92, 205
Fichte, J. G., xiii, xv–xvi
Frank, M., xi, xxxiv
Frege, G., xxi

Gadamer, H.-G., xxxiv, xxxvii
German Idealism, x, xii
Gibbon, E., 110
God, xvii
    and the transcendent basis, xxv
Gospels, 74, 117, 128, 138, 145, 154–5, 187, 200,
    214, 215–16, 217–20
    of John, 48, 49, 52, 58, 74, 99, 118, 128, 138, 145,
    155, 159, 203, 212
    of Luke, 20, 74, 145, 146, 155, 212, 220

Index

Cambridge texts in the history of philosophy